D0615603

Date: 8/22/16

158.125 ROS
Rosenthal, Norman E.,
Super mind :how to boost
performance and live a richer and

PALM BEACH COUNTY
LIBRARY SYSTEM
3650 SUMMIT BLVD.
WEST PALM BEACH, FL 33406

SUPER
MIND

SUPER MIND

How to Boost Performance and Live a
Richer and Happier Life Through
Transcendental Meditation

NORMAN E. ROSENTHAL, M.D.

A TarcherPerigee Book

tarcher
perigee

An imprint of Penguin Random House LLC
375 Hudson Street
New York, New York 10014

Copyright © 2016 by Norman E. Rosenthal
Penguin supports copyright. Copyright fuels creativity, encourages diverse voices, promotes free speech, and creates a vibrant culture. Thank you for buying an authorized edition of this book and for complying with copyright laws by not reproducing, scanning, or distributing any part of it in any form without permission. You are supporting writers and allowing Penguin to continue to publish books for every reader.

Tarcher and Perigee are registered trademarks, and the colophon is a trademark of Penguin Random House LLC.

Most TarcherPerigee books are available at special quantity discounts for bulk purchase for sales promotions, premiums, fund-raising, and educational needs. Special books or book excerpts also can be created to fit specific needs. For details, write: SpecialMarkets@penguinrandomhouse.com.

LIBRARY OF CONGRESS CATALOGING-IN-PUBLICATION DATA
Names: Rosenthal, Norman E., author.
Title: Super mind : how to boost performance and live a richer and happier life through transcendental meditation / Norman E Rosenthal MD.
Description: New York : TarcherPerigee, 2016. | Includes bibliographical references and index.
Identifiers: LCCN 2016006787 (print) | LCCN 2016010923 (ebook) | ISBN 9780399174742 (hardback) | ISBN 9781101983478
Subjects: LCSH: Transcendental Meditation. | Self-actualization (Psychology) | BISAC: BODY, MIND & SPIRIT / Meditation. | SELF-HELP / Personal Growth / General. | SELF-HELP / Personal Growth / Happiness.
Classification: LCC BF637.T68 R667 2016 (print) | LCC BF637.T68 (ebook) | DDC 158.1/25—dc23
LC record available at http://lccn.loc.gov/2016006787

Printed in the United States of America
3 5 7 9 10 8 6 4

Book design by Spring Hoteling

Neither the publisher nor the author is engaged in rendering professional advice or services to the individual reader. The ideas, procedures, and suggestions contained in this book are not intended as a substitute for consulting with your physician. All matters regarding your health require medical supervision. Neither the author nor the publisher shall be liable or responsible for any loss or damage allegedly arising from any information or suggestion in this book.

While the author has made every effort to provide accurate telephone numbers, Internet addresses, and other contact information at the time of publication, neither the publisher nor the author assumes any responsibility for errors or for changes that occur after publication. Further, the publisher does not have any control over and does not assume any responsibility for author or third-party Web sites or their content.

FOR BOB ROTH

CONTENTS

III. BEYOND THE SUPER MIND

Our normal waking consciousness . . . is but one special type of consciousness, whilst all about it, parted from it by the filmiest of screens, there lie potential forms of consciousness entirely different. We may go through life without suspecting their existence; but apply the requisite stimulus, and at a touch they are there in all their completeness, definite types of mentality, which probably somewhere have their field of application and adaptation. No account of the universe in its totality can be final which leaves these other forms of consciousness quite disregarded.

WILLIAM JAMES

Through the repeated experience of settling, a continuum of calmness develops.

PATANJALI

PART I

DEVELOPMENT OF CONSCIOUSNESS

1

A NEW BEGINNING

In my end is my beginning.

T. S. Eliot

Have you ever concluded a project—or thought you had—only to change your mind later? All those feelings you had at the time—premature in retrospect—were genuine: typically relief, mixed (one hopes) with a measure of contentment, though mingled with sadness. It can be hard to say good-bye to ideas and characters with whom you've shared so many hours. Conclusion and closure bring rewards, but also a sense of loss. That is how I felt when I completed *Transcendence*, a book that—like the present one—deals with the Transcendental Meditation (TM) technique and its effects. I thought I had said everything I had to say on the subject.

But I was wrong. T. S. Eliot, quoted above, was wiser: "In my end is my beginning." Exactly so.

I had come full cycle once before with regard to TM. I first learned the technique back in South Africa in the early 1970s, but in the helter-skelter of daily life I let it fall by the wayside. Thirty-five years later (in 2008), challenged by a young patient to renew my TM practice, I did so and have been meditating regularly ever since. After observing beneficial effects of meditation in myself—such as decreased anxiety and reactivity—I began recommending the technique to some of my patients. Many experienced results that were equally impressive—or even more so. After delving into the literature on TM, I was so impressed with its many benefits that I felt compelled to write about it—and do so, once again.

Although both *Transcendence* and *Super Mind* explore the effects of TM, the earlier book dealt mostly with its documented benefits on physical and emotional health, especially in people with problems such as anxiety, depression, addictions, and post-traumatic stress disorder (PTSD). In contrast, this book explores not only the advantages that TM can bring to your task-driven life, but how it can actually result in a new state of consciousness—a word that may seem troublesome to a scientist, but seems perfectly apt for the experiences I will describe.

The founder of TM, Maharishi Mahesh Yogi, outlined several states of consciousness—the three widely acknowledged states (waking, sleeping, and dreaming), and four others, which are summarized in table 1 below and presented in more detail in the notes.[1]

Table 1: The Four Higher States of Consciousness (According to Vedic tradition)

Stage 4: Transcendence—the experience of the Self in the silence of meditation.
Stage 5: Cosmic Consciousness—the experience of the transcendent in activity—traditionally used to express the state in its fully realized, continuous form.
Stage 6: Refined Cosmic Consciousness—a state in which the development of the senses and emotions are at their maximum.
Stage 7: Unity Consciousness—a state in which you experience the transcendental reality not just within yourself, but also within everyone and everything.

I will discuss transcendence (the fourth state) in some detail in chapters 4 and 5, and Cosmic Consciousness (the fifth state) in its fully realized form in chapter 18. When it comes to stages of consciousness beyond stage 4 (transcendence), however, I will speak of them collectively as "Super Mind"—a term that seems well suited to our present frenetic and interconnected era. Indeed, in these stressful times we need to have all our neurons, synapses, and brain circuits at our disposal. I selected the term "Super Mind" because it describes an experience of not only heightened aptitude and problem-solving ability but also a state of emotional sensitivity, empathy, perspective, and diplomatic skills. It is the mind in peak condition, not just momentarily—as we have all experienced—but with a consistency that tends to grow over time.

*   *   *

I first began to get a glimpse of this state in myself and some of my patients soon after publishing *Transcendence* (in 2011). I continued to meditate, and after some time, a new and utterly unexpected set of developments began to unfold, both within my meditating patients and myself. These developments fell roughly into two categories. The first I can best describe as everyday changes in awareness or consciousness: Feelings of stillness, expansiveness, boundlessness, and peace, formerly confined to my meditation sessions, began to seep into my daily life. For a while after meditating, I would sense a pleasant glow about me—and others would notice it.

"You've been meditating, haven't you?" one knowledgeable friend remarked. Or, as I would talk with a patient or colleague about feelings that arose during meditation, I would feel myself slipping into that state of inner expansive calm, often at the same time becoming even more engaged in the conversation. As with so many other experiences I have had that seemed at first unique to me, I later found that this phenomenon—stillness in the presence of activity—is commonplace among long-term meditators.

In tandem with the development of expanded consciousness, my life started to improve in many ways (the second set of changes). And once again, these shifts turned out to be typical in people who have been meditating for months to years—although, as you will see, dramatic changes sometimes occur within days of a person's very first TM session. I will elaborate on this subject later. At this point, let me say simply that life became easier and I became happier—both of which were apparent not only to me but also to my family, friends, and even colleagues. *It is these two sets of changes—developments in consciousness in tandem with improvements in many aspects of a person's life—that I am collectively calling the Super Mind.*

It occurred to me that since the two sets of changes both appeared after I started to meditate, they might well be related. Might developing consciousness—an advanced form of which has traditionally been called Cosmic Consciousness—in and of itself be an agent of change? I wondered. Might the presence of stillness and silence that infuses the daily lives of meditators influence their well-being, and thereby their activities and connections with others? Such ideas are hardly new. They have been suggested by sages for centuries, but now they were arising from my own experience, and I have noticed that one's own experience often overshadows the wisdom of sages and the opinions of experts. Also, we now have tools, in the form of technology and a better understanding of the mind, that can lend solid data to the ineffable wisdom of the ages.

I have always viewed my own mind as a sort of laboratory where novel observations (novel to me, that is) throw me into a fever of curiosity, which has been a driving force throughout my life. That's how it was for me as a young man, when I first noticed my energy and good humor draining away in the short, dark days of winter, then resurging in the glorious light of spring. I had never had such experiences in my native sun-drenched South Africa, and the dramatic contrast between my seasonal responses in the old country and the new one were instrumental to my first description of seasonal affective disorder (SAD).[2] It turned out that I was just one of millions of people who suffer from this condition.

In an analogous way, I became aware that meditation had induced in me alterations in the quality of my everyday consciousness—and all sorts of good things started to happen. Once again, like an explorer who stumbles upon a wonder of nature, I was possessed to find out all I could about it and to share my observations in the hope that they would be of interest and value to others.

So here goes.

CAN IT BE TRUE?

The subtitle of this book makes a grand promise: that TM can boost your performance and help you lead a richer and happier life. I don't know about you, but when I see such claims, I am immediately suspicious, as was a favorite cousin, Lois, who attended a talk on TM that I gave in London. She came mostly out of family loyalty, I suspect, but was sufficiently impressed that she learned the technique herself. When I saw her a year later, she was delighted. She was meditating regularly and credited the practice with helping her get out of a toxic long-term relationship. "I was so surprised," she said, "to find out that you were telling the truth. To be honest, I thought it was just a publicity stunt." (That's what I love about family. They tell you things that others are too polite to say.)

In this book, I will describe many instances of people who have enjoyed the transformative changes that accompany expanding consciousness. These people include superperformers in their chosen field, which I would claim is no accident. I now think that all high performers have in common, knowingly or unknowingly, qualities and characteristics of the Super Mind. That is, they are calm under pressure and uncannily resilient to stress. They take care of their health, set high standards of innovation and creativity, and are not only intensely engaged in their actions but also capable of detaching when need be. They choose their projects carefully, keep the big picture in mind, and ignore trifling details. It is not necessary, however, to be a superperformer in order to develop your Super Mind. What matters is to reach your own potential, not some idealized standard.

I will also present for the first time the findings of a survey of more than six hundred TM practitioners who were asked about the quality of their consciousness and their lives since starting to meditate. I recognize that even if you accept that such beneficial changes can and do occur, you may well ask why they have to come about exclusively through Transcendental Meditation. The answer is, they don't. There are many ways to reach the same destination. I am convinced that almost anybody has the capacity to experience transcendence—that inner awakening of the Super Mind. It is a natural state of the brain, reported by people from many cultures throughout recorded time (as we will discuss). For now, however, let's address an obvious question: if it is possible to access these states by many routes, why do I recommend TM in particular?

Before I answer that question, let me tell you about a series of events that occurred when I was a first-year resident at Columbia Presbyterian Hospital in New York City. Once a week, first thing in the morning, I would have a regular session with my "long-term psychotherapy" patient. These sessions were meant both to help the patient and to teach the resident how to conduct therapy based on psychoanalytic principles, which discourage providing direct advice. My analytic supervisor had been quite stern on the subject. "Don't tell the patient what to do or how to do it," he admonished. "Help him figure it out *by himself.*"

Now, I should mention that these early morning sessions took place in a clinic on the fifth floor of a building in which the elevator only started running later. There was a work-around, however, as one faculty member explained: I should take an elevator up to the fifth floor of a *neighboring* building, where elevators *were* in early morning service. Then, by a labyrinthine route through various corridors, I could connect to the clinic building by an inconspicuous passageway. That made life much easier—at least for me. I would be in place, fresh and ready for the session, as my patient—a middle-aged man— arrived, red faced and panting, after clambering up five flights of stairs. It seemed unfair. Yet I had been sternly instructed not to tell patients what to do or how to do it. So what *was* I to do?

A common strategy, adopted by any bright three-year-old when an authority figure says no, is to seek another authority. That is exactly what I did. I took the question to a different supervisor—one less impressed by psychoanalysis, and in fact rather hostile toward it. I explained my predicament and described the secret passageway. "What should I do?" I asked him. "Tell him, of course," the man replied. "He'll never find it on his own."

Although I agree that it is good to help people find answers for themselves, I also know that there are passageways in life—including the life of the mind—that one is unlikely to stumble on alone, and since that early lesson I always point them out when it seems useful. And so it is with Transcendental Meditation—the simplest and most effortless way I know to access transcendence, the royal road to the Super Mind, and all the benefits that flow therefrom. It is, accordingly, with delight and enthusiasm that I share with you what I have learned about TM, in the hope that you may benefit as much as my patients and I have done.

WHY THIS BOOK AND WHY NOW?

I thought I had said everything worth saying about TM when I wrote *Transcendence*, so you might well ask, what's left to say? *Transcendence* focused on TM as a powerful technique for helping people with problems—for reducing stress and its related ailments. In contrast, the goal of *Super Mind* is to help anybody—including healthy and successful people, and even superperformers—who want to live a richer, more creative, and more fulfilling life. It shows how TM can influence brain functioning beyond mere stress reduction—and open the door to new possibilities.

In these challenging and ever-more-stressful times, we are called upon to navigate a complex world while maintaining our inner equilibrium, a task in which we often turn for help and comfort to the many technological wonders of recent decades. These devices continue to proliferate, giving us unprecedented access to information and a certain type of connection. They can also overwhelm us, however, and gobble up the internal space and quiet in which happiness and creativity flourish. Now more than ever it is time to find a way to expand our internal space, to instill a joyful silence alongside the frenetic activity of our daily lives. It is my hope that *Super Mind* will provide a road map toward that goal.

HERE ARE SOME OF THE KEY QUESTIONS
THAT WE WILL CONSIDER IN THIS BOOK:

- What is "consciousness" anyway?
- Can consciousness be developed and how does that relate to the Super Mind?
- What is the Super Mind and how does it relate to Cosmic Consciousness?
- How does it feel when consciousness develops?
- What are the physical signs of such development?
- What scientific evidence do we have for it?
- What value does the development of consciousness have beyond the experience itself? What are the gifts of the Super Mind?
- Can it help you become more effective, creative, and successful, personally and professionally?
- Can it help you become rich?
- How about greater fulfillment and happiness?

MAHARISHI AND THE BEATLES

The fully realized Super Mind—a state in which transcendence infuses one's daily life in an unbroken flow—has been called Cosmic Consciousness in traditional Vedic teaching. I first heard this term in a rather magical setting—a concert at Radio City Music Hall, where former Beatle Paul McCartney talked about Cosmic Consciousness and incorporated it into a lilting melody, both haunting and uplifting. It was a simple song based on an invitation given by Maharishi Mahesh Yogi directly to McCartney: "Come and be cosmically conscious with me."

McCartney was reminiscing about 1968, when he and the other Beatles went to visit Maharishi in Rishikesh, India. It was a time of turbulence and intergenerational strife but also, in the words of Simon and Garfunkel, "a time of innocence." Back then, "make love not war" and "flower power" were ubiquitous slogans that captured key elements of the era—the increasingly unpopular Vietnam War, the sexual revolution, and the idea that something as innocent as ideals of peace and love may ultimately have more impact than guns and grenades.

From these roiling social currents iconic figures emerged, of whom the Beatles were perhaps the most famous. It was fortuitous that these revolutionary young musicians found their way to an eminent spiritual figure who is key to our story—Maharishi Mahesh Yogi, a man of slight build with a gentle face and long flowing locks. He dressed in the traditional garb of a Vedic monk— white flowing robes—and often wore a garland of flowers round his neck. Maharishi had studied for thirteen years in the Himalayas as the principal student of the great sage Brahmananda Saraswati, known as Guru Dev, from whom he had learned an ancient Vedic technique of meditation

Maharishi called the technique Transcendental Meditation, and he believed it had so much potential to help people that he was determined to teach it throughout the world. In this mission, he was surprisingly successful, in large measure due to his personal qualities. Those around him talked often about his keen intellect (he was a physicist by training), his charismatic personality, his seemingly endless energy and tireless work ethic (he needed just a few hours of sleep a night), the bliss he brought to his work, and his fascination with everything around him. He had thought deeply about the nature of consciousness, both personally and professionally, and was an authority on Vedic teachings. In short, he was both an innovator and a consummate marketer, who brought to both East and West not only a powerful, ancient technique but also a compelling combination of artless innocence and the artful skills of a man of the world.

In retrospect, it makes perfect sense that these iconic figures from two different worlds—the Beatles and Maharishi—would meet up. The Beatles were searching for answers to questions that arose from the conflicts of the times, and Maharishi had an appealing answer. In summary, the message was simply this: Meditate, dive within, and expand your consciousness. In so doing, you will change, and the world around you will follow.

METAPHORS OF CONSCIOUSNESS

Fleshing out abstractions such as consciousness invites the use of metaphors as a way to lend shape and substance to concepts that can seem all too vague. A wise mentor of mine once took this approach in explaining the power of *unconscious* processes in shaping our lives. "The unconscious is like the wind," he said. "You can't see it, but you can tell its effects by the way it moves the branches of trees and scatters the leaves across the lawn."

In considering the conscious mind, we are on somewhat sturdier footing in that, by definition, conscious thoughts and feelings are accessible to us—if we choose to attend to them. But, like unconscious processes, conscious ones also blow around the branches. So another important way to assess our conscious mental processes is by examining what we do with our lives. As the saying goes, "By their fruits you will know them."[3]

This biblical quote brings to mind one of Maharishi's favorite sayings: "Water the root, and enjoy the fruit." He was offering Transcendental Meditation as a way to water the root—to nurture the psyche at its deepest core—while the fruits were the prize that would result from the process. To derive the benefits of TM, that may be all you really need to know. "Meditate and act," Maharishi used to say—and the benefits will emerge in the quality of your life.

If we wish to extend this metaphor further, however, we could consider the development of higher consciousness as all the intervening steps between the root and the fruit. It is these experiences of higher consciousness (which are a joy in themselves), plus all the benefits they bring, that I am collectively referring to as the Super Mind.

Another way to think of consciousness is as the medium through which we move and experience our lives, almost in the way a fish swims through water. And whether that water is clear or murky, fresh or brackish, makes a big difference! Both the quality of our consciousness and the way it affects us are keys to a good life.

Some have also compared our different states of consciousness to wearing different-colored glasses. Red glasses will make the world look red, blue glasses blue. According to this metaphor, the Super Mind allows you to wear colorless glasses—so that you see everything clearly, *in its actual color.*

Given our high-tech environment, it is natural that the effects of TM are often described in terms borrowed from the world of computers and cell phones. People talk about meditating to "reboot" or "reset," and I know what they mean. Often, when feeling stressed and depleted, a single TM session can "recharge my batteries." But over time, two new (and larger) computer-related metaphors have occurred to me—that TM gives me a "systems upgrade" or, better still, a "more powerful computer." In short, a Super Mind. When I think of meditating, I'm not expecting just to relieve the stress of the moment but to nurture the growth of consciousness and to improve the functioning of my mind and the overall quality of my life.

Before going any further, let me clarify a few points about the Super Mind. First, I'm not suggesting that everyone can do anything they want. We all have limitations, which differ from person to person. Rather, I'm referring to an ability to live up to your potential—something that successful people strive to do. Second, I do not see the Super Mind as the end stage of a process, as in: "Now that I have attained a Super Mind, I have arrived!" Instead, I see the Super Mind as a process of continued growth in which the development of consciousness evolves together with increasing success and well-being.

DEFINING THE SUPER MIND

Since I am going to use the term "Super Mind" frequently in this book, it may be useful to define what I mean by it right up front, so here goes: *the Super Mind is a mental state that consists of the development of expanded states of consciousness and that occurs in tandem with reduced stress, better physical health, and the emergence of life-enhancing personal qualities.* Growth of the Super Mind occurs commonly but by no means exclusively in those who practice TM, and can be measured and characterized by the Consciousness Integration Questionnaire (CIQ) (see chapter 7).

A GUIDE TO THIS BOOK

This book is organized into three parts: In part 1, after this introductory chapter, I will tell you about the new science of consciousness (chapter 2)—a set of intriguing developments that have transformed what used to be philosophical conjectures into measurable phenomena, such as EEG (electroencephalogram) tracings. We will consider these new findings alongside ancient wisdom about the growth of consciousness, for which we now also have scientific data.

In chapter 3, I will describe the technique that is, in my opinion, the surest way to expand consciousness—namely, Transcendental Meditation. Chapter 4 deals with the subjective experience of transcendence, and chapter 5 addresses the physiological basis associated with that state.

In chapter 6, I will introduce the Super Mind by describing the mysterious process through which the "repeated experience of settling" develops into "a continuum of calmness," phrases derived from an ancient text, the Yoga Sutras of Patanjali, quoted in the epigraph to this book.

I will then, in chapter 7, introduce you to the Consciousness Integration Questionnaire, developed by my colleagues and me to measure the components of the Super Mind in the same way that researchers measure psychological functions such as depression, happiness, resilience, and anxiety. We administered this questionnaire to more than six hundred TM meditators, with results that are revealed for the first time in this book.

In part 2, I will show you how the gifts of the Super Mind occasionally occur soon, but generally develop over time. These gifts include better physical well-being and mental functioning (chapters 8 and 9), the joys and rewards of being in the zone (chapter 10), and accelerated internal growth (chapter 11). In many situations we are called upon to balance two emotional forces that appear on the surface to be at war with each other—remaining engaged with the world without being overattached when it is healthy to let go. I hope to show you how this delicate balance naturally unfolds as part of Super Mind development (chapter 12). I will then describe the curious way in which people feel luckier after starting to meditate, as though they are being supported by the world around them (chapter 13). Many people are unclear about the distinctions between transcendence and mindfulness—another widely popular and influential form of meditation. In chapter 14, I will compare and contrast these two different types of meditation. In the last two chapters of this second section, I will explain how as consciousness grows, people can almost automatically attain happiness and sometimes even wealth—two things for which so many strive (chapters 15 and 16).

By then I hope your curiosity will be aroused to learn more about how consciousness expands in such a way as to offer these seemingly miraculous gifts. Enter part 3, in which I will also show you how the developing Super Mind can transform people's lives, and how the Super Mind develops to such an extent that they experience this state of consciousness and its benefits continuously through the twenty-four-hour day (chapter 18)—a state that has traditionally been called Cosmic Consciousness. Although this degree of expanded consciousness is by no means necessary to enjoy the huge benefits of the Super Mind, the fully developed form is fascinating to contemplate.

Chapter 19 introduces you to a less typical way in which consciousness may develop—by "transcendent surprises," intense mystical experiences that arise unbidden (and therefore cannot be planned), but that can have powerful long-term consequences. In the final chapter, "Toward a Connected Universe," I will briefly discuss how the Super Mind keeps growing beyond our individual concerns, thereby providing a channel for greater connection between and among individuals, their fellow human beings, and the universe as a whole.

Without further ado, let me welcome you to our journey into developing consciousness and the Super Mind.

2

THE SCIENCE OF CONSCIOUSNESS

Consciousness is the only real thing in the
world and the greatest mystery of all.

Vladimir Nabokov

At the time when the Beatles were visiting Maharishi, I was plowing through medical school. As most medical students can testify, there was and is a great deal to learn, not all of it interesting or even relevant to one's later professional life. Many details that I learned I have long since forgotten; others, no more important, tenaciously stay put. I enjoy, for example, strange-sounding words—so I may never forget the zonule of Zinn or the canal of Schlemm, both obscure but important structures in the eye. Likewise, Latinate terms seem to cling to my neurons—the "substantia nigra" and "locus coeruleus," for example, meaning, respectively, "black stuff" and "purple dot," both small but crucial regions of the brain.

But when I ask myself, what did I learn about *consciousness* at medical school? the answer is, not very much. Our generic patient was either conscious, unconscious, or somewhere in between—concussed, stuporous, obtunded. My psychiatric training was likewise lacking. We did, of course, learn about sleep with its various stages and maladies, and we attended lectures on hypnosis. We also learned about mood, anxiety, and other disorders listed in the latest manual of psychiatric ailments. We were taught to inquire about people's thoughts, dreams, and feelings, and even to make some attempt to understand where they came from and how best to deal with them. As I think about it, though, all of this learning involved the *contents* of consciousness—the subject matter, if you will—not consciousness itself. Consciousness as a topic for study and understanding was not on the menu.

MODERN SCIENCE

In reading the excellent comprehensive review *Consciousness and the Brain* by neuroscientist Stanislas Dehaene, professor of experimental cognitive psychology at the Collège de France, I found that my South African colleagues and I were not alone in those benighted times. According to Dehaene, the word "consciousness" was banned from scientific discourse when he was a student in the 1980s. At that time, as Dehaene put it, "I was surprised to discover that, during lab meetings, we were not allowed to use the C-word. . . . And then in the *late* 1980s everything changed. Today the problem of consciousness is at the forefront of neuroscience research."[1]

A great deal has been written about consciousness, much of it of a speculative and philosophical nature, asking questions such as "Who exactly has consciousness?" Daniel Dennett raises this question in his encyclopedic book *Consciousness Explained*: "Do newborn human babies?" he asks. "Do frogs? What about oysters, ants, plants, robots, zombies . . . ?"[2] In this book I will avoid venturing into such heady terrain. As a psychiatrist and researcher, I am more inclined to the empirical approach adopted by Dehaene and his colleagues.

Dehaene summarizes three fundamental elements that have enabled the transformation of consciousness from a "philosophical mystery into a laboratory phenomenon." These elements are: "the articulation of a better definition of consciousness; the discovery that consciousness can be experimentally manipulated; and a new respect for subjective phenomena."

Let us say that an image is flashed on a screen in front of you—very briefly, so it's below your detection threshold; you will (by definition) be unable to see it. Another way of masking an image so you cannot detect it (even though it is flashed in front of you) is to pair it with distracting images. In contrast, as you can imagine, that same image could be flashed in front of you for a longer duration or without distraction, in such a way that you could both see it and report on its presence.

Researchers have in fact conducted studies in which they presented images in these various ways and measured people's responses, both in terms of subjective reports (what people say they saw) and specific brain changes (for example, EEG and imaging methods). Then, by correlating subjective reports with brain measurements, scientists have been able to establish four EEG signatures that signal consciousness. These are shown in table 2 (below).

As for Dehaene's third element—a new respect for subjective phenomena—

most psychiatrists would probably say, "About time." Clinicians have depended on patients' reports of their conscious experiences since therapy (or medicine, for that matter) first began—sometimes with excellent results.

The table below details four signatures of consciousness, EEG patterns showing that a person's response to a stimulus is consciously experienced.[3] The researchers have a simple way of determining whether subjects experience stimuli consciously or not: they ask. The resulting EEG tracings are measured by electrodes glued to the scalp.

Table 2: Four EEG Signatures of Consciousness

1. The EEG response becomes amplified and involves many brain regions. Based on the differences between EEG responses to a subliminal stimulus (one that is registered unconsciously) versus a consciously perceived stimulus, researchers have compared the impact of these two events to that of a snowball (the unconscious stimulus) versus an avalanche.

2. The EEG response to stimuli exhibits a wave form with several bumps in it, rather like a row of rolling hills. Only during conscious trials (where the subject is aware of the stimulus) do researchers observe an especially large third hill—the so-called P300, which often starts around 300 milliseconds after the stimulus is presented.

3. During conscious trials, the EEG shows "a massive increase in gamma-band power starting at around 300 milliseconds." During unconscious trials, this fast-frequency wavelength generally fades within 200 milliseconds after the stimulus.

4. When stimuli are consciously registered, there is invariably a "massive synchronization of electromagnetic signals across the cortex." Information that reaches the level of consciousness is judged by the brain to be especially important. It therefore makes sense that different brain regions shout out to one another at the same time.

ANCIENT WISDOM: STATES OF CONSCIOUSNESS

Although most scientists ignored the study of consciousness until the late 1980s, sages from many traditions have contemplated the subject for thousands of years. In general, different states of consciousness have been defined in terms of subjective experiences—for example, feelings of stillness, boundlessness, and bliss. Now scientists are using modern technology, such as EEGs and brain-imaging techniques, to try to understand the physiological underpinnings of these states.

While this book focuses primarily on meditation derived from the Vedic tradition of ancient India, including brain changes that occur in TM practitioners, other forms of meditation have also been associated with measurable brain changes. For example, Sara Lazar, assistant professor of psychology at the Massachusetts General Hospital, and colleagues have measured the thickness of the cerebral cortex in twenty long-term practitioners of Buddhist "insight meditation" and fifteen nonmeditating controls by means of magnetic resonance imaging. They found increased cortical thickness in brain regions associated with attention and other mental faculties central to this form of meditation.[4]

There are also many other studies of brain changes associated with different types of meditation, which deserve consideration but fall outside the scope of this book. Aside from a chapter in which I compare and contrast mindfulness and transcendence (chapter 14) and a few paragraphs at the end of this chapter, I have for the most part left the rich and extensive literature on meditations derived from the Buddhist tradition to those far better qualified to write about them than I am.

I will tell you about the brain changes associated with TM in detail in chapters 5 and 18, and also report on my own experiences of being hooked up to an EEG machine, meditating, and seeing—to my delight—that the predicted alpha waves had rolled off my brain and onto the recording paper.

Despite technical developments, I have to say that in our current state of knowledge, subjective reports remain the most precise way to characterize states of consciousness. Technology has yet to catch up.

Three states of consciousness are self-evident: waking, sleeping, and dreaming—though there can be huge variations even within these separate states (for example, efficient and restful sleep versus broken, disturbed sleep). These states of consciousness are accompanied by specific physiological and brain changes. For example, dreaming is marked by REM sleep, a state in which the body is still except for the eyes, which dart rapidly from side to side. The other sleep stages are accompanied by specific EEG patterns.

Beyond the three ordinary stages of consciousness, other states have been observed by practitioners from different cultures and by scientists alike. The eminent psychologist William James, for example, explicitly recognized such different states without which "no account of the universe in its totality can be final."

The history of expanded consciousness in different cultures has been elegantly reviewed in Craig Pearson's *The Supreme Awakening.* In several cultures there is a recognition that expanded states of consciousness can be classified according to increasing degrees of complexity, refinement, or purity. Here is one colorful example featured in Pearson's book:

> Daoist *literature refers to states known as* High Pure, Most Pure, *and* Jade Pure, *corresponding to different degrees of consciousness development.*[5]

I have alluded here mostly to Eastern traditions, but there are also many Western traditions that incorporate meditative elements into their prayers and spiritual practices. Although I will not detail them here, it would be an omission not to acknowledge them.

In this book I have focused on the expanded states of consciousness that arise through the practice of TM according to Vedic teaching for a few reasons: First, TM is a method that I know personally and through direct observation, and also one that science has shown can reliably induce these states. Second, expanded states of consciousness have been a major focus in the ancient Vedic study of consciousness, which has acknowledged and analyzed them for centuries. Third, I have been fortunate enough to have the present-day cooperation of a large number of TM meditators. They have provided me with both crucial data and excellent stories that support and illuminate the observations on which this book is based. Finally, TM is taught in a standardized and reproducible way throughout the world. This enhances my confidence that the progression of consciousness described by TM practitioners in different parts of the world is in fact the outcome of a shared practice, and therefore likely to represent shared brain mechanisms.

According to Vedic tradition, as transcendental consciousness extends beyond the experience of meditation, it enters the waking state where it unfolds progressively.[6] It is this unfolding of consciousness—along with its accompanying benefits—that we are calling the Super Mind. Although this unfolding occurs progressively over time, it may start surprisingly soon after a person begins to meditate, as we shall see.

Before proceeding further, it may be useful to clarify some differences between TM and popular forms of Buddhist meditation, especially with regard to the development of consciousness, which is our focus here. Certain key elements of three major types of meditation are show below (figure 1).

Figure 1

Category	Focused Attention	Open Monitoring	Automatic Self-Transcending
Vehicle	image or profound emotion	breath, body sensations, thoughts, feelings	mantra
Example	loving kindness	Buddhist-style mindfulness (Vipassana)	Transcendental Meditation
Predominant EEG wavelength (cycles per second)	gamma (20–50)	theta 2 (6–8)	alpha 1 (8–10)

As the above figure shows, modern meditation scholars have classified various forms of meditation into three categories: focused attention, open monitoring, and automatic self-transcending.[7] TM falls into the last category. The other forms of meditation generally involve either focus (for example, on an image, the breath, or a thought) or open monitoring (in which the mind is directed to focus on specific stimuli that arise from the senses, the body, or the brain). These latter techniques (both of which fall under the category of mindfulness) differ from TM, in which a special sound, a "mantra," is used in a systematic manner to slow down and refine mental activity—a more automatic type of process than focusing or open monitoring.

According to meditation expert Chris Germer (a clinical psychologist affiliated with Harvard Medical School), altered states of consciousness (known as the *jhanas*) have been part of Buddhist meditation in the past, but this element has been de-emphasized in the last century. Nevertheless, the *jhanas* continue to be taught and practiced. Leigh Brasington, a Buddhist meditation teacher and author of *Right Concentration: A Practical Guide to the Jhanas*,[8] explained to me that these states of consciousness can be accessed by concentrating on as many as thirty different stimuli, including the breath, mantras, or thoughts of compassion and loving kindness. According to him, however, none of them fully coincides with the state of transcendence as I described it to him.[9]

TO SUMMARIZE WHAT WE HAVE DISCUSSED IN THIS CHAPTER:

- Modern neuroscientists have defined consciousness in such a way that it can be studied experimentally.
- Using scientific methods, especially EEG measurements, four specific "signatures of consciousness" have been defined.
- According to ancient Vedic tradition, there are stages of consciousness beyond the three traditional stages (waking, sleeping, and dreaming), which have been described.
- The science of these "higher states" of consciousness development will be detailed in later chapters.
- Elements of three major forms of meditation are presented.

The next chapter provides an introduction to TM—a simple passageway to transcendent consciousness.

3

TRANSCENDENTAL MEDITATION: THE SECRET PASSAGEWAY

Science isn't about authority or white coats;
it's about following a method.

Ben Goldacre

In the introduction I related a minor anecdote involving a secret passageway in a hospital complex. Once I'd been told about it, I was able to breeze into my office for an early morning session, with no need to climb five flights of stairs.

We learn about such secret passageways from our childhood storybooks. In Lewis Carroll's *Alice* books, for example, the young heroine falls down a rabbit hole and finds a key, or steps through a looking glass, each of which gives her access to an absurd wonderland. More recently, consider the magical transitions in the Harry Potter series, where the students of Hogwarts School of Witchcraft and Wizardry step through a special portal in King's Cross Station—unknown and invisible to ordinary Muggles, who see only a brick wall—to board the Hogwarts Express. It seems to be an enduring part of human fantasies that somehow, by acquiring some special knowledge or ability, we can slip through an ordinary-looking object and pass, as if by magic, into an alternative reality.

I would suggest that the real world is also well populated with secret passageways. It would be an enjoyable exercise to inventory them all, but for now, let us consider just one—the telescope. By turning the telescope toward the heavens and observing the moons of Jupiter, Galileo helped upend the prevailing geocentric theory of the universe, according to which all heavenly bodies were considered to revolve around Earth. By developing a method, a truth was revealed. In a more modest but analogous way, a method is needed to reliably access higher levels of consciousness. The method we are principally exploring here is the technique of Transcendental Meditation.

WHY DO TM IN THE FIRST PLACE?

Before considering how to do anything, it is usually worth asking why one should do it in the first place. Here is a list of potential rewards that I have seen in myself and my clients. In several instances, these observations are supported by published scientific studies, which I look forward to sharing with you in the chapters that follow:

- Better physical health (see chapter 8).
- More efficient cognitive functioning—including creativity (chapter 9).
- Improvement in many personal attributes
- Better interpersonal relationships (chapters 11–13)
- Better performance and greater success professionally and financially (chapter 15)
- Greater happiness and self-actualization (chapter 16)

With these benefits in mind, let us consider what learning TM involves.

THE PRACTICE OF TRANSCENDENTAL MEDITATION

Reduced to its basic elements, TM consists of the following:

1. Learning the technique from a qualified teacher. You start by attending an introductory educational session, answering some basic questions about yourself, and meeting with a teacher on four consecutive days for up to ninety minutes on each occasion.
2. Sit comfortably in a chair twice a day with your eyes closed for twenty minutes each time.
3. Think of the traditional mantra that your TM teacher provides for you, in the prescribed way.

That seems pretty simple, doesn't it? Well, it is and it isn't. Let's look deeper.

WHY DO I NEED TO LEARN FROM A QUALIFIED TEACHER?

Like many practices in which precision is important—such as ballet, playing the piano, or martial arts—TM needs to be taught by a qualified teacher. TM teachers have undergone extensive training and are credentialed to help all different types of people acquire the technique as effortlessly and enjoyably as possible. Some people are surprised at how easily they can learn a technique that can rapidly lead to profound effects. Actress Cameron Diaz, for example, says that TM is not only the easiest form of meditation she has ever learned but the easiest *thing* she has ever learned. But since each person has different life experiences, a different brain, and learns at a different pace, the teaching process will proceed differently, depending on the individual—and some people do not get the hang of it quite so easily as Ms. Diaz did. I fell into that category.

The art of properly teaching this subtle form of meditation has been handed down from teacher to teacher over centuries, and modern teachers continue to take their work seriously. I have regarded it as a privilege to be able to learn and benefit from this technique at the hands of some very fine teachers, and would wish the same for my family, friends, patients, and for you, the reader. So I should make it clear at this point that you will not learn how to practice TM from this book—or any other book.

After talking with the student and providing background information, the teacher assigns the student a special sound or mantra. The mantras, which have no meaning, are ancient and traditional to the practice. Over the centuries they have been found to have soothing, positive (the TM teachers describe them as "life-supporting") qualities that are conducive to transcendence. Once learned, the student's practice is checked several times until both student and teacher are confident that the technique has been properly established. The entire course can be accomplished in the span of four days, and then you're good to get started. Periodic check-ins, however, are strongly recommended to make sure that the technique is working well for you. And certainly if you feel yourself struggling with the technique or not getting the desired results, the student should not hesitate to get back in touch with the teacher.

Sometimes the question about why one needs a teacher, which arises frequently, is a polite way of asking, if the technique is so simple, why should I spend the time and money to learn it?

Yes, the technique is simple and effortless, but for many people, learning it can be—at least initially—complicated and confusing! I myself have been guilty of underestimating its subtlety. A central goal of TM is to help the meditator enter a state of transcendence, the key to the Super Mind. In order to do so, proper technique is necessary, and this is acquired by learning from a trained teacher and then checking in with that teacher periodically until a regular and effective practice is established. I have heard many stories from intelligent and sophisticated people who, despite having learned, were not achieving their desired results. A brief consultation with their TM teacher often revealed the source of difficulty, putting the meditator back on track. Sometimes meditators are pleasantly surprised at how a mere canny suggestion (or two) can make all the difference.

Despite having meditated for seven years, I too have been surprised at how much value I invariably find in having my technique refreshed. A few years ago, I had a wonderful experience in this regard. My son, Josh, and I were visiting South Africa for a family wedding and had occasion to stay in Johannesburg for a few days. I visited the TM center there, which is run by Vicki and Richard Broome. (It was Vicki who had first taught me to meditate some thirty-five years earlier and whom I will mention again in chapter 19 when I discuss sudden, dramatic transcendent experiences.) The TM refresher session that she conducted with Josh and me was deep and powerful. In addition, Vicki emphasized an element that had been glossed over in earlier teachings.

"Take a full three minutes to emerge from your meditation session," she counseled. "It is very important, and do so even if time is short and you have to take that time away from the mantra." That seemed like strange counsel to me. Surely the mantra was key to transcendence—and transcendence was the goal! Although I had heard about people occasionally getting headaches if they emerged too quickly, was the three minutes really necessary? And why did she emphasize it so? Only once I began to think more deeply about the Super Mind did I realize that its development depends in good part upon the carryover of the transcendent state into daily life. By allowing a certain amount of overlap between the transcendent and the ordinary waking state, we may foster the easy mingling of these states and promote the growth of the Super Mind. Yet even knowing this, I too often jump up at the end of a session to get on with my tasks. That brings to mind another important role of the teacher: not only to provide us with new information, but to remind us of things we already "know" but may tend to ignore.

Nowadays it is an occasional treat for me to meditate with my friend and TM mentor Bob Roth. When we meditate together, he goes through a special checking procedure in which he assesses my technique. He has me open and close my eyes, and inquires about my state of mind before we launch into our twenty-minute session. Sometimes he is almost apologetic about going through these steps, as if to say, "You know this all already. I hope you're not offended by my reviewing it with you yet again." I'm never offended. I am always grateful. Small elements of the technique can easily slip away through carelessness or distraction. How good it is to be reminded of them. As we begin to meditate, Bob typically says, "Remember, every meditation is different. Each meditation is a new experience because each time you sit to meditate your body is different—tired, fresh, agitated, calm. So take your experiences in meditation easy and take them as they come."

Bob's instructions remind me of "beginner's mind," an expression that comes from Zen Buddhism. "Beginner's mind" refers to looking at a situation with fresh eyes—like the eyes of a child, unencumbered by memories, expectations, aspirations, or other distractions. In the words of the Zen teacher Shunryu Suzuki, "In the beginner's mind there are many possibilities. In the expert's mind there are few."[1] So, in his instruction, Bob is encouraging me to leave behind the prejudice and expectation that comes with experience. And somehow the meditation that follows when I do is deeper, quieter, and easier than ever.

Let's consider two important words that Bob uses when he reviews my technique.

"EFFORTLESSLY"

How can something that promises to transform be effortless? An image used by many meditators to explain this idea is a sled or toboggan ride. For the experienced sledder, slipping down a gentle slope may require little effort because the basic driving force is gravity. But learning how to make small, moment-by-moment adjustments that will see you successfully down the hill does require attention, and the body needs to be engaged. Once mastered, however, sledding is sheer joy, a seemingly effortless slide—as is the case when you meditate. As one experienced meditator described it, "I just close my eyes and go for a long, smooth luge ride."

It is true, however, that practicing the technique does require a different kind of effort—blocking off time in your schedule and setting aside the many competing claims on your day. Having done so, once you sit down and access the mantra as you have been taught to do, you will enjoy an easy ride to wherever the mantra takes you.

Paradoxically, forcing the mantra ("mantra bashing," as one TM teacher-friend calls it) or pushing yourself to get the technique exactly "right" is often counterproductive. Effortlessness, as you will learn in personal instruction by your TM teacher, is the key to successful transcendence.

"INNOCENTLY"

When Bob first said "innocently" in advising me how to approach my meditation, I thought it a strange word to use in that setting. It did, however, resonate with "beginner's mind" in conveying a sense of purity and freshness. It took me a while to understand the meaning of the word when used in the context of TM. Essentially, it means "without expectation as to the outcome." In this regard, TM differs from most forms of therapy, where a goal is identified and efforts are made to attain it. TM can help people in many different situations (as we will see), but only if it is approached innocently—without expecting anything in particular.

As we sit down to practice TM, there will no doubt be many problems percolating away at different levels of our mind, much unfinished business. As these thoughts mingle with the blissful peace of transcendence, they become less bothersome, disturbing, or problematic. The transcendent state experienced during meditation—along with its settling effects on body and mind—will if repeated regularly move into the person's daily life, which will automatically become easier and more fulfilling. What the word "innocently" signifies to the meditator therefore is that it is not necessary to burden one's session with goals or expectations, because you can trust the process.

WHY DO I HAVE TO MEDITATE FOR TWENTY MINUTES EACH TIME?

This is a trick question. You don't have to meditate at all. Many of us have a skeptical or even an oppositional streak (I say that from both personal and professional experience). Why twenty minutes? I have asked myself. Why not fifteen? Or even ten? The simple answer is that over centuries, the twenty-minute duration has empirically been found to work, not only during meditation itself, but in the intervals between sessions. I have often contemplated with appreciation the intelligence of those who figured out the optimal duration for the basic TM technique—long enough to accomplish its goals but not so long as to disrupt the day of a busy person.

We have a tendency to think arithmetically. For example, we might conclude that fifteen minutes would be three-quarters as good as twenty minutes, therefore no big deal. But this thought could be altogether incorrect, for in my experience it often takes the first five or six minutes of a TM session for my mind and body to settle down. (Of course, I speak for myself here; other meditators often have very different experiences.) Then comes a period of stillness, and only in the last third of the session do I enjoy the full bliss of transcendence. Imagine if I were to clip off the last five minutes of a session. It would be like missing the last quarter of a ball game, play, or concert. I'd be missing the best part, which would hardly yield three-quarters of the enjoyment.

Many others have reported a similar need and appreciation for the entire duration of the session. Consider, for example, the comment of movie director Martin Scorsese with regard to his longtime TM practice: "It creates a sense of order, of priority as to what we really should be thinking about . . . finally, in the last six minutes or so, there is a kind of peacefulness that I don't think I've ever achieved before."

But what if it's absolutely impossible to devote twenty minutes to a session? The answer is, of course, to do the best you can. Any amount of meditation is better than none at all.

WHY IS IT IMPORTANT TO MEDITATE TWICE A DAY?

"Why not once a day?" my patients often ask. Of course, that's better than no meditation at all, I concede, but I also echo the sentiments of many experienced teachers who agree that meditating once a day is less than half as good as meditating twice a day. It's almost as though the effects of morning meditation (which is usually the easier of the two to accommodate) wear off by late afternoon. Also, results from our survey of TM practitioners support the value of more frequent meditation in promoting the development of the Super Mind (see chapter 7).

Famous comedian Jerry Seinfeld has practiced TM for forty-one years, and has derived great benefit from it. As he puts it, "I've explored a lot of different things and gotten a lot from all of them, but nothing compares to what TM has done for me . . . especially lately." Seinfeld went on to say that for the first forty years of his TM practice, "I would just do one in the afternoon . . . and that was a very sustaining thing in my life."

"I immediately stopped doing the one in the morning. Couldn't understand why you needed to get out of bed and rest," the comedian observed. Then he met with Bob Roth, who suggested that Seinfeld add a second session in the morning. He did, and according to Seinfeld it has changed his life.

I have interviewed Bob Roth for this book about several aspects of TM and the Super Mind, and those of you who are interested in our conversation can find my questions and Bob's answers in appendix 1 at the end of this book.

Often it is the afternoon TM session that falls victim to the pressures and commitments that pile up as the day proceeds. I remember one occasion when I was visiting a TM teacher on the West Coast of the United States. He and his partner and I had been traveling that day, and we arrived at his home a few hours before dinner. His partner, a delightful woman and a retired pediatric surgeon, was bustling about, taking care of chores, when she turned to me and said, "At the end of the afternoon there are always so many things that seem urgent that I feel inclined to put off my meditation. But what I've realized is that if I meditate first, everything gets done more easily." Her words have returned to me many times, especially as my patients tell me how difficult it is to squeeze in their afternoon session, and I pass on her good advice. I have learned never to miss my afternoon session if at all possible. I feel as though the second session gives me a whole new start on the day, so that I stay fresh and clearheaded throughout the evening. Moreover, by logging in the second session, I maintain the regularity of my practice and reap the benefits of the Super Mind.

Another perspective on the benefits of twice-daily sessions was offered by Elaine, an old friend and fellow meditator (you will meet her again in chapter 17). "It feels like there is much more energy to my meditation when I do it twice a day," she said. "I just can't wait for my next meditation. It's the way I used to feel about sex when I was younger." I could hear the giggle in her voice, and we both laughed long and hard.

CONCLUDING WORDS

According to the classic Sanskrit text the *Bhagavad Gita*, "You have control over action alone, never over its fruits."[2] What this means for our present discussion is that if your actions are practiced and correct, the desired results are more likely to follow. Specifically, if you meditate in the right way, for the right amount of time and with the right frequency, that is all you can control. But in most cases that is enough to enable you to reap the fruits of expanding consciousness—fruits that can sustain you for a lifetime.

4

TRANSCENDENCE: BEYOND WAKING, SLEEPING, AND DREAMING

Become totally empty
Quiet the restlessness of the mind
Only then will you witness everything
unfolding from emptiness
See all things flourish and dance
in endless variation
And once again merge back into perfect
emptiness—

Lao-Tzu[1]

Consciousness has been compared to the ocean—vast and deep, almost boundless. According to this analogy, the ordinary waking state is like the surface of the ocean, which may be joyful and lively, as when sunlight sparkles off the ever-moving waves. But the sea's surface can also be menacing, roiling with breakers, powerful and dangerous. So it is with our waking state and all its moods and contemplations, hopes and fears, triumphs and disasters. It varies! And of course, when we sit down to meditate, wherever we are is always the point at which we begin—our waking state, whatever it happens to be on that particular day, at that particular moment.

So now it is time to meditate, and we sit down comfortably and prepare to take time away from the ocean's surface with all its turmoil. We think our mantra as we have been taught to do, and like a diving bell, the mantra takes us deeper and deeper into our innermost self—at depths to which we may never have given much thought. Down there it is utterly still, and the agitations of daily life are transient. Both body and mind can rest in a special way—different from sleep or other types of rest. Such is the state we call transcendence, the fourth state of consciousness.

When you emerge from this state, you may feel rested in a particular way—one that not only energizes you, but also helps you organize your priorities and focus with renewed enthusiasm.

For those of you who have meditated, these descriptions probably strike a resonant chord. For those who have not, imagine: One minute you are sitting on a chair or couch, and the next minute . . . peace and quiet. Your mind feels perfectly settled and all encompassing, suffused with joy and indifferent to sorrow—all at the same time. That's how it was for me when I first experienced transcendence. It was a state both thrilling in its novelty yet strangely familiar. In retrospect, I should not have been surprised, since the state we access during TM is simply a deep part of ourselves. Perhaps we have seen flashes of it from time to time, or fallen into it accidentally for brief spells. We may not have identified it or given it a name, but once we reexperience it, it is easy to recognize.

As you can imagine, while we are experiencing these profound psychological changes, major shifts are taking place in both brain and body. I am glad to report that we have a good deal of information about these changes— so much so that I have devoted the entire next chapter to discussing them. At this point, however, I wish simply to remind you that everything we experience at the level of the mind is supported by corresponding changes in the circuits of the brain and the workings of the body. With the expected arrival of new imaging techniques and other technological advances, along with more powerful computer systems to analyze the data, we can look forward to exponential growth in neuroscience—including our understanding of meditation. These are exciting times for those of us intrigued by the development of consciousness.

What, then, are the usual elements of transcendence? That was the question I asked a group of students, at Loyola University's Stritch School of Medicine in Chicago, who had learned to meditate. They replied with gusto: stillness, quiet, no boundaries, no thoughts, and bliss. In short, they captured the essential spirit of the state.

Maharishi explained how easy it is to enter transcendence: "To go to a field of greater happiness is the natural tendency of the mind," he wrote. "[T]he mind finds that the way is increasingly attractive as it advances in the direction of bliss." All that was needed to accomplish this goal, he taught, was the regular practice of TM.[2]

As I mentioned in chapter 2, there are many different types of meditation, each of which asks the meditator to do something different, which appears to have different effects on the brain (more about that in the next chapter). Briefly, the three main categories of meditation are focused attention, open monitoring, and automatic self-transcending (see figure 1 on page 19). In "focusing" types of meditation, the meditator directs attention to a specific target, such as a thought, image, or feeling. Loving-kindness meditation is a well-known member of this group. In open monitoring, the meditator directs awareness to whatever is happening in the mind or body, often starting with the breath. TM falls into the third category, automatic self-transcending. "Focusing" does not accurately describe the TM technique. Rather, it is an automatic way of transcending.

With regard to the central role of transcendence, TM differs from most other forms of meditation, which de-emphasize its importance. Nevertheless, the transcendent state is familiar to meditators of many, if not all, cultures. The quote at the top of this chapter, for example, beautifully describes the experience, yet it comes, not from the Vedic tradition, the source and fountainhead from which TM arose, but rather from Taoism—illustrating the universality of this state of consciousness.

As we meditate, both mind and body are effortlessly involved in the process, changing as we move from the waking to the transcendent state. The changes in these two realms are intimately intertwined. For the sake of clarity, I will deal with the changes in body and mind separately in the paragraphs that follow. Please remember, though, that they are happening simultaneously and influencing one another. You might think of them as dancing together.

THE BODY DURING TRANSCENDENCE

One of the first changes to appear in the body during transcendence is that breathing slows down. This slow breathing during meditation is very familiar to me personally. Sometimes while meditating, I wonder how I am getting enough oxygen—but of course it is not a real concern. Maybe we need less oxygen when we meditate because our metabolism slows down—though I know of no good research to support this notion. Of possible relevance: I've noticed that I need to cover my shoulders during meditation so as not to feel cold (which might result from a slowed metabolism), and other meditators have reported a similar need for a shawl or blanket.

Besides slower breathing, there may be other idiosyncratic changes in breathing during meditation. In my case, for example, as I am about to enter transcendence, I often start yawning in great gulps—almost as though I just then realize how tired I am and how welcome the approaching rest will be. Just as people differ in how they fall asleep or wake up, so they differ in how they enter transcendence. And they differ in the physical changes that may occur during transcendence.

If you tune in to your body as you meditate, you may feel your muscles relaxing as your body molds into the chair or couch. This relaxation may be accompanied by relief of any pain due to muscle tension anywhere in the body. Indeed, pains of every kind may ease during meditation—abdominal pains, headaches (even migraines), and sore feet may all improve so much that sometimes, once the session is over, no trace of pain remains.

As I marvel at the far-reaching physical changes that may occur during transcendence, I need to remind myself that TM influences the sympathetic nervous system, a widespread meshwork of nerves that ramifies throughout the body and affects every organ. For example, in my own case, my sinuses regularly become unblocked during a TM session. Perhaps you will also observe some unexpected but welcome physical changes as you meditate.

THE MIND DURING TRANSCENDENCE

Before I go on to describe different ways that people may feel while they are meditating—and even in a transcendent state—I need to emphasize one thing: the quality of your transcendent experiences during meditation may have no bearing whatsoever on how much benefit you get from your regular TM practice.

This is hard to believe because it is natural to think that exotic and esoteric experiences will do you the most good—but there is no evidence to that effect. I remember being quite discouraged because I didn't have such experiences until a TM teacher-friend reassured me and encouraged me to keep meditating. In time I would harvest the fruits, she assured me—and she was right.

Here are a few famous examples of people who report a similar disconnect between their banal experiences during TM and the dramatic results of their practice.

Artist Mindy Weisel credits TM with transforming her from a state of exhaustion and hopelessness into a happy, fulfilled woman. In addition, she believes that TM changed the direction of her artistic career. Before learning to meditate, she had for years been a painter. Within a few years of beginning regular TM, however, she shifted to working in glass and has since become famous for her glass sculptures.

When I asked her about her experiences *during* meditation, however, she replied that mostly she has no thoughts at all, just a sense of openness and space, and a nice feeling that seems to be centered around the front of her head.

Let me close this particular point with a few words from Jerry Seinfeld, whose long experience with meditation (forty-one years as of 2015, and counting) has by his own account changed his life. Yet, here's what he has to say about his meditative experience during his morning TM sessions:

> I'll do the TM before anybody gets up and how does it feel? It doesn't feel like anything. It doesn't do anything. I don't get it. I don't understand it. But here's the difference: At 1:00 p.m. that day, my head does not hit the desk like it used to.

Here we see in the concise, punchy style of a brilliant comedian the powerful effect TM has on his day *despite* how uneventful the sessions themselves feel.

What's going on in the mind while the body is so busy relaxing? First, not all mental changes are transcendent. Ordinary thoughts come and go, as naturally happens when you close the eyes. You're sitting at rest for what may be the first break you're taking all day, and that feels good in its own right. But then the mantra comes, as you have been taught to access it, in a way that may be different each time you meditate.

Now that we have these important points out of the way, let me turn to my friend, colleague, and veteran TM teacher Bob Roth, who explains how the brain works with the mantra in this way: "The mind, by nature, doesn't like to do 'nothing.' The mind likes to think, imagine, visualize, plan. Thinking the mantra engages the mind. And because the mantra has no meaning, the discriminating intellect doesn't have to get involved. And because it is a soothing, life-supporting sound, and you are taught in personal instruction how to use it properly, you are able to effortlessly, naturally, and quite spontaneously access deeper, more abstract, intuitive levels of the mind that are rarely available in the ordinary waking state."

For a while thoughts and mantra may travel side by side, then perhaps just the mantra and then . . . transcendence. You have gone through the looking glass and entered the fourth state of consciousness. It is quiet there. Still. Peaceful. Thoughts may still come and go but sooner or later . . . silence . . . all thoughts have gone. How strange it is to be alert and peaceful at the same time—so alert, in fact, that you could hear a pin drop. Yet in the place where thoughts usually reside—nothing. That's why this state has been called "pure consciousness," because you are conscious in a way that Thoreau has compared to "a still lake of purest crystal," where "without an effort our depths are revealed to ourselves."

Usually, when we think about something, we engage in a process called "duality," in which the person thinking and the thought itself seem like two separate entities. Even when we are thinking about ourselves, duality applies insofar as the mind and that aspect of the self that is the focus of reflection are experienced as two separate entities. In pure consciousness, however, no such division occurs.

The philosopher Martin Buber divided relationships into "I-Thou" and "I-It," referring to profound interpersonal relationships and impersonal ones, respectively. When you transcend, I, thou, and it all blend. There is a feeling of "oneness." As I write about these experiences, I am aware that some people might imagine a sense of loss associated with such oneness, or nonduality. Where is the thou? Where is the it? Won't I feel lonely? You might think so. Yet in conducting many interviews with people who have experienced transcendence, I have never encountered this as an issue.

Once in a while, some people feel minor anxiety on first meditating, perhaps due to the newness of the experience. If that should happen, checking in with your TM teacher usually resolves the matter within a few minutes. For most people, however, the sense of oneness is blissful and relaxing. One's sense of self dissolves into a pleasant emptiness, which eventually fills up again with vibrant thoughts, feelings, and all the bric-a-brac of mental life, as described in the quote from the *Tao Te Ching* at the head of this chapter.

Just as our thoughts come and go, so (at times) do other boundaries, such as our sense of time and space. One person told me that he once lost all sense of his hands, which were propping him up as he sat on the floor, yet had no fear of falling. The sense of time disappearing is also curious. Is it Wednesday or Thursday? How long have I been here? In transcendence, the familiar anchors of time may vanish. Yet somehow the brain seems to have its own alarm clock that tells people when twenty minutes is up. It's not infallible, of course, and if you have an important engagement, you may want to use a meditation app that gives a single faint chime after twenty minutes and then shuts off—unlike an alarm that has to be turned off manually.

One property of transcendence that the Loyola students nailed is the feeling of bliss. It's an unusual word, "bliss," not one we use much in everyday life, perhaps because it has an otherworldly quality. Beyond the components of joy and happiness, for which there are many other words, "bliss" also conveys a sense of serenity and peacefulness. I don't know any other single word that captures all these elements, which together typify the state of transcendence.

A few people dive into transcendence the very first time they learn to meditate (see more about this below), but for most others the state comes more slowly. I fell into the second category, and it was several weeks before I even realized I was transcending. This is an important point to note, because the joys of transcendence are often the reinforcement you need to keep on meditating, especially in the early days. Absent such reinforcement, it is easy to give up, thereby missing out on everything TM has to offer. Here is another place where the input of a good TM teacher can make a crucial difference. Sometimes a small correction in technique can hasten the progression; at other times simple encouragement to persevere is all that's needed. One of my patients, a woman in her sixties, insisted that she was unable to meditate. "I can't even sit still," she said. After some encouragement and simple tweaking of the mechanics, however, she now meditates regularly with her husband and loves it.

The descriptions of transcendence that we've encountered—stillness, peace, unity, bliss—capture many of the standard aspects of the fourth state of consciousness, but there are many exceptions. For example, some people report going into a state where awareness of any sort disappears—until consciousness returns—when, lo and behold! twenty minutes have passed. I know that sounds pretty much like a nap, but having experienced such transcendent states myself, I can say that when I emerge, I do not feel as if I have taken a nap. Although I cannot swear no z's slipped in, I am clearheaded in a non-postnap way, wide awake, and ready to get on with the day. Others have reported similar experiences.

Then there are those who have spectacular transcendent experiences—with the caveat mentioned above, which is important enough for me to repeat: Dramatic experiences are by no means necessary for obtaining the benefits of transcendence. Actually, Bob Roth tells me that many people rarely have experiences that can be readily identified as clear transcendence yet love their meditation practice because it produces such powerful and positive benefits in their lives. The experience of clear transcendence most often comes from twice-a-day regular meditation practice. Although transcendence can start with the first meditation—going beyond agitated thinking to calmer levels of the mind—the clarity and richness of the experience grows over time.

Keep these thoughts in mind as you listen to vivid pyrotechnic descriptions, especially if all *you* may experience is stillness, quiet, bliss, and pure consciousness—which is what happens mostly for me (and which is really quite a lot, when you think of it). It has taken me years, in fact, to fully accept the value of this less spectacular form of transcendence, but now I do finally believe that its benefits are just as profound as some of the experiences you will read about below.

Even so, I must confess that a lingering trace of transcendence envy can crop up. Recently, that occurred when I was visiting with my friend Richard Friedman, a professor of psychiatry at Weill Cornell Medical College and a regular columnist for the *New York Times*. He was telling me about the copper-colored light that infuses his inner space as he practices TM. "I also see phosphenes," he said, referring to dots of light (such as you might see when gently pressing the closed eyelids). My first instinct was to ask, "Why don't I see phosphenes?" But then I reminded myself of how I have changed since I began to meditate—even in the absence of dazzling visuals—and envy turned to gratitude.

One famous example of a spectacular transcendent experience is described by iconic filmmaker and veteran meditator David Lynch, in his book *Catching the Big Fish*.[3] According to him, the very first time he meditated, it felt as though the cable of an elevator in which he was riding had been severed. It was as though he literally fell into a pool of bliss. Some people reading that ecstatic description have felt inadequate in never having had such a thrilling experience during meditation, no less on their very first attempt. As you can see from the above discussion, however, such feelings of inadequacy are unwarranted.

Now that I have issued all these caveats, let's have some fun: here come some colorful descriptions of what transcendence is like for diverse meditators, drawn from responses to the Consciousness Integration Questionnaire (see chapter 7).

It is like a waking dream, an altered state where the mind feels like it is suspended midway in a "flotation tank of consciousness."

fifty-two-year-old man from Johannesburg

It is as though I have put on noise-canceling earphones. I can hear my heart beat in my ears. I am aware only of whiteness surrounding me.

sixty-seven-year-old man from Florida

My senses are ignited. The air is more fragrant. I'm filled with a connectedness with everything around me, living or inanimate. I am overwhelmed with a sense of joy and meaning at being alive.

sixty-three-year-old woman from Maryland

Artists, in particular, seem to have especially vivid transcendent experiences. Here is a description by one of my patients, Moira, a woman in her early sixties.

As I am transcending, I often feel as though vibrant color is washing over me again and again. At other times I feel a sort of pulsating aurora borealis. I describe it that way because the hues are vivid with no hard edges and it moves upwards, filling me with beautiful color. When I have fully transcended, I don't remember too much. Sometimes ideas for my current paintings drift in and out, but mostly I experience a wonderful, restful feeling.

Moira has experienced remarkable changes in the quality of her painting and her life after just eighteen months of meditation. She has realized that she is more interested in representing color than form and has, therefore, simplified the design of her paintings to reflect this new emphasis. Moira has shown me pictures of these recent paintings, and they are indeed spectacular. In parallel with these developments in painting style have come changes in her lifestyle, which she has also simplified so as to emphasize her priorities—a shift she finds more fulfilling the more she continues to reshape her life.

It could be tempting to conclude that the beneficial effects on Moira's art and life are directly related to her dramatic experiences while transcending. Recall, however, the similar transformational effects on artist Mindy Weisel—both personally and in her work—even though her experiences during meditation sound quite ordinary. These anecdotal observations are consistent with brain-wave studies in which the EEG changes seen in meditators bear no relation to how dramatic their transcendent experiences are.

So if *your* experiences during meditation are more like Mindy's than Moira's, don't despair. There is no evidence that spectacular transcendent experiences will advance the development of consciousness—the growth of the Super Mind—any better than less dramatic ones. My own transcendent experiences and those of most of my patients are pleasant but unsensational. What *is* sensational, however, are the effects of those TM sessions—the emergence and growth of the Super Mind. Let me leave the last word on the subject to Maharishi. Someone once asked him if a deeper meditation is better than one that seems more on the surface. Maharishi replied that both are good. When asked why, he said, "Because even in a shallow dive we get wet."

At this point, let us summarize what we have learned so far about the changes in body and mind during a TM session:

- During transcendental consciousness the meditator may experience stillness, quiet, no specific thoughts, disappearance of boundaries (of time and space), and bliss.
- Breathing slows down, muscles relax, and any pain that is present may diminish.
- The actual content of thoughts and experiences during the session is highly variable, but there is no clear association between these thoughts and experiences and the emergence and growth of the Super Mind.

In the following chapter, we will investigate what we know scientifically about the physical and mental changes that underlie the experiences we have during TM sessions in general and during transcendence.

5

THE PHYSIOLOGY OF
TRANSCENDENCE

I shall consider human actions and desires . . .
as though I were concerned with lines, planes,
and solids.

Baruch Spinoza

In the last chapter, we considered the subjective experience of transcendence. The key question I will address in this chapter is, while a person is meditating, what changes can we measure in body and brain that might explain the quiet bliss of transcendence?

At this point, I should probably be explicit that—like most psychiatrists and neuroscientists—I regard mind and the brain as two aspects of the same set of phenomena. Whenever we feel, think, or act, specific neural circuits fire accordingly. We register phenomena of the mind as experiences originating either from within or from the world around us. We measure phenomena of the brain with specific instruments. We use different languages as we shuttle between the two domains of mind and brain, but all the while we understand that they represent one and the same entity.

Because people spend most of their lives experiencing themselves in the framework of the mind—thoughts, feelings, memories, and desires—it is these mind elements that cohere to create a sense of self. Every now and then, though, people become aware that there is a brain operating in parallel with the mind—for example, when you have an EEG or, more commonly, when something goes wrong with your brain and you realize that your sense of self is rooted in neurons, synapses, and circuits. With that in mind, let us examine what we know about the effects of TM on the body, brain, and mind.

LET'S START WITH THE BODY

The German philosopher Friedrich Nietzsche emphasized the wisdom of the body in helping us understand ourselves. William James, known to many as the father of psychology, would have agreed. In his famous essay "What Is an Emotion?" he postulated that when we see a bear in the woods, we run first!—and only then does fear follow. According to him, we are afraid because we run rather than the other way around. As you can imagine, there has been endless debate on this subject, which continues to this day. For present purposes, let us simply agree that measuring changes in the body during meditation may advance our understanding of *both* the physiological and psychological changes that result from the practice.

Besides the remarkable slowing and irregularity of the breath, the most noteworthy physical changes have emerged from measurements of electrical current conducted across the surface of the skin—the so-called galvanic skin response (GSR). The GSR is a sensitive measure of nervous system arousal that increases when a person is tense, anxious, or excited. It is a key measure employed in a polygraph or lie detector. A person afraid of being caught in a lie is likely to feel a spike of anxiety when a sensitive question is posed, and the GSR bounces up accordingly. Of course, the GSR could bounce up for other reasons, and the accuracy of lie detectors has been challenged.

You may wonder why the surface of the skin would be a good place to determine if someone is lying. Well, even though we generally consider sweating as a bimodal bodily function—that is, we're either drenched with sweat or bone dry—in fact the sweat glands on the skin's surface are very finely calibrated to our emotions. When our anxiety level rises even slightly, sweating increases enough to boost the current between two electrodes on the skin (part of the GSR apparatus) and register an upward blip. When we relax, the opposite occurs. In other words, changes in GSR current result from tiny moment-to-moment variations in sweating.

We might therefore expect that when a person meditates and transcends, the overall GSR drops. Oddly, however, just before people enter transcendence there is a clear *uptick* in the GSR. When Fred Travis (a preeminent EEG researcher, whom we will meet again soon) first noticed this paradoxical uptick, he wondered whether there was something wrong with his equipment. He repeated his studies and checked the machinery, but sure enough there it was again—a GSR increase just before a person settles into transcendence.[1]

Upon reflection, Travis's paradoxical finding (increased GSR at the start of a TM session) is not as strange as it may seem. In a parallel way, levels of wakefulness have been found to increase just before bedtime. It's as though the body and brain have evolved to get active and make sure your place of slumber is safe before you let yourself sleep. I often wonder whether something similar is happening as I watch dogs drawing sharp circles in the carpet before they nap. It's as though they are enacting an ancient ritual of digging a safe place where they can settle into the profound canine slumber that is the envy of many a human being.

PROLACTIN: A HORMONE TO TRANSCEND BY

Before we go on to what happens to the brain during transcendence, one other observation is worth mentioning—after meditation there is a rise in blood levels of the hormone prolactin. Prolactin is secreted by the pituitary gland, a structure located at the base of the brain. The hormone has many functions, but of particular interest here is its capacity to induce a state of calm alertness, like what people feel as they enter transcendence.

Thomas Wehr, a psychiatrist and close friend since our time together at the National Institute of Mental Health, observed similar increases in prolactin levels when people were asked to lie in the dark for extended periods, spending the night as our ancestors did before the development of electric lights.[2] Under those circumstances, people experienced sleep not as one unbroken block (as we do in modern life), but as two separate blocks.[3] Between the first and second sleep period, Wehr's subjects lay in a state of calm attentiveness, which a few described as "crystal-clear consciousness." This phrase recalls descriptions of transcendence arising both during TM and in the course of day-to-day living.

What is the function of this calming hormone? Although we certainly don't have a complete answer, we do know that prolactin levels rise in nursing mothers and brooding chickens—both situations in which it is important to remain stationary and calm. There are also human data that suggest prolactin may offer psychological benefits—such as the calmness and clarity of thinking that some of Wehr's study participants reported.

THE BRAIN DURING TRANSCENDENCE

While changes take place in the body during TM sessions, especially during transcendence—slowing down of the breath, relaxation of the muscles, decreased GSR, and increased prolactin—what is happening in the brain? EEG recordings show an increase in the concentration of alpha waves, a slow wave form associated with calm self-reflection. The increased density of alpha waves during transcendence is most prominent in the prefrontal area of the cortex—that part of the brain just behind the forehead,[4] which is known to be important in regulating impulses and promoting good judgment. In the well-functioning brain, the prefrontal cortex operates smoothly in harmony with other brain centers. Indeed, given its central role in the brain's executive functions, the prefrontal cortex has often been called the CEO of the brain. By soothing the prefrontal cortex over time, the powerful fluxes of alpha rhythms may strengthen this important brain structure. We will return to this idea when we consider what happens when transcendent experiences—initially present only *during* TM sessions—begin to pervade a person's daily life.

In a recent imaging study, sixteen experienced TM practitioners were compared with sixteen control subjects using blood-oxygen-level-dependent magnetic resonance. While meditating, the meditators showed increased blood flow to portions of the prefrontal cortex (and elsewhere in the brain), a result consistent with the idea that TM strengthens this executive part of the brain.[5]

Another concept I'd like to introduce here is EEG coherence, which refers to the relationship between EEG patterns in different regions of the brain. The more that brain-wave patterns in different brain regions correlate with one another, the higher the level of coherence. During TM sessions, EEG coherence increases in the alpha range, especially in the prefrontal cortex. Studies in Norway conducted by Harald Harung (at the time, associate professor at Oslo University College) and Fred Travis have found that in both business[6] and athletics,[7] more accomplished individuals showed higher levels of EEG coherence in the frontal regions across several wavelengths.[8] In other words, this increased coherence was found when subjects had their eyes open and were performing tasks. Similar EEG findings occur during the waking state (with eyes open) in those who meditate consistently over time (as we will see in chapter 18).

In summary, the brain changes seen during meditation, in particular during transcendence, fall into two broad categories. First, there are body and brain changes that reflect deep relaxation. Such changes may be the basis of the stress relief that meditators experience, which may begin within days of the first meditation session. This relief then builds in impact over years and probably accounts for the cardiovascular and other health benefits of TM. Second, there are changes in brain rhythms that occur during meditation—notably an increase in alpha-rhythm density in the prefrontal cortex and greater levels of alpha coherence throughout the cortex. These brain-wave changes may explain (at least in part) the many ways in which the brain appears to function better in those who regularly practice TM.

OFF TO SEE THE WIZARD

As I contemplated writing this book, it was clear to me that I would need to pay a visit to the laboratory of Fred Travis at Maharishi University of Management—the wizard in the title of this section, whose GSR research we have already considered. It is fair to say that nobody in the world knows more about the relationship between EEG patterns and Transcendental Meditation. I arrived at Fred's lab, which is housed in—of all things—a yellow-brick building. Fred had just arrived by bicycle and greeted me with his characteristic smile, more impish than wizard-like. He was casually dressed and wearing sandals, and his bicycle helmet was still in place, with bushy hair bursting out on both sides of it. He showed me into his lab and introduced me to his assistant, nicknamed Neo—a character from the movie *The Matrix*—all of which contributed to an exciting sense that I was entering an alternate universe.

Fred left me with Neo, who attached electrodes to various places on my skull and hooked them up to an EEG monitor. First, he asked me to perform a set of computerized tasks while he recorded my EEG responses. Then he had me close my eyes and meditate for ten minutes. In this segment, I was to press a button when I was completely lost in thought before coming back to the mantra. This allowed me to mark specific experiences during the meditation practice.

During that TM session, I had what was for me a unique experience. I felt suffused by light—as though I could see the light of the room shining brightly despite having my eyes closed. After the test was over, I became skeptical of the experience, quizzing myself as to whether I was fabricating it in order to produce a better story for the book. I smiled, however, to think of what a poor job I had done had I intended to be theatrical. How much better,

I thought, if the lights had been colored, vivid, flashing, sinuous! But, no, they looked like ordinary fluorescent office lights.

When I reported my experience and the train of thoughts that followed, Fred responded in a matter-of-fact way: "If you saw light, you saw light," he said, and had no further questions. On reflection, I understand why he was uninterested in the exact phenomena of my transcendent experience. As I pointed out earlier, there is little or no correlation between people's sensory illusions during transcendence and the changes TM will produce in their lives.

After completing Fred's research protocol, I looked over my data with Neo and found that my EEG response to meditation was exactly what it was supposed to be: During TM, alpha rhythms predominated in the frontal areas of my brain, and there was an increase in alpha coherence. As expected, of course—but nonetheless I was pleased. I have done and seen many studies in which the data don't turn out as predicted, so when they do, it is always a happy event.

THE ALPHA, BETA, AND GAMMA OF EEG RHYTHMS

Now may be as good a time as any to tell you a bit about different brain rhythms and their corresponding states of awareness. The correspondences are not rigid, however. Few things in nature are. EEG rhythms may vary across different brain regions at any particular time. So when we say a certain rhythm is associated with a certain state, we do not mean a perfect correspondence. Instead, we are referring to a preponderance of a certain type of rhythm in the majority of people studied.

During my visit to Fred Travis's lab, I had the treat of a private lecture on brain waves by a world-class electrophysiologist. In table 3 (below), I'm delighted to share with you what I learned from him about different brain rhythms and the states of awareness and subjective experiences with which they are most often associated.

The pairings of EEG rhythms with the subjective states shown in this table tell only a fragmentary story, as there are many other subjective states not covered here (such as anxiety, ecstasy, and dissociation, to name just a few). Also, EEG rhythms may be shared by different subjective states.

As the table shows, the alpha rhythm is divided into two bands: alpha 1 or "paradoxical alpha," is associated with TM, whereas alpha 2 is seen when a

Table 3

NAME OF RHYTHM	WAVELENGTH (CYCLES PER SECOND)	SUBJECTIVE STATE
delta	0–4	sleep (deep sleep mostly)
theta 1	4–6	drowsiness/dreaming
theta 2	6–8	internal mental processes, open monitoring
alpha 1	8–10	TM (paradoxical alpha)
alpha 2	10–12	eyes-closed rest
beta	16–20	attending
gamma	20–50	focused attention

person is at rest with eyes closed. Because both types of alpha occur during resting states, you might expect that both would be associated with decreased brain metabolism. Such a drop, however, occurs only when alpha 2 predominates. When alpha 1 predominates, as occurs during TM, brain metabolism actually increases—hence the term "paradoxical alpha." This paradoxical state may reflect the mixed experience so common during TM, in which active thoughts and quiet transcendence may occur at various times—or even simultaneously—during a single session.

Different forms of meditation are characterized by different predominant brain-wave patterns, as one might expect (see table 3 above). After all, each one requires a different type of task. Loving-kindness meditation, for example, is predominantly associated with higher levels of gamma waves, a fast frequency associated with active attention—as expected, given that the meditator concentrates on sending messages of loving kindness toward self and others. Loving-kindness meditation, which derives from the Buddhist tradition, falls into the broad category of focused-attention meditation. In other examples of this type, attention might focus on a mental image—such as a flower, a flame, or a point of light between the eyebrows.

In open-monitoring meditation, people predominantly show increased theta 2 waves in the frontal part of their brains. This makes sense: it reflects the internal processing required to pay close attention to internal experiences—such as the breath—that are central to this form of meditation. Open monitoring and focused attention are often considered to be forms of mindfulness meditation.

The different brain-wave signatures associated with each type of meditation are just one of several elements that distinguish one type from another, and that suggest they are not interchangeable in their effects upon particular people.

LET'S SUMMARIZE WHAT SCIENCE CAN TELL US ABOUT CHANGES IN THE BODY AND BRAIN DURING TM:

- There is an increase in levels of the soothing hormone prolactin in the bloodstream.
- EEG studies show (1) an increase in alpha 1 power in the frontal parts of the brain, and (2) an increase in alpha coherence in the prefrontal cortex.
- There is an increase in blood flow in the prefrontal cortex and elsewhere in the brain.

Just as there are specific EEG changes associated with transcendence, so there are with Cosmic Consciousness—the continuous experience of the Super Mind—which I will discuss in chapter 18. For now, however, let's examine the development of the Super Mind in greater depth.

6

FROM TRANSCENDENCE TO SUPER MIND: AN EXTRAORDINARY TRANSFORMATION

The key to growth is the introduction of
higher dimensions of consciousness.

Lao-Tzu

Over the years that I have meditated, changes have occurred in me that were so subtle that often I couldn't detect them at all—though I did, of course, notice that everyday stresses seemed to bother me less. If someone offended me or was rude, instead of having it out—as I might have done in the past—I instinctively adopted an attitude that the matter could wait till the next day, and in most cases by then the issue didn't seem worth pursuing. People were nicer to me and everything came more easily. But all that felt like no big deal. It took the observations of others—family, friends, and colleagues—to show me how dramatically I had changed.

Before going any further, I feel obliged to say that I have hardly reached some lofty summit of enlightenment. Like everyone else, I'm a work in progress. However, unbeknownst to me, I've made significant gains along the axis of happiness and self-fulfillment. Over time it became clear to me that I meditate for much more than simply stress relief. I meditate also to sustain and advance the changes I have learned to associate with the Super Mind.

I had been encouraging many of my patients to meditate—and a fair proportion followed through with good results. At times we would discuss their meditation experiences during sessions, and I saw in them, as in myself, changes that went beyond relief of stress. Instead, they were more like the progress I was used to seeing from psychotherapy—a growth in what therapists call "ego strengths," by which they mean positive personality attributes. It became apparent that TM was not merely relaxing my patients but also helping them change for the better. Curiously, it was in discussing their experiences of transcendence that I first became aware of mirroring the states they were describing. Specifically, I would begin to slip into a transcendent state during our discussions—a sort of silence during wakefulness. There I was, actively engaged in listening, thinking about what my patient was saying, offering responses when appropriate, but at the same time experiencing stillness. This was, I realized one day, the beginning of my personal awareness of transcendence and wakefulness mingling together *outside of a TM session*—my first awareness of the dawning Super Mind—and an enormous excitement came over me at the experience of this new state of consciousness.

The joy I felt then—and now as I write about it—reminds me of that novel state of feverish bliss mixed with quiet confidence that I experienced when I first became aware of transcending *during* meditation. Allow me to repeat how I described that feeling in *Transcendence*.

> It was a threshold experience, much like the ecstatic day when I realized I could swim, that I could actually take my feet off the bottom of the shallow end and paddle around without sinking; or when I realized—this was before the era of training wheels—that I had pedaled half a block with no one holding on to the bike. In all these cases I needed to persevere before I saw any payoff.

And so it was with the first experience of the Super Mind: I had that same feeling of ecstatic discovery—in the sense, of course, that one might "discover" any natural wonder or work of genius on experiencing it for the first time. Keats expressed that inner state beautifully in his poem "On First Looking into Chapman's Homer."

> Then felt I like some watcher of the skies
> When a new planet swims into his ken;
> Or like stout Cortez when with eagle eyes
>
> He star'd at the Pacific—and all his men
> Look'd at each other with a wild surmise—
> Silent, upon a peak in Darien.

Even now, as I remember those first Super Mind experiences, a stillness comes over me, but along with the stillness, an energy, a focus, a sense of being able to tackle whatever might come my way. My friend Ray Dalio, a decades-long TM practitioner and founder of the hedge fund Bridgewater Associates, describes such feelings well in chapter 15. As Ray puts it, TM has helped him feel like a ninja in the midst of battle, who experiences things coming at him in slow motion so they are easier to tackle one by one.

The thrust of the present book, therefore, is to explore the benefits of TM that go beyond promoting physical well-being and handling stress. Rather (or in addition), my new focus is on the development of consciousness and the many fruits it yields—collectively what I am calling the Super Mind. I'm intrigued to see what happens next, because it is now clear to me that consciousness can keep on expanding. I am convinced that many others share this fascination, and hope that this book will provide a sort of road map to this curious and thrilling journey.

Much of what I am sharing with you is not new. In fact, it comes from Vedic teachings that are thousands of years old. But, as with many great texts, their meaning is not immediately apparent. Some time ago, for example, I came across the following quote from the Maitri Upanishad, one of the Upanishads, a series of foundation texts in Vedic literature.

There is something beyond our mind which
abides in silence within our mind. It is the
supreme mystery beyond thought. Let one's
mind . . . rest on that and not rest on anything
else.[1]

When I first encountered this passage, I immediately fell in love with the description of transcendence embedded in the words "something beyond our mind which abides in silence within our mind." What a subtle portrayal of how it feels to pass through some mysterious portal into another world! It was therefore no surprise that the text should enjoin us to rest on that something. But not to rest on anything else? There I got stuck.

How could that be? I wondered. Surely only a professional pundit or guru could afford such a luxury as resting on transcendence—not a busy person who had a job to do, a family to care for, a living to make. But over time, whenever I reencounter these words, I have come to experience that curious pleasure one gets on rereading a classic as a mature adult that they last read years before. Has that ever happened to you? As a result of life experience, you are now able to appreciate the writing in an entirely new way.

So it was for me with the above quote. I have now grasped that it is possible for the transcendent to be present throughout the day—or parts of the day—even in the midst of ordinary life. So it seems that the Upanishad is referring to Cosmic Consciousness—the fully established Super Mind—and in the course of writing this book I have encountered people who enjoy transcendence throughout each day, even while going about their busy and successful lives.

The progression from transcendence—a state experienced initially only during TM sessions—to the Super Mind, with its many facets, is highly variable from person to person. In some people there is clear evidence of Super Mind development even within the first four days of training. Often these involve changes in perception or profound psychological attitudes that seem difficult to explain purely in terms of stress relief. One ER doctor, for example, was convinced that the critical care unit where she worked had been brightened in some way, either with new lighting or a fresh paint job, neither of which had occurred. After people start to meditate, the world often appears brighter, both literally and figuratively. Such early changes are the exception, however. For most people, the changes associated with the Super Mind occur slowly, subtly, and incrementally. Ultimately, however, their cumulative effect can be powerful and even transformative.

As consciousness continues to develop, some meditators experience the state of stillness during waking, along with its benefits—in other words, the Super Mind—continuously. This far end of the development of consciousness is the subject of chapter 18.

As you will see in the next chapter, which presents the results of a survey of over six hundred TM practitioners, the longer and more regularly a person meditates, the more steadily and progressively the Super Mind develops. This progression has led some meditators to compare the growth of the Super Mind to compound interest: It tends to grow geometrically over time. Certainly that is how it has been for me.

BEFORE PROCEEDING TO THE NEXT CHAPTER, LET'S SUMMARIZE
WHAT WE'VE COVERED HERE:

- With regular meditation, people experience transcendence entering their waking hours.
- The result is an intermingling (coexistence) of transcendence and wakefulness that can be a source of bliss in itself, as well as yielding numerous tangible gifts that we will discuss in subsequent chapters.
- Collectively, the combination of changes in consciousness and the benefits that accrue constitute the Super Mind.
- When a person's consciousness develops to the point where transcendence is present continuously, that person is said to be in a state of Cosmic Consciousness.

7

THE CONSCIOUSNESS
INTEGRATION QUESTIONNAIRE

If you can't measure something, you can't
understand it.

H. James Harrison

A lthough the development of consciousness is an ancient concept—and although Maharishi and others have set forth its elements in richly descrip-
tive terms,[1] it has not to date been scientifically characterized. Can you measure
it? Does it change over time and, if so, how? What are its elements and predic-
tors? And perhaps most important, how does the growth of consciousness affect a person's life? These are the types of questions that have been asked for
other psychological states, and there are established methods for finding out.
Questionnaires have been developed in many areas of behavioral science and
are important for both understanding and measuring such experiences as anxiety, depression, resilience, and happiness. I wondered, "Why not use similar
methods to measure the effect of TM on the development of higher consciousness and the lives of meditators—in other words, on the Super Mind?" To this
end, my colleagues and I constructed the Consciousness Integration Questionnaire (CIQ), which you can find in appendix 2.[2]

Because the development of a questionnaire and survey methods involves
more quantitative elements and statistics than may be of interest to most
readers, I have chosen to relegate technical information to the notes for those
of you who enjoy delving into such things. That allows me to use this chapter
to share with you our most interesting survey findings unencumbered by
technicalities. Also, the most important findings from our survey are summarized at the end of the chapter.

Starting with Maharishi's teachings about higher states of consciousness, Fred Travis, Gerry Geer, and I, along with many other TM scholars, constructed a list of items that we grouped a priori into two subscales that measured aspects of (1) consciousness development (State of Consciousness scale), and (2) the effect of TM on a person's life (Impact on Life scale). The reason for naming the collective responses to questions about these two scales the Consciousness Integration Questionnaire is that one of our major goals is to assess how the development of consciousness (scale number 1) affects and becomes integrated into a person's life (scale number 2). You can find the actual questionnaire (CIQ) in appendix 2, answer the questions yourself, and see how you score on the two different scales. The items in these two scales are also shown in figures 2–5 (below), which show what percentage of respondents endorsed each item as yes and, in those who had had the experience, how frequently.

Although in our survey all these questions referred to the period during which respondents had been meditating, the questionnaire can easily be modified and administered to anybody. For example, it would be useful as a baseline measure before people start to meditate or engage in any practice that might alter their state of consciousness or change their lives. That way they can use the questionnaire to check back later and see how they might have changed.

MEASURING THE SUPER MIND

We conducted a survey, and analyzed data from 607 meditators,[3] referred by various TM centers in the United States and South Africa, using a web-based instrument called SurveyMonkey.[4] Of those who replied, about 80 percent were from the United States and 20 percent from South Africa. The choice of these two locations may seem strange, but they were the two countries where TM teachers were kind enough to motivate their students to complete the questionnaire. Women slightly outnumbered men (52 percent versus 48 percent). There was a wide range in duration of TM practice, with a median of four years. (For those interested in more details about background variables of the surveyed population, see the notes.[5])

Whenever people respond yes to a CIQ item, they are given a choice as to how frequently they experience that item. For analysis purposes, we divided frequency into three categories: infrequent, often, and very often.[6]

As mentioned, we statistically developed two scales by which we assessed the effects of TM on a person's life: the State of Consciousness (see figure 2) and the Impact on Life scales.[7] By means of appropriate statistics (factor analysis) we further subdivided the Impact on Life scale into three factors: (1) support of nature, (2) internal growth, and (3) in the zone (see figures 3–5).[8]

THE IMPACT OF TM ON THE DEVELOPMENT OF CONSCIOUSNESS

The following figure shows the items that constitute the State of Consciousness scale (listed in figure 2 below, along with the proportion of respondents who endorsed each item). The bar graphs in the figure itself show the frequencies with which those who endorsed each item reported each experience. In the three graphs that follow (figures 3–5), data are presented in the same format.[9]

Figure 2

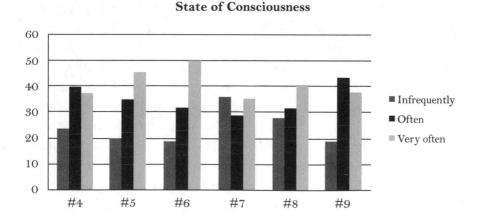

State of Consciousness

Key to Figure 2

ITEM NUMBERS IN THE FIGURE AND BELOW CORRESPOND TO ITEM NUMBERS ON THE CIQ

4. Silent and calm experiences during meditation (95 percent said yes)
5. Stillness during ordinary waking experience (92 percent)
6. A sense that the "real you" is separate from the ups and downs of ordinary life (85 percent)

7. Experiencing the world in more vivid, richly colorful, or fine-grained detail (78 percent)
8. Continuing influence of such vivid experience (61 percent)
9. Changes in quality of sleep (76 percent)

The above items may be familiar to you from your reading, from your own meditation practice, or from both.

At this point, I would like to draw your attention to the last three items shown above: those related to experiencing the world more vividly, and changes in quality of sleep. Then we will proceed to look at other ways in which regular TM practice can influence a person's life.

HEIGHTENED SENSORY EXPERIENCES

On one occasion after my evening meditation, I went for a stroll around my neighborhood. Though it was deep summer, the evening was surprisingly cool—moist after the rain. On my return, I walked up the garden path toward my door and stood for a moment, or maybe several moments, in a space between flowers that had grown tall—taller than me—over the course of the summer.

The flowers had generated moisture, creating a miniature atmosphere of their own. What jumped out at me was the cleome—pink and white spidery blooms, like creatures from outer space—that seemed to reach out to me, while the air stroked my face like a gentle hand. The hibiscus flowers stood aloof.

For a while, standing there, it seemed to me as though time had disappeared so that I, the flowers, and the moist air were all part of a single tapestry.

The heightened experience stayed with me long after I had unlocked the door and entered my house—the vibrant blooms, the cool moist air, and the summer evening were still fully present as I went about my daily chores. And for many days afterward, whenever I passed that threshold to enter the house, I experienced an echo of that state of mind.

I had never been given to mystical experiences, such as the one described above, but meditation has sharpened both my senses and my awareness of the world around me, just as many others have reported. Eventually, as consciousness develops by means of repeated, regular meditation, perceptions often become more vivid, fine-grained, and radiant. Let's hear about such experiences from other TM practitioners who responded to the Consciousness Integration Questionnaire.

Here are some thoughts from psychiatrist Richard Friedman, one of the people kind enough to respond to the questionnaire (he had been practicing TM for about three years at the time):

> It is as though a sensory filter has opened up—more information enters than before. I see things in more vivid, intense, fine-grained detail. For example, recently I was sitting on the stone porch up at my house in the country by myself one shimmering afternoon just listening to the birds and being aware of the light and the clouds. I don't remember how it happened, but I fell into a reverie and realized that I had been sitting there for an hour or more, admiring nature and lost in a rapturous haze. And the day went flying by and I thought to myself, "What did you do today? Oh my God, you didn't do this, and you didn't do that, and you could have." And you know, it didn't matter at all. I was perfectly content with what I had experienced, and it was great. And this from a type A who loves the charge of deadline and pressure. I can only attribute this effect to meditation—or the tooth fairy. You pick.

Several other CIQ respondents also reported experiences related to scenes in nature:

- The thing I noticed the most is that everything appears brighter and clearer, especially the birds flying by and the clouds in the sky. I feel an intense awareness of the beauty of nature.
- Nature ambushes me with breathtaking sunsets.
- I was driving on the interstate and some trees caught my attention. They were just second-growth poplars, nothing special. I had seen them many times before. Yet this time they were vastly different. They were glowing with incredible white light.

Sometimes perceptions concern mundane, everyday objects:

- I was in the ladies' restroom of the meditation hall and my eyes fell on the simple bolt latch on the stall door. It seemed like the most beautiful object. When I spontaneously had that appreciation, I knew my keener perception had kicked in again.
- This morning, during the simple task of making coffee I noticed the refraction of light on water. It was fascinating to me and left me open to the day's delights.

- Recently in Brooklyn, New York, I began to see old bicycles parked on the street, locked to streetlight poles or fences. Even these seemingly simple objects just hit me with a beauty that felt very personal and real.

You can find more about heightened sensory experiences occurring during TM sessions, or arising spontaneously and unexpectedly, in chapters 4 and 19, respectively.

TO SLEEP, PERCHANCE TO WITNESS

In asking about sleep changes (item 9), we were particularly interested in finding out the frequency of "witnessing," a state in which people are simultaneously asleep and aware (see chapter 18 for more about this fascinating phenomenon). We did not, however, want to ask the question in a leading way. Instead, we asked, "Have you noticed any changes in the quality of your sleep or in your experiences during sleep?" I am so glad that we kept it vague, because in doing so we learned about a whole spectrum of interesting sleep-related changes that people report after starting TM.

A large majority (76 percent) reported changes in sleep since starting to meditate. Of these, almost half provided comments that allowed us to identify the nature of their sleep changes.

The most common report was of improved quality of sleep—in general sleep became deeper, longer, and more refreshing. One woman wrote that after her very first TM session she experienced "the best rest I've ever had in my life. When I woke up, I felt like, 'Wow, this is what a real person feels like.'" Another observed, "The quality of sleep is much better with more meditation."

Praise for TM as a sleeping aid took many forms. For example, one person said, "I have not needed to use sleeping pills since the first week of meditation." Several others echoed her sentiment. One happy consumer said, "Sleeping through the night has been worth the entire TM course fee." Some people made a direct connection between falling asleep more easily and the ability to settle down from the cares and worries of the day.

The most dramatic response concerned a woman suffering from severe post-traumatic stress disorder. She wrote:

The effect on my sleep was profound. A year or so before starting to meditate, I had been attacked, strangled to a "near-death" experience, and was having violent nightmares every night. My partner was a TM teacher—and was nearly killed in the attack—and suggested TM as a way to deal with the experience. The nightmares stopped completely within a month of meditating.

Many people described changes in their pattern of dreaming after starting TM, including disappearance of nightmares and the experience of more vivid dreams. Several reported the onset of lucid dreaming, a mixed state in which people are conscious and dreaming at the same time—aware that the experience is a dream, and also that they (their nondream selves) are having it. In a few instances, unrelated people described an aspect of lucid dreaming that was novel to me—the ability to influence the outcome of the dream. As one woman put it:

> While dreaming I sometimes have control. I'm able to consider my options and make decisions that change the outcome of the dream—particularly in recurring dreams that I have had on and off over many years. Also, I do not have as many anxiety-ridden dreams.

Another wrote, "Dreams are more lucid. Sometimes I can change the content if I don't like the storyline!"

The general sense I have from reading all the responses is that after starting TM, sleep becomes an overall more pleasant experience, less beset by insomnia and nightmares. Indeed, for many people it becomes a joyful part of the twenty-four-hour day. Although I could cite many respondents to illustrate this, I will choose just a few.

- I enjoy my sleep. Since starting to meditate, the sleep quality is better. There are fewer unpleasant dreams—in fact, I hardly ever have unpleasant dreams now. While I cannot say that I have "witnessed," I experience the night as enjoyable.
- I will wake up with deep realizations from a dream that seemed more like a vision, which reveals to me qualities of life. I love those dreams/visions because they bring to the surface of my consciousness meanings about relationships, events, etc., that were previously hidden to me.
- I laugh more in my sleep—a happy laugh that comes from my heart and sometimes wakes me up.

As you read these first-person accounts of lucid dreaming and joyful mood shifts during sleep, you may wonder whether these changes represent the beginnings of witnessing, as do I. As you may recall, "witnessing" refers to that state in which people have a sense of awareness even while they are sleeping (see chapter 18 for more details about this intriguing phenomenon). Experienced TM teacher Katie Grose has observed that people first experience witnessing around transitions in the sleep cycle—moments when they're dozing off, moving in and out of dream states, or in those drowsy moments between sleeping and waking. It is possible, therefore, that lucid dreaming (being aware that you are dreaming) may be part of the development of witnessing.

As witnessing progresses, it can expand to fill the entire night. Of the 286 people who provided narrative responses to our question about TM and sleep, a lucky 48 (about 17 percent) reported witnessing. Here are some of their accounts.

> Almost immediately upon starting my TM practice, I began to experience much more vivid dreams than before. That lasted only a few months. The more recent development is an interesting "ability" to somehow be aware that I am asleep and not dreaming. It is somewhat like being awake but without thoughts—a very restful condition. Usually these moments are accompanied by a sense of light, nothing specific, just a comfortable light all around.

> I feel like I'm not really asleep while sleeping, although I wake up refreshed. The difference between waking and sleeping used to be considerable, but now it is so subtle that I can barely tell when I'm about to fall asleep. When waking up, I'm aware of going through a "zone" of intense bliss and come out infused with that first thing in the morning.

> During sleep there is an element of pure consciousness that seems like I am meditating rather than sleeping.

After a person learns TM and practices it for a while, certain "advanced techniques" are offered (for more information about these, see my interview with Bob Roth in appendix 1). Several respondents credited one of these, "the nighttime technique," for improving their sleep and promoting witnessing. If you want to learn this technique you should certainly check it out with your TM instructor.

After reading through all the responses to the sleep question on the Consciousness Integration Questionnaire, I came away with an increased respect for the profound effects of TM on sleep. I am now more inclined than ever to suggest TM to my patients who suffer from insomnia. Sometimes, however, the person in question has already learned but is not practicing regularly. If you are such a person, you might consider touching base with your TM teacher and giving twice-a-day TM sessions a steady try (say for two to four weeks), in order to capitalize on the investment you have already made. The CIQ data, as we shall see below, strengthen the argument for regular practice.

Finally, the sleep data reaffirm for me the value of asking open-ended questions. Had we narrowly directed this question toward the experience of witnessing, we might have missed a trove of valuable information.

THE IMPACT OF TM ON A PERSON'S LIFE: GIFTS OF THE SUPER MIND

Statistical analysis of CIQ items related to the impact of TM on a person's life yielded three factors, which are shown in the figures below. I will tell you much more about each of these in three chapters, named for each factor: support of nature (chapter 13), internal growth (chapter 11), and in the zone (chapter 10).

Figure 3

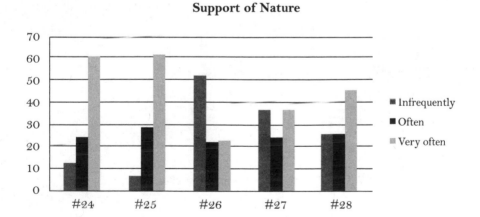

Support of Nature

Key to Figure 3
   24. Healthier choices (85 percent endorsed)
   25. Changes in relationships (89 percent)—almost all favorable*

26. Others notice changes (72 percent)
27. Changes in finances (55 percent)—almost all favorable*
28. Feel luckier (72 percent)

*In those instances where questions were deliberately left ambiguous (as in changes in relationships), narrative comments were read to get a sense of the direction of change.

We use the term "support of nature" to describe the sense that things are going your way more easily. You have more "good luck." The universe actually seems to cooperate! It has been suggested that this effect comes about, as the Super Mind grows, because you are more effectively able to harness the forces passing through you, both from within and outside yourself. People seem more willing to help you. Chapter 13 is devoted to this concept, "support of nature."

Figure 4

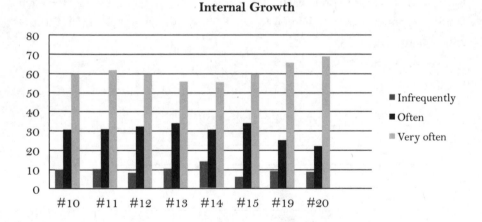

Internal Growth

Key to Figure 4

10. Increased mindfulness (94 percent endorsed)
11. Improved level of well-being (94 percent)
12. Improved recovery from unpleasant events (95 percent)
13. Improved response to pleasant events (84 percent)
14. Not as overly attached to things (88 percent)
15. More fully present and engaged (91 percent)

19. More content with who you are and what you have (90 percent)
20. More empowered to be your authentic self (90 percent)
29. Greater connection with community, the world, or universe (85 percent; no frequency question associated with this item)

Figure 5

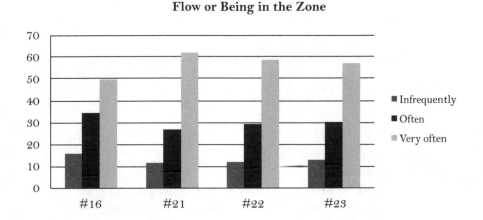

Flow or Being in the Zone

Key to Figure 5

16. Being in the zone (85 percent)
21. Improvement at work (86 percent)
22. Easier to get things done (85 percent)
23. More productive or creative (83 percent)

PREDICTING THE DEVELOPMENT OF THE SUPER MIND

What predicts the development of consciousness? By using appropriate statistics—in this instance multiple regression analysis—the CIQ tells us that two background variables are significantly associated with *both* growth of consciousness and the impact of TM on a person's life—in other words, growth of the Super Mind—*duration and frequency* of TM.[10] This is precisely what experienced meditators and TM teachers will tell you: practice regularly and over time to enjoy more regular transcendent experiences and growth of the Super Mind.

In addition, the more consciousness develops, the greater the impact TM has on a person's life (and vice versa).

If you would like to see how you fare on both CIQ scales, you may find it interesting to complete the CIQ yourself (see appendix 2).

Before moving on, let's summarize what we have learned from the Consciousness Integration Questionnaire.

- The Consciousness Integration Questionnaire has twenty-five items, of which six items can be grouped into a State of Consciousness scale and nineteen items into an Impact on Life scale, which collectively measure the Super Mind.
- The Impact on Life scale can be divided into three factors: *support of nature*, *internal growth*, and *in the zone*—each of which will be explored in its own chapter.
- The questionnaire appears in full in appendix 2, along with scoring directions that will enable you to measure your own scores on the two scales.
- The scores on both scales—your Super Mind score, if you like—tend to increase with length and frequency of practice. In other words, regular TM practice over time is the best way to cultivate the Super Mind.
- Growth of consciousness and impact of TM on life are strongly correlated.

Now that we have explored the development of consciousness, let us consider what this development can do for you. Welcome to part 2, "Gifts of the Super Mind."

PART II

GIFTS OF THE SUPER MIND

8

CONNECTING BODY AND MIND

There is more wisdom in your body than in
your deepest philosophy.

Friedrich Nietzsche

Take care of your body. It's the only place you
have to live.

Jim Rohn

After *Transcendence* was published, there was a time when I toured with
my friend and fellow meditator, the filmmaker David Lynch. David had
written *Catching the Big Fish*, a charming collection of insights drawn from
his own life and art, which acknowledges his debt to meditation. The event
was usually structured so that I would speak first and he would follow. I was
the straight man, and he got the laughs. He would begin by saying, "When I
first started making movies, some people found them rather dark, and suggested that maybe I should see a psychiatrist." Then he would point at me and
say, "Now I travel with one." As you can imagine, we had a lot of fun—and
the audience seemed to enjoy it as well.

Whenever David was my fellow speaker, you could always tell that a
large proportion of the audience had been drawn to the event because of
him—artsy-looking young men with long hair and notepads, and chicly
dressed young women—all aspiring artists and filmmakers, to judge by the
intensity of their gaze. It was to these people that he addressed his talk, which
started more or less as follows:

"There is this myth about the artist," he said, "as someone suffering and starving in a garret. That's really all about getting girls. A guy thinks that a girl will see him suffering and hungry, so she'll feel sorry for him and make him a bowl of soup and soon they'll be eating together, and one thing will lead to another. And *then* he'll start creating! Well, as a means to creativity, this is pure fiction. If you're high up in a cold garret and you're starving and have a migraine headache, abdominal cramps, and diarrhea, I can assure you, you're not going to get any worthwhile art accomplished. On the contrary, in order to be creative it is important that you feel well, that your body is rested, and that you are well nourished both physically and emotionally."

David was right, of course. Physical well-being is a prerequisite for creativity—as well as for other aspects of what we might consider a good life. Robert Sapolsky, professor of biological sciences and neuroscience at Stanford University, has written extensively on the many negative effects of stress on both body and brain—in fact, enough to fill an entire book, the highly readable *Why Zebras Don't Get Ulcers*.[1] These far-reaching effects should come as no surprise if you consider that stress promotes cardiovascular disease, and healthy blood vessels are necessary for carrying oxygen to every organ of the body. In the next chapter, we will further consider the effects of stress on the brain and brain functioning.

For a vivid illustration of the mind-body connection, consider the following vignette.

MEGAN FAIRCHILD: THE HIGH PRICE OF PERFECTION

Few worlds are as fiercely competitive as that of professional ballet. Out of thousands of young girls who set their hearts on becoming a principal dancer in a major dance company, only a handful succeed. Megan Fairchild is one such success story: accepted into the New York City Ballet at seventeen, a soloist at nineteen, and principal at twenty, her career trajectory was an aspiring ballerina's dream. What might be less apparent to such a starry-eyed neophyte, however, is the tough landscape that has to be repeatedly mastered in order to achieve and maintain that level of accomplishment. As Megan puts it:

The world of ballet is almost impossible because it's about being perfect . . . there's never a moment where "that's enough." . . . It's a pressure cooker. We've grown up together, but we're also pitted against each other for roles.

At a certain point in her career, the unthinkable happened—she began to have fainting spells. When she became stressed, she would faint. And the fainting caused her to worry about when she might faint next. Clearly, she could not continue as a ballerina with such an affliction.

It was at this point that her ballet mistress suggested she look into TM, which she had practiced for some time. After her first TM lesson, Megan immediately felt a sense of the energy in her chest settling down, as though she was on "a different wavelength." After a few days, her husband said, "You're a completely different person." Soon she no longer felt as though her husband had to manage her emotions. She managed them herself.

On one occasion, when her dog bit her finger, which began to bleed, Megan felt as though a fainting episode might occur, but her system restabilized itself, and she was fine. At the time of this interview, she had had no fainting episodes for two years.

STRESS, HEALTH, AND THE SUPER MIND

The ancient Romans gave us the aphorism *mens sana in corpore sano* (a healthy mind in a healthy body), and there has been general agreement about this idea ever since. It is true even at the most basic level: If you feel sick, you are not going to enjoy your life. If your blood vessels are blocked, too little oxygen will flow to your heart, brain, and other critical body parts, resulting in pain and disability.

On a more subtle level, however, a healthy body supports flourishing in *all* ways—at work and in your personal life. Likewise, physical disturbance may signal or promote distress and dysfunction. That tension you feel in your neck and shoulders comes not only from being hunched over your computer all day but also gets compounded every time your boss shouts at you or something goes wrong—or even *might* go wrong. It can feel like a screw being turned in your muscles. Why haven't you met your numbers? The muscles tighten over your temples. How many times must I tell you not to do it that way? Now you feel it in your lower back. How will you get it all done by the end of the day? The corrugator muscles in your brow wrinkle your forehead into a frown, sending distress signals back to the brain, which registers anxiety and despair.

*   *   *

As we set out to understand the effects of TM on the life of a meditator, it is useful to appreciate its impact on the body. Perhaps nowhere is this better documented than in the case of high blood pressure, which has been called the silent killer, and for good reason: "silent" because you can walk around for a long time, unaware that your blood pressure is far too high; "killer" because high blood pressure can and does lead to heart attacks, stroke, and death. Often high blood pressure is treated with medications, but now the American Heart Association (AHA) has also approved Transcendental Meditation, specifically, as a complementary treatment for high blood pressure; the AHA also endorses TM, not only as a supplement to, but also as a substitute for, certain other medical approaches, depending on the circumstances.

One thing that fascinates me about the TM blood pressure studies[2] is that hundreds of study subjects meditated in the morning and the evening, while blood pressures were taken at various times of day. So it is apparent that the vascular effects of TM persist for several hours after meditation. Changes in a person's brain and neurophysiology no doubt support this profound effect on the heart and blood vessels. Insofar as blood pressure changes may occur within months of starting TM, these findings are yet another clue that the relaxation of the nervous system that extends beyond TM sessions and into the day (physical evidence of expanding consciousness) begins soon after a person starts TM.

Researchers have wondered how this lowering effect on blood pressure might be mediated. The most likely explanation involves stabilizing the sympathetic nervous system, which (as you probably know) orchestrates the so-called fight-or-flight responses. For our ancestors, the triggers for such responses might have been a snake in the grass, an orangutan attack, or an enemy army surging over the nearby ridge. Although incidents such as these are now happily rare, for most people our well-adapted sympathetic nervous system can still respond in the same manner. Faced with a threat, it kicks all systems into high gear and mounts a massive response—for fight or flight. The body settles down only after the threat has passed—assuming the individual survives.

By contrast, nowadays, stress is most often relatively minor—but repetitive and frequent: for example, deadline pressures, financial concerns, family worries, an aggressive driver cutting you off on your morning commute. The results, however, are often cumulative and can be disabling. Just as when Gulliver woke up in Lilliput to find himself immobilized by thousands of tiny threads, any single one of which he could easily have snapped, so his modern-day counterparts feel overwhelmed by innumerable minor stresses. Taken together, they may be so overwhelming as to trigger a fight-or-flight response—for example, in people who work long hours under deadline pressure, or people who have to make snap decisions in an environment where mistakes can be costly (such as the ER or financial sector). In these situations, the sympathetic nervous system may not have time to settle down before the next stressor hits, so it eventually remains cocked and ready, waiting for the next blow. I remember that clenched-fist feeling from when I was on call as an intern. At the end of the day I would retire to the doctors' dorm, go to bed, and try and catch some sleep. But instead I would toss and turn, wondering, "What's the point of trying to sleep when at any moment I can be jolted awake by the phone?"

Researchers have tested the response pattern of the sympathetic nervous system in both TM practitioners and nonmeditating controls in two separate studies. In each, researchers exposed their subjects to a disturbing stimulus and measured its impact on the sympathetic nervous system by the galvanic skin response (GSR), which we discussed in chapter 5. In one study, David Orme-Johnson and colleagues used startling noises as the stimulus,[3] while in the other, by Daniel Goleman and Gary Schwartz, the stimulus was a grisly occupational safety movie, which contained bloody images of what might befall the careless worker.[4] Both studies arrived at the same conclusion: Meditators showed a sharp rise in GSR when exposed to the disturbing stimulus, followed by a crisp return to baseline. In nonmeditating controls, however, the GSR response was not only slower to rise and fall, but showed further false alarm spikes, indicating a sympathetic nervous system unable to fully settle down even after the threat had passed.

One way, therefore, to understand the health benefits of regular TM practice is as a surge protector for the sympathetic nervous system, one that buffers the meditator against the recurrent onslaughts of modern life.

In *Transcendence* I summarized the many ways in which TM can protect our bodies and remedy our aches and pains, our suffering and distress. I refer the reader who is interested in a more extensive review of these benefits to my earlier book. For now, let me just inventory the benefits and summarize the most impressive findings. As I look over the list, I am still amazed by the dozens of high-quality articles on which these findings are based. Depending on the strength of available data, I have divided benefits into "solid bets" and "intriguing possibilities."

Solid Bets

CARDIOVASCULAR BENEFITS (ASIDE FROM REDUCED BLOOD PRESSURE)
SUPPORTED BY AT LEAST ONE CONTROLLED STUDY:

- Reduced risk of heart attack and stroke in people at risk
- Increased longevity
- Decreased atherosclerosis in carotid arteries
- Increased sensitivity to circulating insulin
- Delayed left ventricular enlargement

Intriguing Possibilities

CONDITIONS FOR WHICH THERE IS ANECDOTAL EVIDENCE OF BENEFIT:

- Headaches, including migraines
- Involuntary movement disorders, such as Parkinson's disease and Tourette's syndrome
- Other pain syndromes

The data favoring the life-extending cardiovascular benefits of TM, spearheaded by researcher Robert Schneider of Maharishi University of Management, are particularly impressive. In a retrospective study of death records of people who had been randomly assigned to short-term studies of TM versus health education, after ten years those in the TM group had 23 percent lower mortality from all causes, and 30 percent less cardiovascular mortality.[5] These results were all the more amazing because the researchers had not followed their study subjects after the initial trial, and thus had no idea whether those in the TM group had continued to meditate.

To the researchers' credit, they followed up their retrospective study with a randomized controlled study of African American men and women fifty-five years and older, all of whom were at risk for cardiovascular problems. Again, some patients received health-education counseling, while others learned TM. After an average of five years,[6] Schneider's team analyzed patient records for what is known in the trade as "hard end points"—heart attacks, strokes, and (the hardest end point of all) death. Once again, reduction of catastrophic outcomes in the TM group was astonishing—a significant 45 percent for all end points combined. This finding was all the more amazing because all the study subjects were also receiving standard treatments, such as medications to reduce high blood pressure and cholesterol, plus diet and exercise counseling.

In one especially fascinating controlled study, Amparo Castillo-Richmond at Cedars-Sinai Medical Center in Los Angeles and colleagues found that TM can actually help reverse the progression of cardiovascular disease.[7] Using a special type of ultrasonography[8] in 138 people with high blood pressure, they examined the thickening of the internal lining of the carotid artery—the crucial pipeline in the neck that feeds blood to the brain. The results: In the control group, the arterial linings continued to thicken over a six- to nine-month period, while the reverse occurred in the TM group. The arterial linings in the new meditators actually became less thick, more normal!

I have often thought that I would willingly take some nasty medicine twice a day if it would reduce my risk of early death so dramatically. Yet as those of you who practice TM know—and those non-meditators who have read the earlier chapters may want to consider—TM is pleasant medicine indeed. As comedian Jerry Seinfeld has pointed out, one of the great mysteries about TM is why people who take up the practice and benefit from it ever choose to stop. I think the explanations are sometimes quite banal. People get busy, and other priorities displace meditation. If you think about the long-term benefits, however, you may be less likely to let such a valuable resource slip away. Another reason why people stop meditating is that their technique may become rusty, and therefore the experience becomes less rewarding.

Although one of the advantages of TM is the ease with which it can be learned and practiced, there are also subtle tricks to getting the most out of it. So if you find that your practice is less beneficial and refreshing than it once was, don't hesitate to contact a nearby TM center (www.tm.org) to have your technique checked. Remember, after your initial payment, all subsequent assistance is free!

THE SUPER MIND: A KEYSTONE HABIT FOR BETTER HEALTH

We are what we repeatedly do.

Aristotle

As Aristotle pointed out thousands of years ago, our lives are shaped by our habits. For better or worse, they make us who we are. In a way this concept resonates with the whole theme of this book. If you meditate and transcend twice a day, the stillness, peace, and even bliss of regular transcendence brings these qualities into your daily life. The state of transcendence becomes established in waking, sleeping, and dreaming. As this process advances, external events no longer overshadow your inner experience of your own unbounded transcendent self.

But there are many other habits that are also important to our health and well-being—from brushing your teeth in the morning to flossing them at night. Indeed, it can be daunting to think of all the things we need to do to maintain our physical, emotional, and financial health. In the Consciousness Integration Questionnaire, therefore, we asked people whether, since starting to meditate, they had made healthier choices in their lives—such as discontinuing bad habits or initiating good ones. Overall, 85 percent said yes, and on further questioning of those who said yes, 60 percent said they had done so "very often," and 25 percent said they had done so "often."

The list of bad habits people reported having quashed is encouraging. As one man who responded put it:

I used to smoke. I don't smoke anymore. I used to drink alcohol. Now I have an occasional glass of wine. I used to eat junk food. Now I prefer healthier alternatives. I used to stay up late at night. Now I go to bed before 10:00 p.m.

One woman chose to emphasize eating behaviors:

I started eating more healthily. I was a sugar junkie and decided that had to stop. I started eating more vegetables and fruits, cut out the sugar, and lost thirty pounds. Also, I have been exercising regularly.

Here is one further candid example offered by a woman:

When I started TM I drank a lot of coffee, had used some drugs and alcohol, had some casual sex, stayed up till all hours randomly, neglected my nutrition or dieted without sense, used profanity gratuitously, was very nervous around men, was often depressed, and compared myself unfavorably to others. I was not happy in my skin but practically bursting out of it sometimes in a state of torment. All these habits of action, thought, and emotion fell away over time with the TM technique without my trying to change one of them.

In *Transcendence* I summarized the impressive literature on the value of TM in helping people with different types of addictions. A monograph by David O'Connell and Charles Alexander[9] devoted to research in this area includes studies of people addicted to alcohol, drugs, and cigarettes. In all these areas, those who meditated recovered more successfully than those assigned to control groups.

The three examples of CIQ respondents shown above are intriguing both in their similarities and their differences. In the first, the man simply tells us that a series of habits changed for the better. In the second, a woman made a resolution: "I was a sugar junkie and decided that had to stop." She then implemented a plan to carry out the resolution successfully. But in some ways the third example is the most astonishing of all: a cluster of unhealthy habits just seemed to fall away, *with no active effort.*

I have often encountered such stories as this last woman's in response to TM. A celebrated case, for example, is radio-show host Howard Stern, who spontaneously kicked a three-and-a-half-pack-a-day cigarette habit within one month of starting to meditate. More impressive, perhaps, he didn't relapse even after breaking his ankle, which would normally have been an excuse for resuming the habit. Twelve-step programs for all manner of addictions, be they to substances or behaviors, recognize the value of meditation in one of their steps (Step 11).

A friend of mine, a TM teacher who used to smoke, told me that he had asked his own TM teacher whether he should quit smoking. The teacher responded, "Don't stop smoking. Just don't smoke when you don't want to." My friend found that he stopped buying cigarettes with his accustomed regularity, then turned to friends when he felt like smoking. They soon became irritated with his constant bumming, and asked him why he didn't buy his own. "Because I'm trying to stop smoking," he said. "Well then, stop," they responded. And he did.

HITTING THE PAUSE BUTTON

Although it is difficult to stop smoking or quit any addiction—whether to a substance or a behavior—the development of the Super Mind seems to decrease the need for whatever the fix might be. One way to understand why is to recognize that we all try to regulate our internal state. For example, if we are tired at work, we may drink coffee. If we are hyper at the end of the workday, a glass of wine may appeal. Twelve-step programs recognize four internal-state adjectives that pose a danger to the addicted person—"hungry," "angry," "lonely," "tired"—conveniently remembered by the acronym HALT. In fact, there are many fluxes in our state of consciousness that can prompt us to seek out dysfunctional remedies (alcohol, tobacco, Ben & Jerry's, drugs, gambling, etc.!). HALT is a useful reminder in the face of temptation—to try and correct the underlying urge—such as being hungry, angry, lonely, and tired—in a healthier way.

The Super Mind provides a different, ongoing type of "halt"—a built-in ability to take a few moments to pause . . . and consider what you want to do next, instead of just doing it. Pamela Peeke, assistant professor of medicine at the University of Maryland, who is an expert in treating people with food addictions and a TM practitioner herself, agrees and often recommends TM to her patients. "It helps people hit the pause button," she says. When it comes to addictions, unwanted behaviors are often driven by impulse. If the impulse can be delayed, the action can more readily be averted. Although it might feel as though you will "burst out of your skin," like the TM practitioner in our survey, the inner peace that comes with regular meditation somehow provides reassurance that your skin won't in fact burst. Usually a voice inside you, one that is part of a steadily growing Super Mind, tells you that you'll probably be just fine.

Settling down our internal state helps eliminate the cascades of bad solutions. By helping us stay calm in the face of challenges, alert during long shifts at work, and engaged even with no stimulation, we can feel steadily good and function well. I should emphasize here that just as the Super Mind is usually not an all-or-none phenomenon, so these controls and safeguards are not watertight. Over the long term, how well we do will depend on our levels of stress, the quality of our lives, and (importantly!) the regularity of our meditation and other healthy habits.

Peeke, in her book *The Hunger Fix*,[10] refers to certain areas of the brain to explain how this shift may occur: "Every one of my clients can benefit from TM because it strengthens the functioning of the prefrontal cortex (PFC), which is necessary for survival." The PFC is that part of the brain just behind the forehead, which is known to be essential to good judgment, wise decisions, and effective executive functioning.

Peeke points out evidence that her patients' rewards systems (brain-pleasure circuits mediated by dopamine receptors) are hijacked by the foods to which they are addicted—just as occurs in people addicted to drugs.[11] The hijacked dopamine receptors weaken important PFC functions, such as the ability to delay gratification and make good decisions.

In wondering where TM might exert its powers in the brain, one other region worth considering is the deep-seated central part of the brain called the basal ganglia, which go back very far in evolution. The basal ganglia have been shown to influence the development of habits in all animals, including humans. So although we have no direct evidence to this effect, it's a fair speculation that TM may help foster good habits by coordinating the functioning of the basal ganglia.

Charles Duhigg, author of the useful and highly readable book *The Power of Habit*,[12] has labeled those habits that influence other habits—making it easier to stop bad ones and embrace good ones—"keystone habits." (The keystone of an arch is the vaguely triangular piece at the center-top that holds all the other stones in place.) In my practice, I often encounter people who would like to improve aspects of their lives but don't know where to start. I frequently suggest they begin with a keystone habit—and, as you can imagine, TM readily comes to mind. Other keystone habits include going to sleep and waking up at regular hours, getting enough sleep and light, regular exercise, a good diet, and limiting the use of alcohol and stimulants.

It is easy to see how an improvement in daily habits would translate into better health—and fewer medical expenses. One study led by Robert Herron, a researcher formerly associated with Maharishi University, who examined the medical expenses paid by an insurance group in Quebec, found that after starting TM, people incurred significantly lower medical costs.[13]

It is clear, then, that the regular practice of TM over time can induce all manner of useful improvements in physical health, though precisely how such diverse changes come about is somewhat mysterious. It is easy to attribute positive changes to "stress reduction"—and that is true, as far as it goes. But as I consider the complexity of changes that TM induces in both mind and body, that explanation seems too simplistic. My mind drifts back to those book tours I took with David Lynch.

I would talk about how TM helped me feel calm and relaxed so that "I didn't sweat the small stuff." David felt otherwise. On one occasion he exclaimed, "When Norman says that TM makes him calm, I want to puke. I don't want to be calm! Artists want to keep their edge, energy, and drive. And this is what TM gives you—a great reserve of energy, access to ideas on a deeper level, and tremendous happiness in the doing."

As you think about all the health benefits that accrue with the development of consciousness, you will perhaps agree that the benefits of TM can take us beyond that ancient Roman ideal *mens sana in corpore sano*—a healthy mind in a healthy body. Now we can aspire to a Super Mind in a super body.

TO SUMMARIZE THIS CHAPTER BEFORE WE MOVE ON:

- A healthy body is necessary for optimal mental health and development of the Super Mind.
- Stress is a major contributor to a wide variety of illnesses.
- Extensive studies show the benefits of TM on high blood pressure, cardiovascular health, and longevity.
- TM may also be helpful in alleviating other physical conditions.
- TM helps our body come into balance, and this is relayed to us in the form of greater physical well-being. This provides an important foundation for emotional balance. Development of the Super Mind involves both physical and emotional balance.
- Improved habits and healthier choices, which accompany Super Mind development, add to the other physical benefits.

In the next chapters, we will shift from considering the effects of TM on the body to the effects on the mind.

9

BUILDING A BETTER BRAIN

Promise me you'll always remember: You're
braver than you believe, and stronger than
you seem, and smarter than you think.

A. A. Milne

A re we smarter than we think, as A. A. Milne suggests? And if so, how do
we gain access to the assets we have and make the most of them?
Throughout this book, we will encounter people who say that TM has
boosted their capacities, enabling them to live fuller, more successful, and
more enjoyable lives. In this chapter we will examine some of the evidence,
both anecdotal and experimental, suggesting that TM may indeed enhance
certain brain functions. If so, that would explain some amazing stories.

REMEMBRANCE OF THINGS PAST—AND PRESENT

The house was packed at the upscale Urban Zen in New York City, where
Cameron Diaz was guest of honor at an event hosted by the David Lynch
Foundation. Looking as radiant as ever, Diaz, a regular TM practitioner, was
dressed casually in black, her blond hair swept across her cheek, as she engaged warmly with the audience about her experiences with TM—such as
this one:

It was about ninety degrees in the Valley, at the Los Angeles Zoo
parking lot, under a tent, in a car, under lights, with the windows
up and no air-conditioning. It was about a thousand degrees in the

car. And I had a monologue and I couldn't remember my lines—lines that I knew. I knew I knew them. I'd said them a million times, and I couldn't access them. They're completely lost in . . . wherever they go. And I realized all of a sudden, I went, "No, I need twenty-five minutes. I just need twenty-five minutes." I ran back to my trailer and I rebooted. I did my twenty-minute meditation. And I came back to the car and I could see all those poor grip guys—they're all sweating, holding heavy equipment. They're looking at me like, "I hate you. Get your lines right, woman, so we can get out of here." I mean really like the evil eye. And I didn't want to let them down, and I wanted to be able to do my lines. But after I had gone back to my trailer and rebooted, I came back and I nailed it. I was like, *Done, thank you very much.* And we were out of there, I have to say, in like twenty minutes.

Diaz held the audience at Urban Zen spellbound as she described the power of TM as a technique for mining memory.

Her description of retrieving her lost lines is at once foreign (After all, how many of us have been on a movie set at the Los Angeles Zoo?) and scarily familiar. How often have you searched for a word, telephone number, or the first line of a familiar poem, only to find that it is . . . sometimes there and . . . sometimes not. We are left asking: where did it go and how can we bring it back?

Diaz's story also resonates because most of us have a sense that our brains hold a vast storehouse of buried treasure, and that if we could only unearth it more efficiently, we'd be far better off. It is this sense, perhaps, that has led to the urban myth (thoroughly debunked) that we use only 10 percent of our brains (though many are the self-help tomes that promise to unlock the missing 90 percent for the price of a few lattes). Although these percentages seem silly to anyone with even a modest knowledge of the brain, the idea contains a germ of truth that has perhaps given traction to the myth: we *do* have untapped potential, so perhaps we *can* be smarter than we think.

Although nobody can say for sure why a person forgets something at one moment, then remembers it later, we do know that stress can affect memory in ways both good and bad, and we have some ideas about the underlying brain structures at work. In fact, once again our old friend the prefrontal cortex (PFC) appears to be involved. Studies in animals have shown that specific neurochemical pathways, when activated by excess stress, cause profound impairment of the PFC.[1] Specifically, too much dopamine and norepinephrine are implicated. By reducing stress, TM may lower the concentrations of these two key neurotransmitters in the PFC, thereby improving cognitive functions— such as remembering lost lines in a movie script.

This effect of improved brain function when stress is reduced may remind some of you of the so-called inverted U-shaped curve, which shows how small amounts of stress or anxiety can boost performance but large amounts can make it worse. If you consider the declining limb of the inverted U (that part of the curve where anxiety is increasing but performance is decreasing), it is easy to see how TM could decrease stress and reduce key neurotransmitters in the PFC, thereby making the brain work better.

Whatever brain mechanisms were at work on that memorable day at the LA Zoo, we will never know. But the bottom line is that twenty minutes of TM restored Cameron Diaz's memory rapidly and completely. She had instinctively reached for the right remedy, and it worked.

Many other performers who practice TM have recommended doing meditation before tackling a stressful task. Megan Fairchild, principal dancer for the New York City Ballet, does her TM before every performance, as does Tony Award–winning actress Katie Finneran. So does actor, singer, and dancer Hugh Jackman, who says: "I meditated before I hosted the Oscars. I meditate before I go onstage. I meditate in the morning and lunchtime when I'm on a film set. It's like it resets." And director Martin Scorsese routinely meditates before facing another grueling day on the movie set.

But here is an obvious fact: You don't have to be well-known or a performer for TM to work. Anybody who has learned TM can take advantage of these observations. I can imagine an architect, schoolteacher, first responder, librarian—anyone, really—benefiting from TM at the start of the day. If you are a regular meditator, you are already at an advantage because the stillness of the Super Mind is already part of you, residing alongside your everyday activities. And if a crisis comes up, you can expand that advantage by taking a TM time-out.

DRIVEN TO DISTRACTION: ADHD AND THE SUPER MIND

Before leaving the topic of memory, let's consider a few other examples of improved memory apparently resulting from TM. A woman friend of mine, a medical student, has found that TM greatly improves her ability to remember the volumes of information her course work requires—but for a different reason. She has been diagnosed with attention deficit disorder, a condition that makes it hard to maintain focus. As you can imagine, if you have trouble focusing on something, you will not do well at remembering it. Problems with attention interfere with both storage and retrieval of memory. One benefit of TM has been to still her overactive mind—even when she is not meditating—which has helped her focus better and thereby be more successful in retaining what she studies.

Although there have been no large controlled studies of TM specifically for attention deficit/hyperactivity disorder (ADHD) at this time, one small pilot study on ten distractible students between the ages of eleven and fourteen was conducted by Sarina Grosswald, Bill Stixrud, and colleagues at a school in the Washington, D.C., area.[2] Although the study was small and uncontrolled, its results drew rave reviews from the staff, who observed that the students not only concentrated better but were less impulsive. One boy, for example, who could barely sit still in his chair at the beginning of the study, was able to concentrate long enough to read an entire book—to the astonishment of his mother. Another boy told Bill Stixrud, a D.C.-area neuropsychologist and longtime TM practitioner, "Before learning TM, when someone would bump into me in the hall, I would hit him. Now I ask myself, 'Should I hit him or not?'"

In a separate controlled study, Fred Travis and colleagues investigated the effects of TM on the EEG in eighteen students, ages eleven to fourteen, who had been diagnosed with ADHD.[3] In prior work on ADHD in adolescents, it had been established that the severity of symptoms is highly correlated with a certain EEG function known as the theta/beta ratio (a simple ratio between two EEG wavelengths): the worse the symptoms, the higher the ratio.[4] In the study by Travis and colleagues, the eighteen students were randomly assigned to practice TM or wait for three months before learning TM. Their EEGs were measured at the start of the study and at the end of three months (just before the controls learned TM). As predicted, the researchers found that the theta/beta ratios in the TM group declined significantly over the first three months compared to the control group (see figure 6 below). Once the control group learned TM (after three months), its theta/beta ratios also declined.

Bottom line: the effects of TM on both ADHD symptoms and the EEG are apparent after three months of practice.[5]

Figure 6

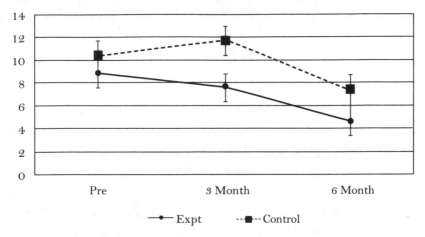

Theta/Beta Ratio

THIS CRAZY WORLD OF OURS

You don't need a formal diagnosis of ADHD, however, to lose focus in a world that offers so many distractions. As one of my friends puts it, "These days I think we all have a little ADHD." The old adage, "More haste, less speed," is part of the problem. In our attempts to "multitask," we often get less done, not more. But inefficiency in multitasking may be the least of our worries. Worse still is a common tendency to sacrifice essentials when we try to juggle less important things at the same time—like making sure that the text we are sending our BFF (best friend forever) is sufficiently witty while driving through a red light. When you multitask, you lose perspective—a potentially fatal mistake. Research shows that we *think* we can multitask and stay effective, but we're wrong. The fragmentary attention paid to each task makes it more likely that no task gets done correctly. And that's where the Super Mind comes in: It slows us down, making us less frantic while sharpening our alertness and focus. The result is improved concentration and ability to prioritize.

Bill Stixrud rails against the "mind-racing, mind-scattering, and mind-numbing effects of our extensive use of technology" that he sees in his daily practice. He adds, "We need to build in antidotes to constant stimulation, and TM is a hugely important antidote." He knows this not only from clinical observation but from his own experience. Here's how he describes it:

As I meditate, I remember what's important. Sometimes I think I should stop my program early to take care of urgent matters, but then I realize that there will be time to take care of everything, and the most important thing is for me to finish my meditation. As I do so, things sort themselves out in my mind and fall into better perspective. It always pays for me not to interrupt my meditation, but to see it through and reap its rewards.

On a personal level, I can't believe how nowadays I can usually locate my cell phone and other important objects that once would have gone astray in a fog of distraction. While my ability to retrieve lost objects is still far from stellar, somehow I am more attentive and less often mislay them. Also, I enjoy slowing down enough to do things properly. It feels less frenetic, more satisfying. We will explore the issue of attentiveness further when we address the relationship between transcendence and mindfulness in chapter 14.

WORKING MEMORY

Even working memory, which many regard as difficult to improve, may yield to the powers of TM, as evidenced in a patient of mine, David, a successful businessman. David has always prided himself on his excellent working memory—a function required, for example, to remember a telephone number long enough to find a pencil (Where did that pencil go? I know it was here just a minute ago!) and write the number down. David came to me because he was depressed, and I treated him with antidepressants and psychotherapy. After a few months, both he and I considered him fully recovered in every way—except for his working memory, which had previously been excellent. Now his memory was perfectly adequate for everyday life, but when it came to remembering long strings of numbers for short intervals, he realized he had lost his old talent—until he learned TM. Within the first few weeks of practice, his memory skill came back, and the timing of its welcome return coincided exactly with his starting to meditate.

REMEMBERING THINGS YOU DON'T KNOW YOU'VE FORGOTTEN

My last example of the beneficial effects of TM practice on memory is quite unusual. How often have you remembered something that you didn't know you had forgotten? That actually happened to a friend of mine who, along with her husband, had traded in their old car for a new one two days before the event I'm about to describe. Both highly competent professionals, they had methodically swept through the old car (once at home and once at the garage) and removed all trash and debris, as well as everything they wanted to keep—or so they thought. Two days later, while doing her morning TM, my friend suddenly remembered the E-Z Pass attached to the windshield, hidden behind the rearview mirror—and still in the car. It was a job to retrieve it, but well worthwhile to prevent further expenses from accruing.

I find this story a good example of Super Mind functioning because it is a simple and clear illustration of how things sometimes surface during meditation that elude us in the clear light of day. As the Super Mind develops, such insights occur more frequently even outside TM sessions. This story is a good bridge to our next section, on creativity, a function that depends in part on the unexpected insights and novel connections that arise unbidden and mysteriously, and may be critically important to solving problems.

THE SUPER MIND AND CREATIVITY

Creativity is intelligence having fun.

source unknown

One highly prized aspect of intellectual functioning that many of us would love to cultivate is creativity. And certainly many creative people seem drawn to TM—raising the question of how this practice, *and* the resulting Super Mind, might contribute to creative development. By "creative" I mean having the ability to make unexpected connections, either to see commonplace things in new ways—or unusual things that escape the attention of others—and realize their importance. The next phase in the creative process is the audacity to hold on to this new realization—often in the face of opposition or ridicule—and then pursue and realize the idea despite obstacles.

I have had the good fortune to discuss creativity with some highly accomplished and creative TM practitioners. To a person, they credit TM with making them more creative—at times dramatically so. Among others, I interviewed the great classical guitarist and longtime TM practitioner Sharon Isbin. She had told me exactly the best time to meet in her apartment on Manhattan's Upper West Side, overlooking the Hudson River, so as to avoid the banging and drilling of construction workers remodeling nearby apartments. After discussing the value of TM in softening her response to the incessant racket, we moved on to a wide range of topics. When I asked whether she thought TM had enhanced her intelligence and creativity, here is what she had to say:

> I suppose intelligence is hard to quantify, but whether you're writing an article, learning or performing a piece of music, or preparing a speech, all those things require tremendous focus and access to your talents and abilities at the highest possible level. And I do feel that TM has not only made me better able to use my own inner resources but has also made me more creative. Very often in a TM session, either in the middle or at the very end, I suddenly have the answer to a question I've had. Or I get an idea that I've never thought of before, and I think it's a *fantastic* idea! And it happens during TM. So for me that proves that TM is a process that enables and encourages and nurtures creative thinking.
>
> As a musician, I ask, what is creativity? It's a complex thing to explain, but somehow when you're writing or speaking, you suddenly think, "Well, that was a good idea. I never connected this thought with that thought before." And it's just flowing and it's happening and you're kind of amazed yourself at what's coming out of you. The same thing happens with music—I'll be playing and suddenly there is a twist of a phrase or a nuance and you just feel that melting sense of beauty. It might be something that you've never done before, and it just happens. That's creativity as a performer. As a composer, creativity is different because you're actually dreaming up these notes, as a writer would words on a page. So all of these things, I feel, reflect the power of TM.

Creative works sometimes advance by great leaps, but more often by a series of small decisions, each one guided by the creator's overarching vision of the desired outcome. The details cumulatively fall into place to achieve the completed work. That is what I learned from two TM practitioners who are creative giants in their respective fields: Ray Dalio, founder of Bridgewater Associates, and Martin Scorsese, a great American film director. Both are longtime TM practitioners, and both attribute their creative success to TM's influence. Dalio points out that in his chosen career—dealing with the world's financial markets—success comes from making a number of good decisions over time. Likewise, Scorsese talks about the importance of getting all the details right—for example, picking just the right piece of music to accompany a specific scene—in order to make a great movie.

UNBLOCKING CREATIVITY

My personal experience resonates with these stories. It is impossible to count the number of insights, both small and large, that have occurred to me while meditating or shortly thereafter. Here's another curious observation along these lines. Sometimes I sit down to write but the words just won't come. As writer William Styron put it, "The syrup won't pour." Often when this happens, I do my TM, and when I return to my desk, something has come unblocked. Mysteriously, the syrup pours freely. Over a longer time frame, within the eight years since starting to meditate, my efforts at writing have become steadily smoother. I am clearer about what I want to say, the right words flow, and the writing gets done more easily. And many others in widely varying fields have told me similar stories about how they rely upon TM to unblock them when they feel creatively stuck.

In an important controlled study performed in Taiwan and published by David Orme-Johnson and Kam-Tim So, three groups of adolescents were as-signed to practice TM versus a control condition.[6] The details of this impor-tant set of studies are presented more completely later in this chapter. At this point, however, it is worth noting that one of the tests used to measure the ef-fects of the different interventions was the Test for Creative Thinking–Drawing Production, which is considered a measure of whole-brain creativity. Based on the three studies, the participants who practiced TM exhibited a far greater increase in creativity than the controls over the course of the study.

An obvious question is, what is happening at the level of the brain? Some clues may come from the work of Fred Travis and colleagues, whom you met in chapter 5. You may remember that these researchers showed that *transcen-dence during meditation* develops within months of starting TM, along with the associated brain-wave changes, such as increased alpha waves and increased frontal alpha coherence. On the other hand, TM-associated brain changes that show up when the eyes are open—that is, *in the presence of dynamic activity*—take longer to develop. This latter group of brain changes include:

- EEG coherence in the frontal parts of the brain, not only in the alpha frequency but also in the faster beta and gamma frequen-cies, which are associated with performing a task.

- Increased alpha power—which suggests internal stillness even when people are performing tasks—a key feature of the Super Mind.
- More efficient use of the brain, as measured by its electrical responses to various types of tasks (these are covered in greater detail in chapter 18).

It is important to realize, however, how much we don't know about brain function and how much remains to be discovered to explain the amazing cognitive effects of TM. I emphasize EEG changes because that is where most of the brain-related TM research has focused. But it is worth considering the possible role of other brain systems—including some not yet described. Take, for example, the recently described "glymphatic system"—a term coined by Danish biologist Maiken Nedergaard, who has led the research into this area at the University of Rochester medical school—which rapidly drains waste products, such as amyloid, from the brain.[7] Studies in mice have shown that such clearance of the brain's waste products speeds up during sleep,[8] which researchers have hypothesized may explain why sleep is so restorative. For all we know, TM may exercise its effects via this system—and/or a myriad of others. But even without any understanding of its mechanism, the remarkable cognitive effects of the technique are obvious, as many TM practitioners will attest.

FIELD INDEPENDENCE

One quality that creativity requires is "field independence"—the capacity to generate ideas from within, without being unduly dependent on the influence of others. It is this aspect of brain functioning that has struck Walter Zimmerman as most improved since he began TM. A decades-long meditator and former TM teacher, Zimmerman saw this effect a few years into his meditation, when he scored high on a test that assesses the extent to which people are independent of distraction in their visual fields.

Now a highly successful energies trader, Zimmerman finds his field independence to be an invaluable asset. He sees the bulls carried away by their euphoric belief that stocks will never stop rising—until a sharp market decline lands them in despair. He sees the bears selling too soon or investing on the short side for too long, only to end up crestfallen when shares keep rising. Field independence enables Zimmerman to watch the market with both interest and detachment, as emotions rage on all sides. He makes his calculations on particular buys and sells based on experience and the ever-changing data as he watches events play out—a type of creativity that involves insight into patterns, numbers, and human psychology.

As you may have noticed, field independence sounds a lot like the Super Mind, where stillness enters the psyche and a person is unshaken by external fluctuations. Zimmerman compares himself to the central figure in Hermann Hesse's famous novel *The Glass Bead Game*. In this novel, an elite group of intellectuals play out a game of enormous complexity. So it is that Zimmerman describes his field independence, which allows him to retain a valuable measure of calm detachment while at the same time actively and successfully engaging in his complex profession. The parallel between his work and his life was clear to me (as I'm sure it is to him).

CREATIVITY AND THE CIQ

To close our examination of expanding consciousness and creativity, let us evaluate our findings from the Consciousness Integration Questionnaire. A great majority (83 percent) of respondents reported increased creativity since starting to meditate, of whom 57 percent and 30 percent said their creativity was enhanced very often or often, respectively. Here are some of their narrative responses, selected because they highlight various aspects of the creative process, which the respondents linked directly to practicing TM.

- I've always had a lot of ideas running through my head, but I could not pin them down when I needed them. Everything would get jumbled, and then I would get overwhelmed. Now I feel like I have a filter or filing system in my head that helps me sort through my ideas and organize them. After my meditation my creativity increases.
- I'm much more productive and have begun creative works that I had only imagined in previous years. I had a concept for one film almost ten years ago, but only after meditating for a few years was I able to complete it—and it all came about effortlessly.
- Before I started meditating, I was a music composition student who had a really hard time composing. Shortly after learning to meditate, that changed, and these days there is very little difficulty in any kind of creative work. It just flows out all the time.

- I get more done in less time—less procrastination. I do things well the first time so there is less do-over. Now I'm doing three jobs and writing a book, and somehow it all gets done.
- I always wanted to be an artist. I graduated from high school at sixteen, went to college at seventeen, and wasn't prepared for it at all. I was afraid of failure and afraid of success. I dropped out and didn't make any art again until I learned to meditate. Now I'm a nationally exhibited sculptor and I hope one day to earn my living with my art.
- Since meditating, my creativity has grown from the spewings of a distressed person to the outpourings of a wealthy imagination. My creativity is no longer needed for personal catharsis. It comes instead from insight, delight, and deep feeling. I am more productive because I know what doesn't matter and what does.
- Psychiatrist and *New York Times* columnist Richard Friedman sees a clear improvement in the quality of his columns since starting to meditate. One aspect that distinguishes his more recent columns is that they are "more provocative and intriguing, creative and daring. I'm less worried about whether others think they're interesting and haven't checked as much with others. I just do them."
- One painter said, "When an artist makes a mark on a canvas, he feels a resonance with that mark—whether it works or not, produces the desired effect, pleases or disturbs. Since starting to meditate, I have felt a greater resonance and connection with my paintings, which has given me a lot of pleasure."

LET US, THEN, COUNT SOME OF THE WAYS BY WHICH PEOPLE SAY TM HAS IMPROVED THEIR CREATIVITY:

- It helps them sort out and organize information, turning sketches of ideas into fully formed works of art.
- It gives rise to new ideas, new connections, and new emphases (Wow, that thought is more important than I realized!).
- It helps the creative person figure out where to begin (the leading edge of the problem) or what to do next.
- It helps people get started (overcoming procrastination) and

complete projects—both common impediments to creativity, which are often related to anxieties (such as fears of failure or success).

- It promotes the flow of ideas and actions (more on this subject can be found in chapter 10, "Being in the Zone").
- It shifts the axis of motivation from fear (if I don't succeed, something bad will happen) to enthusiasm (won't it be great to have my first show?).
- It gives people the confidence to take risks.
- It enhances the joy of connection to one's creative works.

Clearly, many different brain functions must be involved in expediting these happy outcomes. The controlled studies described and discussed below provide some insight into what these specific brain functions might be.

Anecdotes aside, let us consider now two of the most impressive studies that connect meditation to various brain functions. They were conducted in two countries thousands of miles apart, Taiwan and the United States. Both sets of researchers were interested in the same basic question: If one takes a group of essentially normal young people and teaches half of them to practice TM while the matched other half receives a control treatment, what differences, if any, will you find in their psychological function six to twelve months later? Put differently, can TM not only normalize brain functioning in people with problems—as has been shown in numerous studies (for example, in people with anxiety)[9]—but also enhance brain functioning in healthy individuals? Two sets of studies in two different countries sought to answer this question.

A TRIO OF TAIWANESE STUDIES

Three remarkable experiments were conducted by psychologist David Orme-Johnson and his graduate-student collaborator, Kam-Tim So (both associated at the time with Maharishi University), who published their results in 2001.[10] These three studies involved three separate groups of Taiwanese students: Two groups were in high school, while the third attended a technical school just above high school level. A total of 362 students were involved. In all three studies, conducted over six to twelve months, the same six standardized psychological tests were used (see table 4, below).

Table 4

NAME OF SCALE	FUNCTION MEASURED
Spielberger State-Trait Anxiety Inventory (STAI)	Anxiety, both as a state (the mood of the moment) and a trait (a more stable index).
Cultural Fair Intelligence Test (CFIT)	Fluid intelligence, which correlates with executive functions mediated by the prefrontal cortex and also with academic achievement.
Inspection Time (IT)	Speed of information processing at the step where a stimulus is transferred to short-term memory.
Constructive Thinking Inventory (CTI)	"Practical intelligence," which is thought to predict success in love, work, and social relationships.
Group Embedded Figures Test (GEFT)	Field independence, which means the tendency to generate thoughts and ideas based on internal, as opposed to external, processes. This test predicts academic achievement if one controls for fluid intelligence.
Test for Creative Thinking–Drawing Production (TCT–DP)	Said to measure whole-brain creativity.

Let us consider each of these experiments in turn. In the first, 154 students of average age 16.5 years were divided into three groups: Those who were interested in participating in the TM study were randomly assigned to TM practice or napping (for an equal amount of time), and those with no interest in learning TM constituted a third group. After six months of TM practice, those in the TM group significantly outperformed the nap takers on six of the seven measures (remember that the STAI yields two measures of anxiety) and the no-interest group in every respect—seven out of the seven measures.

In the second experiment, also in Taiwan, 118 slightly younger female students (average age 14.6 years) were randomly assigned to three groups: TM, contemplation meditation, and a no-treatment control. The two types of meditation were taught by two different teachers, both of whom practiced and believed in the form of meditation they taught, which helped control for expectation and placebo effects. After six months, the TM group significantly outperformed the no-treatment control on six of the seven measures, and proved significantly superior to the contemplation group on five out of seven measures (including state and trait anxiety). The contemplation group outperformed no-treatment students on two out of seven measures. Besides replicating several findings of the first experiment, this experiment tends to confirm that not all types of meditation produce equivalent results.

In the third experiment, 99 male vocational guidance students (average age 17.8 years), all of them majoring in technical drawing, were randomly assigned to two groups: TM or no treatment. After one year, the TM group significantly outperformed the no-treatment group on all seven measures.

To put these results in perspective, it is highly unusual in behavioral studies for an intervention to outperform the control condition across the board, on most if not all measures, *and* in three separate studies. In other words, these strongly positive studies essentially replicated one another. As someone who has looked at many behavioral studies, I find these results astonishing, both in the breadth of their findings and their consistency across studies.

In order to assess the effect of TM versus control, the researchers pooled the data from all three studies. You may recall that in behavioral sciences, an effect is considered to be large at 0.8 units or more, medium at 0.5, and small at 0.2 units.[11] The effect of TM versus controls ranged in magnitude from 0.77 to 0.34, as shown below, with the order of effect size being from highest to lowest:

- Creativity (0.77)
- Practical intelligence (0.62)
- Field independence (0.58)
- State anxiety (0.53)
- Trait anxiety (0.52)
- Inspection time (0.39)
- Fluid intelligence (0.34)

Overall, then, after six to twelve months of TM practice, there was a large effect on creativity; a medium effect on practical intelligence, field independence, and state and trait anxiety; and a small-to-medium effect on inspection time and fluid intelligence.

The researchers sent the paper documenting their findings to *Intelligence*, one of the top journals in the field. My guess is that the reviewers thought the data looked too good to be true, because they took two years to publish it!

One value of publishing in a high-profile, peer-reviewed journal is that it enhances one's confidence that the data are genuine.

Besides the credentials of the authors, the prestige of the journal, and the diligence with which the reviewers scoured the data before accepting the manuscript, there are other reasons why I find these findings credible. Over the past decade, I have seen hundreds of TM practitioners (myself included) who have improved—sometimes dramatically—in creativity, field independence, and practical intelligence. In addition, when it comes to intelligence, it is not only important how smart you are but also how well you deploy your intelligence. As we have already discussed with regard to memory, being overstressed, frenetic, or distracted seriously impairs function. The same applies to other aspects of intelligence—and all can benefit from slowing down one's internal pace while retaining alertness and acuity.

MEDITATING AT A MILITARY ACADEMY

Norwich University—the military college of Vermont—is the oldest private military college in the United States. You might not expect it to be the site of a study on the potential benefits of TM on officer trainees—but it was. In 2011, Carole Bandy, associate professor of psychology at Norwich, began a randomized controlled study by inquiring which entering cadets might be interested in participating. A total of seventy fresh recruits, familiarly known as "rooks" (short for rookies), expressed interest. Of these, sixty (about three-quarters of whom were men) were entered into the study and randomized either to receive TM training or to serve as controls. Both groups received their military training and other studies as usual.[12]

By way of background, here is how Bandy describes freshman training at Norwich:

> It is an incredibly stressful time for the students, and they must undergo training that is very unfamiliar in our culture. A lot of it is psychologically unfamiliar as well. They have to look straight ahead, to obey commands, and they can't look at their officers. They have to walk and eat in certain ways. And they do all of this while at the same time beginning their college courses, which are considerably harder than high school.

Those in the TM group were taught to meditate in the week before they started training, and they went on to practice TM twice a day, seven days a week, as a group. At baseline, both meditators and controls took a large battery of tests. These included questionnaires and physiological tests, such as EEGs, eye tracking, and behavioral tasks. Follow-up data were obtained on both groups after two and six months of TM training. At the same time, EEG and eye-tracking measurements were also repeated.

A full replication study was carried out in the second year on a new batch of cadets.

At the time of this writing, only the questionnaire data are available for discussion, but it is already possible to say that the results are remarkable: In the first year, at the two-month mark, every instrument showed significant changes in favor of the TM group. Specifically, there was a significant decrease in self-reported depression (as measured by the Beck Depression Inventory),[13] as compared with controls—even though these scores were normal at baseline. In other words, there was no evidence that these cadets were depressed on arrival at the college. There was also evidence of decreased stress (as measured by a stress scale), and state anxicty (as measured by the State-Trait Anxiety Inventory, or STAI,[14] which is mentioned above). Although most differences between TM practitioners and controls became evident after two months, trait anxiety (another output of the STAI) took a little longer to register a difference, which showed up at the six-month mark.

The widely used Profile of Mood States (POMS)[15] showed a highly significant decrease in overall mood disturbance for the TM group. At the same time, all positive aspects of personality improved.

Positive affect (feeling) was associated with increased constructive thinking. Not surprisingly, cognition (thinking) and affect were found to be interrelated. There was evidence of increased emotional coping, as measured by the constructive thinking inventory and increased behavioral coping.

Those in the TM group were also found to have increased resilience at the two-month mark, as measured by the Dispositional Resilience Scale (DRS-15),[16] which is a very stable scale. Interestingly, at baseline the Norwich University students scored in the same range as US and Scandinavian college students on this measure. In other words, regular TM practice appears to boost levels of resiliency significantly above levels normally found in college students.

Overall, constructive thinking as well as behavioral and emotional coping (as measured by the Constructive Thinking Inventory) increased significantly as well.

Almost all the changes in the TM group were apparent at two months, and all continued and increased as of six months.

And here is an amazing fact: all the findings obtained in the first-year study were replicated in the second-year study.

At the end of the first year, the TM platoon was graded number one out of sixteen platoons, which is not all that surprising when you think of the ways in which they outstripped the controls. It is, however, a nice validation of the pencil-and-paper tests.

David Zobeck, the TM teacher who taught the cadets, was kind enough to share some of the experiences of those who had been assigned to the TM group and are now progressing in their military careers. Here are a few typical comments.

- Todd, a rising senior, who since the study has become a regular meditator, says that during stressful situations and under duress, he is able to slow down his mind and make more thoughtful decisions as opposed to being influenced by emotions. (Do you detect the strengthened prefrontal cortex at work here?) He also says that his exam results improve when he meditates, and that he needs less sleep. (Zobeck adds that the candidate officers can get to bed as late as 11:00 p.m., have to be up by 5:00 a.m., and are generally sleep deprived.) Todd concludes that TM will be a "magnificent tool for active duty" when he enters the navy.

- James, one of the first rooks to learn TM, has since graduated from his training and course of study. He says: "It's really clear to me there's a tremendous energy boost after meditation. TM contributes to my resiliency and stamina. It removes a fog from my brain. It acts as a reserve for me; I never get tired. There's no doubt in my mind that TM makes me clearer in everything I do." At the time of this writing, James is in the US Navy and getting his master's degree online.

- Forrest, a lieutenant, finds that TM helps with his physical training: "When I meditate before I do my physical workout routine, I always have better results because it removes stress from me. TM brings me profound calmness of mind."

- Andrew, currently a second lieutenant, reports similar improvements in focus and academic work, but adds: "The thing I most note is that TM increases my creativity. I write music, poems, and stories. When I meditate my writer's block disappears immediately, I am more organized and am able to get in touch with more expanded levels of my mind."

As Zobeck talks, extolling one candidate officer after the other, his devotion to his students is obvious. "I can't separate them," he says. "It's like looking at a galaxy—they're all stars. If I made fifty more phone calls, I could give you fifty more sparkling results."

I find it interesting that all these study subjects were not troubled people to start with. They were normal students in Taiwan and officer candidates in Norwich, the latter group being chosen for particular hardiness (and validated as normal according to standardized tests). In all these cases, a simple conclusion is inescapable: the regular practice of TM—and the resulting development of the Super Mind—can boost positive psychological qualities (such as positive mood, cognitive functioning, and resilience) and decrease negative ones (such as depression and anxiety). To a behavioral-science researcher, these five data sets, replicating one another as they do, are astonishing. In fact, I would say that Transcendental Meditation is one of the most potent interventions for enhancing well-being and functioning that I have encountered in more than thirty-five years as a researcher and practicing psychiatrist.

In the chapters that follow, we will further explore the gifts of the Super Mind. As we do so, bear in mind the many physical and psychological (brain-related) benefits of TM, which are the basis of these gifts.

Before proceeding further, it may be useful for us to review some of the highlights of this chapter:

- Based on two sets of controlled studies, conducted on two continents and more than a decade apart, TM has been shown to outperform a variety of control conditions in boosting a wide array of psychological skills in physically and mentally healthy young people.
- These studies, performed in Taiwanese schools and at a US military university, found that TM enhanced the following mental abilities: creativity, practical intelligence, field independence, state and trait anxiety, mood, resilience, and coping.
- Numerous anecdotes suggest beneficial effects of TM on creativity and memory.

10

BEING IN THE ZONE

In sports, you have to let the zone come to you
by being as present as possible, and having as
much focus and concentration as possible—
then all of a sudden, you're in the zone.

Barry Zito

It was the 2012 National League Championship Series—the semifinals. The San Francisco Giants were up against the St. Louis Cardinals, down three games to one in a best-of-seven contest. This was game five—do or die—and the Giants' Barry Zito was on the mound. Zito had been a rising star as a young pitcher with the Oakland A's, had been named to the American League All-Star team three times, and won the prestigious Cy Young Award as the best pitcher in the American League (2002). He was then signed by the Giants in a much-publicized multimillion-dollar contract. Once with the Giants, Zito had had his share of struggles, but now he was back on top, and the fate of the series depended, really, on how he performed under intense pressure. For any pitcher, the stakes could not have been higher.

Barry and I had become friends after the publication of *Transcendence*. He and his wife, Amber (then his fiancée), had learned TM and were meditating regularly. As a result of our friendship, I became interested in baseball for the first time, having grown up in South Africa where, in deference to past British connections, cricket was all the rage. (When I arrived in the States, my friends laughed when I talked about watching "a baseball match" on TV. Everybody knew it was a game, not a match—I had exposed myself as a foreigner.) But now, slowly, I learned the subtleties of the game, especially from the pitcher's point of view. The mechanics of the fastball and curveball—

previously mere figures of speech—now became intensely interesting, and I enjoyed the trickiness of the changeup, which looks like a fastball but bamboozles the hitter by moving more slowly.

Now my attention was riveted as I watched my friend unleash these weapons on the enemy, acutely aware that the battle between pitcher and hitter is as much a match of wits as a physical combat. Here is how Barry describes that fateful game:

> We were down three games to one, playing in St. Louis, in an underdog situation. With Cardinal fans filling the stadium, they had the home field advantage. They had a dominant lineup, a ton of playoff experience, and had won the World Series the year before. And so, that was the biggest opportunity I'd ever had as a pitcher in my career. Instead of getting ahead of myself and trying to figure out what was going to happen in the game or after the game, my goal was to be as present as possible with every pitch, and not to let one pitch slip by without my thorough intent to focus and do my best. If I could do that, then regardless of the outcome, I could sleep well that night.

The opposing pitcher was Lance Lynn, who according to Barry, "had had a couple of really good years with St. Louis, and so I think all the oddsmakers had St. Louis kicking our butts that day."

As I watched the game, I became completely lost in the unfolding drama. As though by magic, Barry's pitches seemed to be going exactly where he wanted. Some change had come about within him that was apparent in his pitching. Here's how he describes his inner experience as he recalls it some two years later:

> I think the most difficult thing for a pitcher—and also for people in life—is staying really present with the task at hand, especially if there's a lot of meaning given to that task. For example, if that task could advance or demote you in any way. A lot of times we start to lose focus in the moment and have too general a perspective. So in that game, my focus was laser sharp on just every throw I made. Warming up before the game, warming up in the bull pen, I put as much focus as possible on every pitch, every throw. And that carried on into the game. So I felt like time was moving very slowly. And in pitching and in baseball we try to slow the game down, because the

game can speed up on you very quickly. It can feel like it's going much faster than it would to someone who's just watching from the stands, and when that happens, you have less control.

Barry was kind enough to answer some of my questions about his inner process as a pitcher during that critical game. Here are my questions and his answers:

NR: HOW DID YOU MAKE THE GAME "SLOW DOWN" FOR YOU?
BZ: I just stayed with my breath as best I could. I used a methodical breathing pattern, because when the game speeds up, you start to breathe too fast. So I breathe real deep. And I think the reason that the game went slowly for me is not because I tried to make it go slower, but because I just had so much intent and presence, with every single pitch. So it seemed like there was a full minute between every pitch I threw, where in reality it was probably fifteen or twenty seconds.

NR: DID YOU FEEL AS THOUGH YOU WERE 'IN THE ZONE' DURING THAT GAME?
BZ: Ah, yeah, definitely. That's right. And the tricky thing about the zone is that when you get into it, as soon as you become conscious of it, usually you're not in it anymore. So people in sports say things like, "You have to let the zone come to you by being as present as possible, and having as much focus and concentration as possible—then all of a sudden, you're in the zone.

Barry's observation about the zone reminded me of transcendence, in that if you're asking yourself whether you're transcending, you're not. When he said, "You have to let the zone come to you," that reminded me of the effortlessness of TM practice. Barry agreed, saying: "Yeah, in both situations you can't force it because it'll never happen if you try."

NR: IS IT ENJOYABLE BEING IN THE ZONE?
BZ: Yes, but in a way that I think is different than people might think. It's not like, "Wow! This is so fun!" It's enjoyable because you're just so totally connected to your task. The enjoyable thing is executing the task exactly the way you want.

NR: WHAT ELEMENTS ARE INVOLVED IN EXECUTING THE TASK IN THE ZONE?

BZ: Specifically for pitching, you have to be very calm, just completely relaxed, and let your muscle memory that you've worked on for years take over. You have to focus on the target and on the pitch you want to deliver. Essentially, it just becomes about you and the catcher's glove. Everything else goes away.

NR: IF THERE'S SOME PERSON OUT THERE WHO WANTS YOUR ADVICE ON HOW TO GET INTO THE ZONE, WHAT WOULD YOU TELL HIM OR HER?

BZ: I would say that you can't guarantee you will be in the zone. All you can guarantee are the things within your own control. And more times than not, when you execute those, you'll find you're in the zone. So I would say to have a slow breathing pattern that keeps you rooted in the present moment—and also keeps your body very relaxed and loose. But the biggest thing is to be aware of yourself *in the present.* If you find yourself jumping into the future or going back to the past, reset and focus on what's important *now.* There's an acronym that we talk about in baseball—WIN—What's Important Now? Because when you're on that mound and you have a pitch to deliver, it doesn't matter what happened before, and it certainly doesn't matter what's going to happen in five minutes, or even five seconds. All that's out of your control. The only time that's in your control is *now.*

Barry had been practicing Transcendental Meditation for about two years at the time of the playoff game against the Cardinals. I asked him whether he thought his TM practice had helped him get into the zone and succeed at baseball. Here's his response:

Yes, absolutely. Mastering yourself is what it's all about when you're out there on the field, and managing all the distractions—the different voices that come up—can throw you off kilter. And TM for me is a really great practice because it allows me to become familiar with being quiet internally, and being in the present moment—just with the mantra—and allowing whatever's going to happen to just happen. You know that old adage, "Control the controllables, and let the chips fall where they may." It's a lot like TM, where the only thing you control is the mantra. Then everything else just happens around us.

Barry relates the effects of TM on his game to its effects on his life:

I think TM is great, because it gives us the opportunity to slow down in our lives a couple of times a day. If it feels like things are swirling around us, we can go to this quiet place and allow everything to calm down inside.

When you're doing TM, a lot of times you may have had a rough day. You might be thinking about a family situation or something at work, or maybe someone's health is in jeopardy. And so things are racing in your mind. So you give yourself an opportunity to settle down for those twenty minutes when you just access that mantra and let everything else fall by the wayside.

NR: AND HOW DOES TM AFFECT YOU IN YOUR EVERYDAY LIFE?
BZ: It's easier to make the adjustment when you feel yourself starting to speed up, to engage with an issue too much, or to fixate on the past. TM gives you a toolset, in a secondary-benefit type of way, where you're able to access an awareness that you normally wouldn't have if you didn't take the time every day to slow down.

Although we didn't mention it by name, it was clear that Barry was talking about the Super Mind—the infusion into his baseball practice and his daily life of the silence and stillness that unfurl from his practice of TM. Swirling thoughts and distractions settle down. The brain becomes more coherent even when the eyes are open. And if you need to be in the zone, it is easier to get there.

Incidentally, Barry and the Giants beat the Cardinals 5–0 and went on to win the National League and the 2012 World Series. Barry's stellar performances were credited by teammates, the press, and fans alike with saving the season. Barry's pitching that day was a brilliant illustration of the value of being in the zone.

THE ZONE: KEY ELEMENTS

Although Barry Zito's description of being in the zone is typical, let us consider a few other people in sports, as well in the performing arts, for whom this state of transcendence in motion plays a crucial role. As we do so, watch out for some of these key elements that Barry has already captured in his description:

- A state of calm alertness
- Intensity of focus
- Being in the present
- A state of confident well-being
- Permitting well-rehearsed automatic processes to hold sway without overthinking them
- A high level of effectiveness

Being in the zone is important for sportsmen and sportswomen, especially those few at the very top of their fields. Competition is fierce, so every move and every second counts. Here are a few famous descriptions by legendary champions.

Roger Bannister, who first broke the four-minute mile, writes the following about his historic performance:

My legs seemed to meet no resistance at all, as if propelled by some unknown force.

We seemed to be going so slowly! . . .

I was relaxing so much that my mind seemed almost detached from my body. There was no strain. . . .

I had a moment of mixed joy and anguish, when my mind took over. It raced well ahead of my body and drew my body compellingly forward. I felt that the moment of a lifetime had come. There was no pain, only a great unity of movement and aim. The world seemed to stand still, or did not exist. . . .

I felt at that moment that it was my chance to do something supremely well. . . .

I knew that I had done it before I even heard the time.[1]

Another example of a superb athlete explaining how it feels to be in the zone comes from tennis great Billie Jean King, who describes "the perfect shot" as follows:

I can almost feel it coming. It usually happens on one of those days when everything is just right, when the crowd is large and enthusiastic and my concentration is so perfect it almost seems as though I'm able to transport myself beyond the turmoil on the court to some place of total peace and calm. I know where the ball is on every shot and it always looks as big and well-defined as a basketball. Just a huge thing that I couldn't miss if I wanted to. I've got perfect control of the match, my rhythm and movements are excellent, and everything's just in total balance.[2]

I am indebted to Craig Pearson, an expert in expanded states of consciousness, for including these personal descriptions by these two great athletes in his book *The Supreme Awakening*. Pearson draws connections between the states of consciousness that the athletes describe and our understanding of Cosmic Consciousness (the 24/7 Super Mind).

In commenting on Bannister's description, Pearson writes, "In Cosmic Consciousness, one's awareness is grounded in transcendental silence, unshaken even in dynamic activity, and one's physiology functions in a dual mode, restful even while active, much as Bannister describes."[3] In commenting on Billie Jean King, Pearson again references her "effortless superior performance, the inner quietude, the transcendent happiness,"[4] which suggest glimpses of the Super Mind.

Now I have no evidence that either Bannister or King ever practiced TM or any similar form of meditation. This seems like a good moment, therefore, to emphasize that the Super Mind can develop in many different ways—and perhaps superb athletes in all sports are more inclined to develop such powers as a result of their specific training and disciplined practice toward a goal.

Let us turn now to another area of human endeavor where being in the zone is important and highly prized—the arts.

THE ZONE AND THE ARTS

As part of researching this book, I spoke to several people in the arts, all of whom are also solid and established TM practitioners, and asked them whether their meditative practice has helped them stay in the zone. Here are some of our exchanges.

I asked actor, singer, and dancer Hugh Jackman whether he could relate to the expression "being in the zone." Here's what he had to say:

I totally relate to it. I'm a frustrated sportsman, really. And the ability to be at your peak in any endeavor is the ability to find measure, to be able to manage all sorts of desires and expectations, pressures from outside, other people. Pressures can motivate to an extent, but for most people they become debilitating, because you lose that sense of relaxation. And in my job, relaxation and the ability to be present—which are totally strengthened by meditation—are the keys. In fact, relaxation is the power that is everything.

I asked Tony Award–winning actress Katie Finneran whether getting into the zone is an important part of her work. Here's what she had to say:

One million percent. In fact, sometimes if I lose myself onstage, I'll do something very similar to TM to get back into listening and back into the present moment. I know when I'm exhausted onstage and can't wait for the play to be over, that I'm *not* in the zone. And I know when I've lost track of time and suddenly the play's almost over, that I *am* in the zone. And TM helps me more than anything. It's the only tool I can use that helps me get back into the moment—especially on film, because in film or television people can see *everything* that you do. So you don't want to do too much, because the camera always picks up all of it. I find that doing TM right before I shoot always helps me make an honest choice.

Fascinated at how Katie uses TM before going onstage, I asked her to say more about it.

I don't go onstage until about fifteen minutes after the show starts, so I'll get my hair done, and I'll come back over and I'll meditate. And after that, it's almost like I don't have to be there. I know the show, so that once I get into the character and into the zone, everything seems taken care of. If I'm trying too hard, then it's just a struggle. It's exhausting, and I won't get my laughs or I won't get my message across, and the show might not go so well. But if I can get into the zone—and TM is a huge part of that—the outcome is almost none of my business. I've already done all the work, so I just have to be present.

We met classical guitarist Sharon Isbin in the last chapter, where she described the effects of TM on her creativity. Here she talks about how it promotes her feelings of being in the zone:

If I'm playing at my very best, I'm in a kind of trancelike state. I'm not thinking about what I had for breakfast, about who might be in the audience, or even what finger goes where. I'm immersed in the flow of the music. I'm at one with it, and feeling the energy from the audience, from the music—they all kind of combine into one. That is a process that I feel TM has facilitated in many ways, because when you are meditating and in that state of bliss, you are at one with the energy of the universe. And that's similar to what I feel when I'm performing at my best.

Megan Fairchild, the principal dancer with the New York City Ballet whom we met in the last chapter, credits TM with "helping to keep me out of my head." Sounding very much like Barry Zito—or any artist or athlete who depends on executing spontaneous virtuosity—Megan says, "The dance just happens to you. Your body's got muscle memory and your body just goes. It's much more enjoyable."

THE ZONE IN EVERYDAY LIFE

Until now, we have considered the zone as it affects people with special talents. If I were to leave it there, however, I would be doing a terrible injustice, not only to the topic, but also to the legions of people who live regular lives and have regular jobs but nevertheless enjoy being in the zone. I am a case in point. I often walk briskly around my neighborhood. My route is unvarying, eliminating the need to think of where I'm going. If it is not too hot or cold, especially if I am blessed with a gentle breeze, my mind goes into a zone that fits many of the elements of the descriptions we have heard— calm alertness, focus (on something), confident well-being, a well-rehearsed automatic process conducted without overthinking. I see many familiar faces. We greet one another in passing. I cannot pretend to know what they are thinking, but many are smiling blissfully. Could they also be in the zone? I wonder.

A transcriptionist friend of mine (who happens to be a TM practitioner) tells me about the bliss she feels as her fingers fly effortlessly across the keyboard. Words move from the voice on the audiotape to the growing manuscript. It is a fluid, effortless, exhilarating process that feels very much like transcendence—calm yet focused, and boundless with regard to time and space. It is an example of transcendence in the midst of action—in other words, the Super Mind. Yet clearly she is also in the zone—another example of how these two states of mind overlap with each other.

To understand the value of regular TM practice in helping people to be in the zone, we looked once again to our CIQ responses. We found that a large majority—85 percent!—of meditators reported that they have felt more "in the zone" since starting to meditate, and 82 percent of those who responded yes reported feeling this way either often or very often. Nor was the feeling confined to extraordinary activities. Rather, it was part of these people's everyday experience. Here are some examples:

- "Be here now" is a phrase that encapsulates how I feel when I am engaged in most activities. There is pleasure in activity no matter how simple and mundane.
- Often during work, I move from issue to issue smoothly, effortlessly. I feel very effective, like the work is effortless.
- If I'm out in the woods taking pictures of birds or animals, I'm completely involved.
- I feel more alive, more connected to myself and what is around me. It's pure pleasure. I was cutting vegetables the other day in the flow; I've never cut vegetables like that before, but I hope it happens again.
- Doing the dishes is more fun than it used to be.

The term "flow" has been popularized by author Mihaly Csikszentmihalyi, professor of psychology and management at Claremont Graduate University, in his book by that name.[5] The concept, however, is very old, going back to Confucius and Taoism, perhaps even earlier. The ancient Chinese term used to describe flow is *wu wei*, which means "spontaneous virtuosity"— highly skilled actions performed effortlessly because they have been preceded by years of practice. In Vedic teaching, the term "spontaneous right action" has a similar connotation.

THE "IN THE ZONE" FACTOR

You may recall that when we analyzed the responses to all the questions in the CIQ that measured TM's impact on a person's life, three factors emerged: (1) in the zone, (2) internal growth, (3) support of nature.

Four items made up the "in the zone" factor: Besides those we have already dealt with in the last chapter and this one, two other items fell into the zone cluster and are worth considering: "improved work and endeavors," and "greater ease at getting things done." These items were positively endorsed by 86 percent and 85 percent of respondents, respectively, almost all of whom said they occurred often or very often.

Their unscripted answers were often very similar to one another and can be summarized as follows:

- Everything is easier
- Work less and accomplish more
- Better focus
- Better organization
- Better prioritization
- Less hampered by anxiety
- Mundane activities are less boring
- Can persevere for longer
- Easier to switch gears
- More efficient
- Better people skills make the work environment easier
- More drive and commitment to work

If you think of the last chapter and consider how many skills and brain functions are sharpened and expanded in those who practice TM over time, it makes sense that work would flow more easily and be more productive. We will return to these observations in later chapters, particularly chapter 15, "Meditate and Grow Rich." For now, however, let's move to our second CIQ "impact on life" factor—internal growth.

TO SUMMARIZE THE POINTS IN THIS CHAPTER:

- Survey data and anecdotes—including some from high-performing individuals—suggest that TM helps people to "stay in the zone."
- This may relate to the automatic nature of TM practice, which may be reflected in the automatic and effortless virtuosity required in performance.
- To date there are no controlled studies that speak to this point.

11

INTERNAL GROWTH

There were times when I could not afford to
sacrifice the bloom of the present moment to
any work. . . . I grew in those seasons like corn
in the night, and they were far better than any
work of the hands would have been.

Henry David Thoreau

How do we grow? Whether we ask this question in relation to physical or
psychological change, the process is a mystery. How does that little
baby who turned to us for every need now lead a life as an independent adult?
I know we fed and clothed the child, took him or her to school, pointed out
right from wrong, attended soccer practices and parent-teacher conferences.
But still—from there to *here*? What a miracle! And, for that matter, each of us
has undergone a similar transformation from total dependency to reading the
words on this page.

And how do we know that we've grown? Even on a physical level the
changes are often subtle, which is why there are those marks on the door or
closet with dates showing when they were scratched, close together till the
adolescent growth spurt (thank heavens!)—and then no more dates, because
the person being marked lost interest and moved on to other things. Growth
is more easily perceived when there has been a longer interval. I remember my
parents' friends saying to me, "I can't believe how you've grown! The last time
I saw you, you were just *this* high," with a hand held three feet from the ground.
"It shouldn't be such a surprise," I would think. "After all, that was twenty
years ago." Now I'm the one who feels amazed when I see my friends' children
grown up (but I *do* try to restrain myself from making similar comments).

Internal growth—which is the subject of our present discussion—is even harder to come to grips with than the inches. Even when we know we have matured and developed, how do we separate the effects of time from those of some specific intervention? As a psychiatrist, I am often faced with this question. It is, after all, highly relevant. Should I continue the same approach or make some change? You can never know for sure, but one guideline I often turn to is the trajectory of change. If I see sudden growth after a particular intervention, it is reasonable to infer that the two have some relation—especially if the patient backslides when the intervention is withdrawn.

In chapter 9, "Building a Better Brain," I described some controlled studies of TM's effects on key psychological variables that are important for personal change. Elsewhere in this book (including in this chapter) I must rely more on anecdote, since studies are lacking. Once again, we will look to the Consciousness Integration Questionnaire and supplement these data with in-person reports. In all instances, I will try to dissect the potential connection between the unfolding Super Mind and a person's internal growth. In this regard, we should bear in mind how the regular practice of TM improves the workings of the mind. Memory, mood, cognitive abilities, and resilience all flourish beneath its gentle but powerful influence. We will watch these qualities come into play in the following sections.

RESILIENCE

It is not the strongest of the species that survive, nor the most intelligent, but the ones most responsive to change.

Charles Darwin

Resilience, the capacity to rebound from unpleasant experiences, is an area in which many TM practitioners notice the biggest difference. In responding to the Consciousness Integration Questionnaire, no less than 95 percent of TM practitioners report improvement in resilience, and almost all of them say it happens often or very often. The following comments are typical:

- Things that used to "push my buttons" may give me a brief twinge, but then I let go of them and return to my calm center.
- I don't hold on to anger as much. Things pass more quickly, like

a ball that is pumped with air. It hits the ground and bounces right back to where it was dropped from.

- I am much less reactive to everyday stresses. It is quite obvious that I do not feel upset at things that used to bother me, and I realize that this or that problem is really so minor as to be almost funny, or in some cases I can see it's not even remotely about me.

- I am a pleaser and I hate it when people are angry at me. But since meditating, I am able to see that the anger has little to do with me—and it's easy to shrug off.

Often people feel their new resilience physically as well as psychologically—like this man:

Since starting to meditate, I notice that negative emotions in my body dissipate more quickly.

Some people realize how much TM helped them to process angry feelings only after they stop regular meditation—and return to their old, irritable selves. Later many of them start meditating again, for which their family and friends are often grateful. More than one CIQ respondent pointed out that their more measured responses help those around them as well. As one woman put it, "I get less upset and have fewer triggering moments (exponentially so). And I'm also able to address other people in their moments of stress, to bring calm and peace to a situation."

You may recall that in experiments in which people were exposed to alarming noises or violent movie images, meditators showed crisp sympathetic-system responses (as indicated by a sharp rise in the galvanic skin response, which then settled down briskly). In contrast, nonmeditators showed slower recovery, followed by several "false alarm" blips in the GSR (see chapter 8). A parallel distinction appears to apply to emotional reactions, as the following response indicates:

The ability to discriminate when to take something seriously and when to "let it be" is very useful. Although I *do* still get angry, it often seems like I'm having the "right" emotion and there is a positive outcome. More and more, however, things that used to bother me seem inconsequential, and I'm able to see situations in better perspective.

Some people have used their responses to bad traffic as an index of their TM progress—like the man who wrote:

> Although I was interested in TM for a long time, taking the step to actually learn required a dramatic, somewhat ridiculous experience with road rage—where *I* was the raging person. I now use road situations as a barometer of my change. I'm happy to report that road rage is never an issue now. I let everything go, and even when there is some incident on the road, I actually feel *good* afterward, knowing how little it affects me.

I have treated several people with anger management problems and have found TM to be extremely helpful as part of their program. This last example illustrates one obstacle that an angry person has to surmount in order to seek help: to develop the insight that the problem with anger is internal.

In working with people who have trouble managing their anger, it's often a big hurdle to move them past thinking that their rage is legitimate, even justified! "Why, anyone would react that way! It was outrageous!" They may know that their reactions were exaggerated, yet think they were totally reasonable—that the insult was intolerable and demanded a strong reaction.

Part of the goal of therapy is to help the person understand that even when the anger itself is justified, an exaggerated response can still be disastrous, for them and others. I ask (gently) whether being right is worth a traffic accident or a punishing skirmish with another angry person—not to mention the chronic wear and tear on their nerves, blood vessels, and heart. In fact, according to one report by a group of cardiologists, chronic anger can be as harmful to the heart as eating unhealthy foods or smoking.[1] By helping people distance themselves even from legitimate provocations, TM and the resulting inner stillness can prevent these personal and physical adversities. Mellow people are better able to choose their actions and reactions.

Stability in sympathetic nervous system responses, as shown by the GSR studies mentioned above, is an important part of the Super Mind, and has its counterpart in greater emotional stability as well. This would be predicted based on observations that go as far back as William James, who in his famous paper "What Is an Emotion?" emphasized the important role of the body in generating emotions.

Some people actually seek out anger or other forms of drama in order to stimulate themselves. Once the thrill of the drama passes, the resulting emptiness spurs them to repeat the cycle by seeking out further drama. Once the body and mind settle down—a key element of Super Mind development—this desire subsides. As one woman who responded to the CIQ put it, "I feel less connected to other people's drama. I'm aware of it, but quite frankly less interested in it."

Of course, we all enjoy a good drama when we go to the movies or theater, read a mystery or a thriller, or watch a favorite team play its fiercest rivals. We root for the "good guys," and we want to see the "bad guys" get bested, busted, or (in the case of thrillers) even killed! It's all part of the fun. But for many people, drama plays a far more central part in their lives. They use it as a way to fill a sense of emptiness and boredom. Drama can even become addictive, consuming most of a person's waking hours. Those who are so inclined can readily find drama 24/7 in the form of online shopping, gambling, video games, fantasy worlds, imaginary romances, and sexual liaisons. And that doesn't even take into account everyday life!

There is no need to stay stuck in the muck, though. As the woman mentioned above observes, since starting to meditate regularly, she has become less interested in other people's drama. Presumably she now pursues personal happiness and fulfillment rather than feeding on the turbulence, titillation, pain, and suffering of others.

The peace and harmony that enter the psyche as part of Super Mind development make drama less interesting. Then, as with many other addictions, the need for a quick fix falls away naturally.

For our last quote on resilience, let me share the response of one TM teacher, who paraphrased a famous metaphor that Maharishi used to describe the change in reactivity that accompanies the growth of consciousness:

Activity was once like a rock being scraped against another rock. It left a deep impression, and there was lots of friction. Then it became like a line drawn across the sand—very little friction. The impression didn't last, and was easily swept away. Then daily activity became like a line drawn across water—almost no friction, and whatever impression was left, awareness immediately settled, barely disturbed at all. And now it's becoming more and more like a line through the air—super fluid, no resistance, no impression.

LUCID IN ECSTASY

My greatest wish: to remain lucid in ecstasy.

Albert Camus

Many years ago, long before I started meditating, I was interviewed on the *Today* show for one of my previous books. A media-savvy friend briefed me over the phone as I was riding the train to New York. "Remember," she said, "you're not on till that camera starts rolling. They can cancel you for breaking news right up to the very last minute, and you have to be ready for that." Many other instructions and caveats followed, along with the kind reassurances that a good friend offers. The interview went fine. It was apparent why the astute and lovely talk-show host was so successful, and I understood how many guests must fall in love with her during their five minutes of fame.

But after the show, while traveling back to D.C., my mind was racing. Millions of people must have seen the piece! Why wasn't my agent doing more to publicize the book? Where was the publisher in all of this? (The interview had come about through a friend—no thanks to my agent or publisher!) I was full of righteous indignation, and when I arrived home, amped up on Amtrak coffee, I called my agent and gave the poor woman an earful. After that exchange, although I apologized and tried to make amends, things were never the same between us.

Now, with the benefit of hindsight, I think back on the experience with amusement. How illogical my behavior was—not to mention unkind! What did I expect the agent or publisher to do, especially on the very day of the show? As a result of sleep deprivation and caffeine, coupled with the self-importance that can flourish when you are under klieg lights and too many people are fussing about you, my physiology and sense of self were destabilized. As a consequence, my thinking was off and my behavior ill considered and impulsive.

None of that would happen today. Experience and meditation—especially the latter—have settled my physiology and given me a far better perspective on my tiny role on this very small planet for this infinitesimal space of time in our vast universe.

The reason I offer this example is to illustrate that good things—as well as bad—can threaten our equilibrium. Strange as it may seem, winning the lottery, becoming suddenly famous, and other strokes of good fortune can be paradoxically stressful. As Camus's quote at the head of this section suggests, it can be harder to remain lucid in ecstasy than in adversity.

A happy majority of respondents to the CIQ (84 percent) reported that they had noticed a change in their reactions to pleasant or positive experiences since starting to meditate (and of those, 90 percent said that this was noticeable often or very often). In their narrative comments, prevailing themes were greater equilibrium, more gratitude, and more positive feelings, which they experienced not only as a reaction to favorable events but as coming from within. Here are some examples that illustrate the tempering effects of TM on positive experiences:

- I enjoy positive experiences, but I know that they come and go just like unpleasant ones.
- I am more at peace and quiet during compliments or positive experiences.
- I am far more receptive to the good and hardly affected by the bad. My life no longer has extreme peaks of ups and downs.
- I still very much enjoy success, pleasure, etc., but the difference now is that I don't find myself hyperventilating (so to speak) over such things even when they are prodigious.
- I rarely become "overecstatic" about things any longer. I am convinced this is a good thing, as I'm no longer carried away by overwhelming emotions, either positive or negative. On the other hand, I am able to enjoy simple, pleasant things in a deeper, somewhat slower way.
- I'm no longer on a roller-coaster ride.

You may recall from the last chapter that in the Taiwanese controlled studies, TM enhanced resiliency (as measured by standardized tests) to a greater degree than control conditions.

WHO ARE YOU REALLY? THE QUEST FOR AUTHENTICITY

Be yourself; everybody else is already taken.

source unknown

This above all: to thine own self be true.

William Shakespeare

The call came a little late, and I realized I had turned off my cell phone, which registered a missed call. Then the landline rang. I asked if it was Hugh, and a man's voice with a familiar Australian accent said, "Yeah, man, I'm sorry about that. I had a wrong number and some lady answered the phone and then I got your voice mail." The friendly tone was the sort one might expect from a neighbor inviting you over to a barbecue—not a world-famous movie star, which it was. Hugh Jackman is one of the most respected actors, singers, and movie stars working today. Yet from beginning to end of the interview, his manner stayed the same—friendly, candid, down-to-earth, and authentic.

HUGH JACKMAN: STRIPPING AWAY THE MASKS

Hugh offered to be interviewed for this book because of the powerful influence TM has had on his life and his desire to let others know about the practice. At the time we talked, he had been practicing TM for twenty-two years. Here is the transcript of our conversation, lightly edited for flow and clarity.

NR: HOW HAS TM CHANGED YOUR LIFE?

HJ: I would say possibly equal to marriage and kids—I would put it right up there, in terms of things that have affected my life. I was always very curious and very much a searcher, but soon after I started meditating, I felt I gained a true understanding of myself and was no longer just being reactive to events that came my way. I felt a sense of calm, a sense of purpose, of finer energy in things I did. I think I had been quite an external person, living very much outside of myself, either for validation or just from stimulation, until through meditation I started to find what I call home, or a sense of my true nature or true self. So TM is one of the greatest gifts I could have, and I continue to practice it.

NR: IT SOUNDS LIKE YOU'RE DESCRIBING A CHANGE IN YOUR CONSCIOUSNESS. IS THAT A FAIR DESCRIPTION?

HJ: I would describe it more as a *revealing* of consciousness—that through meditation on a daily basis, I get to strip away the masks that we build— that I build for myself, small and large—to reach more a feeling of my true self: Oh, this is who I really am. This is how I can experience life. Oh, I see. It's just something simpler, finer, and more powerful. So the moment you say, "change in consciousness," I sense there has been a change, but the change brought me back more to my true nature as opposed to an acquired nature.

NR: I'VE SEEN YOU MENTION ELSEWHERE A FEELING OF AUTHENTICITY THAT IMPRESSED ME AS A POWERFUL ELEMENT IN THE CHANGE.

HJ: Yeah, and let's not forget I'm an actor, so a lot of my life is putting on other masks and other personalities and looking into them. But, of course, for the actor the real power is finding authenticity no matter what character you're playing—and being. You cannot really move forward as an actor until you understand who you are as a person, and understand yourself—that that is the most powerful book in the library, so to speak. And then you branch out to understand others. So authenticity is something that actors in particular—but I think anyone in a creative field— would call the holy grail. And certainly I find that, through meditation, [my personal authenticity] has increased for sure.

NR: IT'S INTERESTING THAT YOU'RE THAT MUCH MORE IN TOUCH WITH WHO YOU REALLY ARE—AND THEN THERE ARE ALL THESE CHARACTERS YOU PLAY, WHO ARE PROBABLY VERY DIFFERENT FROM YOU. YET TM HAS HELPED YOU ACCESS THEM. IT SEEMS A BIT PARADOXICAL.

HJ: I totally agree. It's one of the great ironics, mysteries, and for me a very, very powerful example of how not to get caught up in the illusion of things. And it *is* paradoxical, because I believe—and this may through meditation have become clearer to me—there are more things we have in common than separate us. Even though I do play characters, I study human nature and the differences in personalities, traits, or natures of different people. But the more I do this job and the more I meditate, the more I see the unifiers that connect us all. And when you start from that basis, then there is great joy in playing different characters, great joy in the variety.

Right now I'm thinking of the example of cooking. I do love to cook. In one sense it's all food, and if it's nourishing, it's something wonderful that can connect people. And yet I like to make different dishes! We like to enjoy different things. So the more I understand the things that unite us, the more I seem to understand the variety.

NR: COOKING SEEMS TO BE A VERY GROUNDING ACTIVITY. HAS TM HELPED YOU DEAL WITH FAME, WHICH IN MY OBSERVATION CAN BE VERY TRICKY TO HANDLE SOMETIMES?

HJ: I started meditating before I was famous—probably four years before I had any level of fame. So TM was fairly well rooted in me as a practice, and although this is a simplistic way to describe it, TM had given me the idea that we find our real existence beneath the surface, or a more powerful, deeper, more meaningful existence than whatever is going on in our life. Whether that be fame, health, illness, or any other kind of experience, that is not the true essence of life. So, yes, there are tricky parts of fame. And there are wonderful parts. But through meditation I've found that from the moment fame happened to me, I could kind of see it for what it is—an experience that will go away at some point, and also that it is not real. So I'm glad that I had meditation first, and that I didn't get famous until I was in my late twenties, because maybe I had a deeper understanding. I'm not sure, if I was eighteen and fame was thrust upon me, that I'd have been able to handle it so well.

Hugh Jackman is by no means alone in observing that TM helps one develop a sense of authenticity. In response to a question on the CIQ, "Since starting to meditate, do you feel more empowered to be your authentic self?" 90 percent of respondents said yes. Of those who responded in the affirmative, 90 percent said they had observed the quality in themselves often or very often. Here are some typical responses:

- I feel more comfortable in my own skin.
- I am not as afraid of what people think of me, even close friends and relatives.
- I am who I am. I don't worry anymore if I am going to upset someone or say something "wrong." If I say something I don't end up agreeing with later, I apologize.

- I've started owning who I am and being proud of who I am much more since starting to meditate—imperfections and all.
- While I sometimes succumb to social pressures and my own need to please, I am much more aware of the perfectly legitimate choice to simply be myself in most situations. While this may sound unremarkable, this awareness of choice for the "natural way" has been incredibly empowering for me. And, yes, I have started to exercise that option more and more frequently.
- My guiding principle has become being true to myself. I used to have lots of rules . . . No more.

As one might expect, some people pointed out that other life influences—such as growing older or psychotherapy—have also helped them become more authentic. So it is important to recognize that no useful practice, TM included, operates in a vacuum. Rather, these practices work collaboratively with other constructive forces in a person's life.

AND WHO DO YOU WANT TO BECOME?

Although the Super Mind helps people remove their masks, TM's effects are actually even more far reaching: Expanding consciousness can also help you truly *change*—to develop into the person you want to become. All of us are aware of things about ourselves that we would like to change. Yet change is difficult, often requiring special methods or techniques. TM is a powerful technique for change, not only as a direct result of the stress relief that follows each session, but also via the sustained expansion of consciousness over time.

Let us pursue this question (becoming a different person) a little further with Hugh Jackman and Lindsey Adelman, whom you will meet shortly. Hugh Jackman talked with me about how TM had produced a personal transformation in his own life. I then raised something he had said in another interview—that people often use the word "stress" when they mean fear—and asked him whether TM had made *him* less afraid. Here's what he had to say:

I think what TM made me do was become *aware* of my fear. I was a very anxious kid in many ways. I had a lot of fears. I was afraid of heights; I was afraid of the dark; I was afraid of what people thought—and I hated the prison of that fear. I hated being stopped. I wanted to be able to do everything. So I hated not being able to jump off a cliff with my mate 'cause I was scared of heights, and I hated it when they made fun of me 'cause I couldn't do rock climbing. I hated that I didn't want to do roller coasters. I hated that I was afraid to go camping on my own in the bush at night. All these things I saw as limiting. So I had a fear *of* the fear.

I found that with meditation, my anxiety levels dropped considerably. It seems to me that the mind is fuel to the fire of fear. The mind can make us worry about things beyond their measure. And the great thing about meditation is that twice a day, I have this sense or feeling that the monkey mind just calms down.

So I have less fear; there's a kind of cap to it. At the same time, I've seen that because I'm afraid of fear, I sometimes deny it and say to myself, "Oh, I'm not afraid of this, I'm fine," as a way of hoping that'll make it go away. Meditation makes you see very clearly what goes on in your mind, its machinations. So in some ways I see more of it—the low-level anxiety—because I'm more aware. And the high-level anxiety just calms down.

Here, then, we see the effects of calmness entering the daily consciousness of someone who used to have a lot of fears but has now mastered them to the extent that he's comfortable stepping out onto a world stage. Like several other performing artists we have encountered, Hugh Jackman frequently meditates before stressful performances and major events—like going on set or hosting the Oscars. But even without that TM-fueled extra boost of confidence, he remains someone who handles himself with grace and ease, regardless of whether he is on a screen in front of millions, granting an interview, or cooking dinner for family and friends.

LINDSEY ADELMAN: SUBTLE BUT PROFOUND

Let us turn now to Lindsey Adelman, a Manhattan-based designer who specializes in creating artistic chandeliers, has been doing TM for years, and credits her practice with allowing her to grow both personally and professionally. Here is what she has to say about the changes she has experienced, having meditated for seven years at the time of our conversation:

I would describe the overall effect of TM as being both subtle and very practical at the same time. It's very profound and gives me a completely different perspective on life. Practically, it's allowed me to manage things with more ease, so I don't really get knocked off my tasks. I don't feel overwhelmed by work and surprises in life as much as I used to.

And on a much bigger level, it has allowed me to feel fuller all the time, fuller in a way I never really knew was possible. It's been like finding an endless well of deep bliss. Before, I used to really thrive on the highs I would get, whatever that high meant, so I would just plan the highs. It could be just about anything, really. So my life had a rhythm of going down from these peaks, and then waiting for the next peak to feel good again. Now it feels much more like I love normal. I'm so enthusiastic about the most normal day in the world.

Lindsey marvels at how something that someone might have said to her could "potentially send me into the most foul mood." On occasion, when she checked to find out what the person *really* said, she found that the offending comment was either innocuous or even complimentary—and should have had an opposite, positive, effect on her mood. It still mystifies her "to think that a human being could be so thrown off by what another person says—or what you think they said. That almost doesn't happen anymore when I'm practicing TM every day. I feel so like myself, at a general level between medium and high all the time."

"And what was your general level before starting to meditate?" I asked.

In the extremes, from very, very low to very, very high. Now it is more steady. On the upper end of the positive scale, I get this feeling of optimism, belief, and trust. I don't expect that people will take advantage of me, and I'm not really worried about people getting sore at me for some reason or other.

Often nowadays, when people say something negative to me, I realize they're pretty bent out of shape. It's easier for me to distance myself and realize this might not be completely about me—but I also ask what my part in it might have been. That level of complexity wasn't accessible to me before. It adds a lot of contentment to life that I am able to separate out my contribution from the other person's, to have empathy for the other person without taking it personally.

Besides giving her a better perspective on life, TM has allowed Lindsey to be her best self. She has become more outgoing and open with others, including her staff. As she puts it:

> This is not the kind of person I've always been. Most of my life I tended to be private and reserved, keeping my creative side to myself because I was comfortable that way. TM has enabled me not to be afraid to let my talents shine—and that encourages others to do the same! It also helps me hire people who are comfortable with their talent, because they see they won't have to play it down or up. I can give them anything and allow them to make something spectacular with their own hands because we all know they are capable of that—just as I can just put the energy of something *I'm* good at out on the table.
>
>   I'm also more comfortable with my weaknesses. I'm well aware of what I'm not versed or accomplished in—and what I'm not even trying to get better at. We work as a team. TM has helped me connect the dots, get people to collaborate, describe the direction I want them to take and let them go. My work life is not an ego trip at all. It's much more exciting.

Although working in a totally different field, Lindsey, like Hugh Jackman, emphasizes the importance of authenticity. "When you cover up what you're not good at, it can create a personality that is full of shame, insecurity, and faking it." By allowing her to shine while acknowledging her shortcomings without apology, TM has helped Lindsey become more authentic and more consistently happy.

Internal growth, the second major factor to emerge from the analysis of the CIQ, is such a large area that its tendrils stretch throughout many chapters of this book. For now, however, let's conclude by returning to Henry David Thoreau who is quoted in brief at the beginning of this chapter. Here is the full quote, in which this pioneer of transcendence attributes his internal growth to allowing transcendent silence to enter his daily life at Walden:

> There were times when I could not afford to sacrifice the bloom of the present moment to any work, whether of the head or hands. . . . I sat in my sunny doorway from sunrise till noon, rapt in a revery,

amidst the pines and hickories and sumachs, in undisturbed solitude and stillness, while the birds sang around or flitted noiseless through the house, until by the sun falling in at my west window, or the noise of some traveller's wagon on the distant highway, I was reminded of the lapse of time. I grew in those seasons like corn in the night, and they were far better than any work of the hands would have been.[2]

TO SUMMARIZE THE ELEMENTS OF THIS LAST CHAPTER BEFORE PROCEEDING:

- Internal growth is one of the factors that emerged from the analysis of the CIQ's Impact on Life scale. It is a broad concept because as the Super Mind develops, so do many specific positive traits, some of which are highlighted in this chapter.
- In reviewing our survey data and anecdotes, we see evidence that TM enhances resilience and authenticity.

12

ENGAGEMENT AND DETACHMENT: A DELICATE DANCE

You have control over action alone,
never over its fruits. Live not for
the fruits of action, nor attach
yourself to inaction.

Bhagavad Gita[1]

Not too tight and not too loose.

Attributed to the Buddha

I have twin sisters or, I should say, I had twin sisters—two years younger than me. One died recently; one survives. My sister Jenny lived in South Africa for sixty-two years, until she developed a rare type of cancer. Shortly after diagnosis, the doctors thought the cancer had been completely removed, and that the prognosis should be excellent. But they were wrong. One morning, just weeks later, I woke to find an e-mail from my brother-in-law in South Africa, addressed to me and my sister Susan. The CT scan report was attached and could not have been worse. The cancer had spread throughout her body.

Everyone concerned did everything they could. Susan rushed to be at her twin's side. Jenny's family in South Africa rallied around. The doctors tried their best. I scoured the Internet for the latest information on this dreaded malignancy. I spoke to Jenny every day for as long as she was able to come to the phone. Many in her situation would have found reason to be bitter (she had been looking forward to enjoying retirement, grandchildren, traveling with her husband). Now this future was looking less likely. Yet she was stoical. "What is happening here is just bad luck," she said. "Do you want me to come?" I asked. "No," she said. "I'll tell you when I want you to come."

I wrote to a world expert on her kind of tumor, asking his advice. He replied with kindness and such information as was available. Even at the time, however, I discerned a pessimistic tone to his letter, which turned out to be fully warranted. I was on a late-night phone call when I saw Jenny's number pop up on the caller ID. I calculated that it must be 4:00 a.m. in Johannesburg. The call could mean only one thing.

Susan was on the line. "I'm afraid to tell you," she said, "but we've just lost our darling sister."

Grief hit me like a punch to the gut. I felt wails wrenched out of my lungs and screamed in ways I could not have imagined possible. The body did what it needed to do.

A thousand details followed. People were incredibly kind and supportive. I flew home. Whatever my grief was, Susan's was worse—by a whole different order of magnitude. Along with Jenny's husband, she had nursed her sister through the last few terrible days. But Jenny had left her—and us—with a final gift. "Whatever happens," she said, "I have had a wonderful life. I have no regrets."

I walked around Jenny's house and garden, with its cottage where my mother had lived. I entered the cottage and tried to recapture all the memories it contained. "You can still smell Mom there," Susan had said. I couldn't, but I saw her everywhere—and the flowers Jenny had planted to give her something lovely to look at. African birds flew by and swooped down to grub around in the grass—the long-beaked ibis named for its squawk, "Ha–dee-da!" and the crested grey go-away birds, named for their shriek, "Go away! Go away!" Family and friends came and went. We tried to comfort one another. Prayers were held; rituals observed. Then it was time to return.

And return I did. Something irreplaceable had been lost. I felt it every day. Jenny had been so vibrant—funny, larger than life, she filled a room—and now she was gone. It was hard to believe. At the same time, I had much to return to—my life here in the United States: loved ones, patients—and this book about a subject so meaningful to me. My loss and my life required me to attach and detach at the same time: to hold on to Jenny, yet little by little to let go of . . . I'm not sure what. But something that would make the pain better.

I recall seeing a documentary about a mother elephant who had lost her calf a year earlier, on the way to finding water. Returning along the same path the following year, when she passed her daughter's skeleton, she buried her trunk in the crevices of the skull as though trying to relive their broken bond. The rest of the herd stood by respectfully until she was done with her reminiscences. Then, slowly, they all moved on. Life required the mother elephant to negotiate the balance between attachment and letting go. And so it was for me. My TM practice and the changes in daily consciousness that flow from it have helped me to manage (more or less) the delicate dance between engagement and detachment, between loving and accepting the necessity of loss, between caring intensely and retreating from the abyss into which emotion can engulf us.

"Live not for the fruits of action," the *Bhagavad Gita* urges us (as quoted earlier). We all did what we could to save Jenny. We should not punish ourselves for failing. "Nor attach yourself to inaction," the great text goes on to advise. We acted. We were—and are—all actors on a vast stage, playing our parts to the limits of our abilities. Sometimes we succeed, sometimes not, but act we must.

It is this delicate dance that is the subject of our present conversation.

Let us consider another story, less tragic than the loss of a loved one but important nonetheless—and common. It involves the tricky balance between engagement and detachment, played out every day in millions of romantic relationships.

A friend and colleague of mine, a physician in his midfifties, decided to learn TM in the aftermath of his divorce. Dating again for the first time in decades was a curious experience for him—in equal parts exciting and daunting—as he pursued the dual goals of having fun and searching for a new partner. After several dates with one promising candidate, he became aware that she would repeatedly become close and intimate with him, then withdraw emotionally. Since he liked her a good deal but disliked feeling jerked around, he gently questioned her about his observations. She acknowledged that she had previously been dating another man. She was clear that she wanted to end the prior relationship, but felt there was unfinished business between them. And that was interfering with her ability to engage with a new boyfriend as fully as she would like.

In the past, my friend says, he would have regarded her withdrawal as a challenge and tried to force things, hoping that he could *make* them work out (too much engagement). Alternatively, he might have blamed himself for the repeated setbacks and dropped the relationship without discussion (too much detachment). Now he saw things differently, and he credits TM with giving him "a wise mind," which enabled him to reach an understanding of the situation as it was yet to leave room for a way to go forward. He told his friend that he liked her, but that it would be best if she could complete the unfinished business with her previous boyfriend. Then she could feel free to circle back to him if she was still interested.

We see here the delicate dance of engagement and detachment at work. Essentially, he was able to remain engaged emotionally with his lady friend, keeping the door open to further development of the relationship. At the same time, he realized that things could not move forward while she was still holding a candle for the other guy—all he could do was maintain a healthy detachment. In the past, he would have been too anxious to sit with the ambiguity, too insecure to see clearly that the lady's mixed signals did not necessarily have anything to do with him, and too needy to let this attractive woman go without "putting up a fight" for the relationship. His "wise mind"—which we might call his Super Mind—allowed him to negotiate these emotional currents with a grace and equanimity that would formerly have been unthinkable.

I will close this section with one final story. It concerns Julian, an architect in his midthirties, married with four children. He has been practicing TM now steadily for four years and has noticed changes in both engagement and detachment—in different spheres.

Here's how he puts it:

One result of meditation for me is being able to get up after twenty minutes and feel more connected to the world, more available to people—especially my wife and children, being in the moment with them—and much more a part of everything, instead of being kind of stuck in Julian's land. I'm more in tune with what's going on with my wife—not only more available to her but more connected emotionally to her and everything that's going on around me.

At the same time as Julian has been more connected with his family and the world, he has recently become less attached to material things, which he describes as follows:

I would constantly need to be buying things such as new shoes, going off to the mall to buy something—I don't know what, it almost didn't matter. We always had trouble managing money, my wife and I, because we were both shopaholics. For me, I think wanting something new was part of a need to feel happy, and attaching that happiness to whatever I was going to buy. Of course it didn't work. I'd feel a bit happier for a short while, until the next trip to the mall. And I don't spend money like that anymore, really. I mean, I buy my coffee in the morning and my lunch, but I don't ever feel the need to go buy something in the way I used to. I sense my attachment to materiality dissolving. Even today, as I was driving into the parking lot (I drive a Jetta wagon), I saw all these BMWs and other nice cars and thought to myself, "I could drive this car for the rest of my life. I think I'm going to stick with this one as long as it runs."

Julian and I have talked about these changes often. He has a clear understanding of expanded states of consciousness—a stillness that has entered his daily activities, a separate type of consciousness that operates alongside his sharp focus on his work and personal life. He credits this new type of consciousness with helping him lose interest in the momentary thrill of a new purchase or other type of "fix." In place of transient highs, he is enjoying ever-increasing success in his profession and a solid satisfaction in his marriage and family.

In the next section of the book, I will explain in detail how the transcendence that occurs during regular meditation begins to infiltrate your daily life, thereby accounting for many of the amazing effects that I am describing in this section.

At the time when I was training to become a psychiatrist, engagement and attachment were always emphasized. To love and to work, those were the two great psychological goals emphasized by Freud. "Only connect," is the famous quote by novelist E. M. Forster, carved in stone on a monument to the great writer. In Western culture, as in my training, connecting, loving, and attaching have been seen as signs of health. By contrast, the word "detachment" has had a faintly pathological odor. If you were "detached," you were unfeeling and uncaring, apart from humanity. That was the great crime of the protagonist in Albert Camus's *The Stranger*: he lacked feelings.

As I gathered experience, however, both as a psychiatrist and in life, I realized how common a problem it is to be *overly* attached, and others were arriving at the same insight. *Women Who Love Too Much*[2] became a number one *New York Times* bestseller in 1990, raising awareness of the prevalence of obsessive relationships and the pain they cause both women and men.

And just as twelve-step programs developed to help people detach from substances to which they are overattached, so there are similar programs for those addicted to behaviors such as gorging on sugary foods (as we saw in chapter 8), sex, gambling, and basically anything that can overstimulate the neurotransmitters of the brain's reward circuitry. Chemicals such as dopamine, endorphins, and anandamide have all evolved to feed the reward centers and encourage beneficial behaviors. It is easy therefore to see how mood-altering substances that mimic these endogenous chemicals—such as cocaine, opiates, and marijuana, respectively—and mood-altering behaviors can so easily become addictive.

It is now widely recognized that overattachment to relationships and addictive behaviors can be just as unhealthy as addictions to substances. To combat such addictive behaviors, detachment is often necessary, though difficult. Members of Al-Anon, for example, who come to meetings for help in dealing with their alcoholic relatives, are encouraged to "detach with love." They are taught how to negotiate a delicate balance: engaging with the people they love but without contributing to their addictive behaviors (as by giving them money) and the disasters that often follow.

In the Consciousness Integration Questionnaire, we included two separate questions that asked people whether, since starting to meditate, they had become (1) more present and engaged, and (2) less overly attached. Surprisingly, while 91 percent said they were more fully present and engaged, 88 percent said they were less overly attached. Apparently, they now find that loving engagement does not require overattachment.

In responding to the question about engagement, many people referred to being present and "in the moment," a subject we will pick up again in chapter 14, "Transcendence and Mindfulness." Here are some of their responses:

- I'm bringing an intensity to the moment. There is a "quickening," a clarity, an "unveiling" to each situation as my attention falls on it.
- There is pleasure in the moment now. I enjoy what I'm doing when I'm doing it, and find that I am so much better at doing those things too!

- I have a sense of the sacredness of the moment, and the experience of living and breathing. Very clear, not intellectually, but in terms of experience.
- And to think I was "sleepwalking" my way through life before.
- I used to dread the "chores" one has to take care of to live in this world. Now I enjoy whatever there is to do. Laundry. Cooking. Cleaning. "Well . . . I still hate vacuuming but I've learned to do it really fast and get it over with."

As far as not being overly attached is concerned, a number of people described how easily they can jettison "stuff," which they had formerly cherished. Here are two examples:

- It was quite easy to throw out or give away 90 percent of my stuff when I last moved. This included giving to family members some highly treasured heirlooms with great sentimental value to me. I wouldn't have been able to do that twenty years ago.
- I was in the film *Pulp Fiction*—a small part. I used to be attached to that fact as if it was so important and a part of my identity . . . LOL. Now I joke about my fun little part and even pawned my cast jacket to the show *Pawn Stars*, whereas before that jacket was a part of me, and some of my friends said I was crazy to give it away.

Nowadays the problem of hoarding has entered the public eye. We realize how very many people are literally unable to part with things that the impartial observer would classify as junk. Yet to the hoarder these relics of times gone by—for example, boxes of old newspapers—are seen as treasures. Although reality TV has turned the problem into a sort of comic spectacle, hoarding can in fact be tragic.

How nice it would be if the stillness that enters the lives of regular meditators could bring some peace to those people afflicted with hoarding (not to mention their beleaguered family) and help them to let go of their stuff. Here is a comment from one CIQ respondent suggesting that such a happy outcome may be possible:

It sounds self-contradictory but I simultaneously enjoy things more and feel less dependent on things for happiness. I am simplifying my life because I know excess possessions are just a burden.

Some people mentioned a shift of attachment from wealth and material objects to family and valued activities. Others pointed out that they are now more discriminating in their attachments, choosing to let certain people go while remaining connected to others.

In trying to explain just how he now experiences detachment, one man said, "The feeling of nonattachment is really obvious. It is not cognitive; I don't decide to be nonattached. It just happens."

For some people who responded to the CIQ, detachment was part of their growing resilience, helping them anticipate and avoid situations likely to create turmoil. One woman, for example, observed, "I'm better able to discern when I am attached to something that is none of my business or will create inner turmoil that is unnecessary or unproductive." Another said, "I used to get disappointed easily because I put too much weight on events." Another woman echoed the sentiment: "I used to become upset whenever I lost, damaged, or broke something of value. I would stay upset for a long time. Now the chagrin is much less intense, and it soon fades away. I have a stronger sense than before, both that these unfortunate incidents are part of life and that in my life I have had more than my fair share of good luck."

Some people specifically pointed out that they have experienced detachment with regard to control issues—in themselves or others. For example, one woman wrote, "I was in a relationship with someone who possessed controlling tendencies for two months until one day something clicked, and I took myself out of the situation without any regrets." For another woman, it was letting go of her own need to control that was important. As she put it:

I still have my opinions but view them as just that——my opinions, and I don't feel compelled to push them on others unless asked. Then I simply state my view without a lot of emotion. People used to say I was very outspoken and forceful, but lately I've received comments to the reverse.

Another woman stated it very simply: "I am less likely to try to control outcomes, and more likely to take it as it comes."

One man tried to reconcile the combination of engagement and nonattachment he has experienced since starting to meditate: "I desire less and less, and find satisfaction in the simple pleasure of daily living. I am enjoying my retirement and yet there are still conflicts that occasionally arise. When these happen, I don't seem to get emotionally overinvolved. I am pleased at how quickly conflicts seem to resolve themselves."

Although in all of these people, one has the sense of the Super Mind at work, in some instances it is so beautifully expressed as to be almost palpable. Here are a few examples:

- I realize more that I'm not a job, salary, degree, or a name. I am part of something greater.
- It is a nice detachment, not a detachment where you tune things out, but one that allows you to be yourself (Be your Self) while enjoying the world around you.
- I have a great love and appreciation for things around me, but I also seem to be quietly detached from things. I see the world as flow.
- Emotions are still there but don't overshadow the essential me. Love has become real and tangible. It is not so much an emotion as the glue that holds the cosmos together.
- Things come and go. Consciousness is the reality. I still have desires and enjoy things, but if they happen or do not happen, it is just fine.

In all these instances we see the balance that is such a welcome aspect of Super Mind development. Our emotions tend to knock us about as we navigate through life. The development of the Super Mind steadies us like the ballast in a ship. We still feel joy and pain, get excited, pursue goals and dreams, but alongside those forces that shove us about, a calmness develops that allows us the critical balm of detachment.

DEALING WITH DEATH

Everybody has got to die, but I always believed an exception would be made in my case.

William Saroyan

To live a thoughtful life requires coming to terms with death—including the prospect of our own inevitable demise. Some people, however, prefer to sidestep the task. A friend of mine, for example, a middle-aged woman, frequently visited her mother who was in the final stages of heart failure. On one of her visits, the daughter, Freda, asked her mother, "Do you think we should talk about dying?" The mother thought for a moment and said, "Do you know anything about dying, Freda?"

"Not really," Freda replied.

"Well, neither do I," said the mother. "So what's there to talk about?"

At the other end of the spectrum are those who remind themselves of dying every day (or night) even when they are in good health. Two famous cases are the poet John Donne and the actress Sarah Bernhardt. The former is reported to have slept in his own coffin and worn his own shroud—extreme behavior even for the time but understandable from the man who wrote "Death, Be Not Proud." Bernhardt, who also frequently slept in a coffin, claimed that it helped her better understand her tragic roles.[3]

These two methods of facing death (denial versus regularly climbing into a coffin) are extreme forms of a universal dynamic: We fear death. From an evolutionary point of view, this fear is a good thing. It helps us stay vigilant and thus to survive and, in the process, to be more successful in passing on our genes. From a psychological point of view, however, the fear of death can haunt people, interfering with our ability to make the most of our lives.

While the process of dying presents a challenge to our ability to engage pari passu with letting go, it is the *fear* of death that concerns us here. Can the Super Mind help soften this dynamic, which for some people can become a painful preoccupation?

I first thought about the effects of TM on how we deal with death when talking with my friend Richard Friedman, the psychiatrist and *New York Times* science columnist you met earlier in the book. He had several salient observations. Since starting to practice TM, he said, he had become less afraid of dying. He has also become less worried about immortality in the form of his legacy. Finally, when he learned that a friend was making a feature film about life after death, he realized to his surprise that despite being a hard-nosed scientist, he had become more open to this possibility. All these changes in relation to his thoughts on death have developed since he began to practice TM.

Lena Dunham, the hugely successful young actress, writer, and creator of the TV comedy *Girls*, is a longtime TM practitioner who says that TM has helped her come to terms with her fear of death. She explains it as follows:

> I think that meditation connected me to a part of myself that felt eternal and whole and not affected by . . . changes . . . because it's very deep and instinctual, but that's been something that's provided me a lot of comfort. I no longer wake up every day thinking, "Is today the day I'm going to die?" It's part of my consciousness, which I think

and believe is healthy, but it's not as fear-based as it once was, and that's definitely been a product of meditating.

In developing the Consciousness Integration Questionnaire, I took observations such as Richard Friedman's and Lena Dunham's into account in formulating the following questions:

Since starting to meditate, have you been less afraid of death?

Since starting to meditate, have your ideas about the possibility of life after death changed in any way?

Let us see what people said in response.

FEAR OF DEATH

Of those who answered the Consciousness Integration Questionnaire, most (72 percent) wrote that since starting to meditate, they had felt less afraid of dying.

Those people who followed up with narrative responses fell into the following self-reported basic categories:

1. Complex after-death theories, religious or otherwise, that protected them against a fear of death.
2. Decreased fear, attributed to various experiences.
3. Decreased fear, attributed directly to TM. Of this group, I found most interesting those people for whom their answer to the question was a happy surprise.

Let us set aside for now categories 1 and 2 and focus on the last category. Here are some remarks by others who report feeling better about the unpleasant matter of dying since learning TM:

• I have no fear of death. Through meditation I have lost a fear of a number of things. One day I simply noticed that the fear has just gone. Death is neither desired nor feared.

• I would even say I'm not concerned about dying. There is still the natural self-preservation impulse, but the concept of death doesn't bother me.

• I was having severe anxiety about aging, sickness, and death. It was regular and debilitating. My doctor wanted to prescribe medicine for it. But within a few months of meditating, it was 80 percent gone. After a year, completely gone.

- Yes, although I haven't thought of that question until it was asked here.
- I can answer yes to this easily, but we will see what actually transpires when I am really faced with a situation.
- With cancer reminding me of the importance of life, the meditation has helped me very much to put death on a back burner.
- I am markedly less fearful of several things, including death, since I started meditating. One of the most dramatic for me is flying. When I was young, I absolutely loved flying. Later I developed great anxiety about it and didn't fly for most of my adult life. Since meditating, that fear has completely dissipated. I am so thankful and happy about that as I have an adventurous spirit and that fear was a huge roadblock for me.

To be fair, here is the one contrarian response.

- I am now more afraid of death. I don't know if this is related to meditation or my increasing age.

Woody Allen famously wrote, "It's not that I'm afraid to die. I just don't want to be there when it happens." I thought of his quote in reading the questionnaire responses of those who distinguished between fear of suffering and fear of death. Here are a few examples:

- It is just a passage through a door; I am afraid of suffering, not death.
- Death? Ha! An old friend, just shuffling off another layer. Pain is the gent I despise.
- Yes!!!! This is one of the first deeply emotional things I noticed when I started practicing TM!!!! Very soon after starting TM, I lost the fear of death. I'm still, of course, afraid of suffering, but not of death.

A few people suggested that the repeated transcending that occurs when one meditates regularly may habituate the mind to the concept of letting go of waking consciousness in such a way as to make the prospect of death less frightening. Here is one example:

> I realized something after experiencing the rapturous transcendental state so many times in the last thirty years: It's almost as if I "die daily" . . . I experience this deep sense of peace and bliss during meditation so I've concluded that death is like meditation. . . . Death doesn't seem to matter any longer then.

Maharishi himself suggested this connection, noting:

> When life leaves the body, it is the breath leaving, like transcending. For one who has been accustomed to this experience for many years, the transition is easy, painless and blissful, not catastrophic. Dropping the body is like letting a bird out of its cage.4

A curious example of someone who discovered the ability to transcend by repeating his own name silently to himself—and who made the association between the experience of transcendence and decreased concern about death—is the poet Alfred Lord Tennyson. Here is a firsthand report of this experience, excerpted from a letter that found its way into William James's *Varieties of Religious Experience*.

> A kind of waking trance—this for lack of a better word—I have frequently had, quite up from boyhood, when I have been all alone. . . . All at once, as it were out of the intensity of the consciousness of individuality, the individuality itself seemed to dissolve and fade away into boundless being, and this not a confused state but the clearest, the surest of the surest . . . utterly beyond words—where death was an almost laughable impossibility, the loss of personality (if so it were) seeming no extinction, but the only true life. . . . I am ashamed of my feeble description. Have I not said the state is utterly beyond words? . . . There is no delusion in the matter! It is no nebulous ecstasy, but a state of transcendent wonder, associated with absolute clearness of mind.5

I find this account fascinating for reasons aside from the poetic words: First, it shows how in unusual circumstances someone can stumble upon a word—in this case one's own name—and use it to enter what sounds very much like a state of transcendence. Second, it is a lucid description of how it is possible to be intensely engaged (in this instance with the state of transcendence) and at the same time detached from one's own mortality to the point that death is "an almost laughable impossibility."

Taken together, our questionnaire data and personal accounts indicate that TM both facilitates detachment and enhances engagement, which is one of life's great joys. These attributes of expanded consciousness extend even to accepting the prospect of death. A plausible mechanism for such acceptance is that the regular practice of transcendence allows the meditator to detach from the fear of loss—even the loss of one's own life. Such detachment can help a person let go of one's last remaining treasure—life itself—while remaining engaged in the process of living as long as body and mind permit.

TO SUMMARIZE THIS CHAPTER'S FINDINGS:

- One of life's challenges is to balance the emotional requirements to be engaged in life and its pursuits while, at the same time, avoiding overattachment—to relationships, ideas, course of action, or life itself.
- Based on our survey responses and anecdotes, TM appears to promote the delicate balance between these apparently opposing needs.

13

SUPPORT OF NATURE

May the road rise up to meet you.
May the wind be ever at your back.
May the sun shine warm upon your face
and the rain fall softly on your fields.
And, until we meet again,
may God hold you in the palm of His hand.

traditional Irish blessing

As we move through life, most of us have the sense that no matter how hard we try, there will always be elements we can't fully control, such as our looks, intelligence, health, and a myriad of other factors. Hopefully, sooner or later we come to terms with the hand we're dealt. But the sweepstakes don't stop there. We still have to deal with another huge variable, one that can trump all other playing cards—luck. Lady Luck, the luck of the draw, the luck of the Irish are just a few of the many images that luck conjures up. My mother used to say, "You should only have luck," an acknowledgment of the importance of this overwhelming influence on the trajectory of a person's life. I have little doubt that every culture must have its traditions for attracting good luck (a horse shoe, a ladybug, a wishbone), for not losing good luck (knock on wood), or for averting bad luck. My grandmother and her sisters recommended attaching a concealed red ribbon to a baby's diaper to avert any evil eye that an envious onlooker might cast in the infant's direction.

I first saw the Irish blessing in this chapter's epigraph hanging on a friend's kitchen wall. You can imagine the layout: plain wooden frame, white mat, Gothic calligraphy, adorned by a large four-leafed clover, perhaps with a leprechaun staring from behind. But the text captured the essence of the matter: luck in the sense that sometimes everything seems to go your way, while at other times nothing seems to go right.

In analyzing the results of the CIQ survey, we found that almost three-quarters of respondents (72 percent) said they felt they had been luckier since starting to meditate. That was one of the items that made up the "support of nature" factor. Other items grouped under that factor included changes in relationships and finances—predominantly favorable (89 percent and 55 percent, respectively); the item "others noticed the positive changes" in 72 percent of the respondents. Yet one item endorsed by the large majority (85 percent) of CIQ respondents may explain, at least in part, the rest of these items—healthier choices.

That leads to the question, "Does luck really enter into it at all or do we make our own luck?" In other words, we're all subject to the forces acting upon us, but perhaps our state of mind (or Super Mind) influences our attitude, judgment, and actions, which in turn influence our luck.

What, if anything, can we do to influence our luck? And what does TM have to do with it? There are no controlled studies that speak to the support of nature, so we will need to depend here on anecdotes, fortified by survey data from the Consciousness Integration Questionnaire. Assuming that support of nature is a common experience among TM practitioners (as it seems to be), I will consider what factors might play a role in this happy phenomenon and how the elements of the Super Mind with which we are already quite familiar might contribute to those factors.

The curious phenomenon of support of nature in the context of TM came to my attention when I interviewed Anna, a Scottish litigator, for an earlier book, *Winter Blues*.[1] Anna had learned TM specifically to help with her symptoms of seasonal affective disorder (SAD) and had found it to be highly beneficial. Despite strong initial skepticism about the practice, at the recommendation of a credible friend who had "raved about TM," Anna told me, "I was so stressed out with a case at that time, you could have scraped me off the ceiling. I thought, 'What do I have to lose by doing TM other than the money?'"

To Anna's surprise, TM helped not only with her winter depression, but also with her temperament in general. I have excerpted the following paragraphs from *Winter Blues*:

"I still don't understand the logic of it, but the technique works for me. Even though I still dislike the winter, I can cope with it. . . . ? I used to spend a whole lot of energy getting my knickers in a twist. Now I'm not as uptight about little things, and if I start along that path, I stop myself more quickly. Even though I'm not walking on air, life has improved across the board." Including her luck: Read on!

Although others don't know the secret of Anna's transformation, they have certainly noticed it. According to Anna, "My opponent in a trial said, 'You're not your usual jangly self,' and my clerk asked me if I was on medication because I was doing so much better. If I miss my TM for a while, people can tell the difference, even over the phone. I am much quicker to rile, angrier, and jangly." On the other hand, when Anna does her TM regularly, she says:

Everything seems to fall into place. People are nicer to me because I am nicer to them. I get more the luck of the draw. For example, shop attendants are more likely to be helpful to me. Recently, when I traveled to a small town and was trying to find the court, I saw two parking wardens, and though they are not my favorite people—delighting as they do in issuing tickets—I asked them for directions. Not only did they show me where the court was, but they went to look for a parking space for me where I needn't pay and walked ahead of my car, showing me the way. Who has ever heard of a parking warden doing that?

I was reminded of Anna when I was about to board an airplane some time ago, several years after I had begun to practice TM consistently. Luggage regulations allowed for one carry-on and one "personal item." There were also strict size restrictions. Although I didn't know exactly what they were, I knew them to be variably enforced and as I viewed the two largish items I was holding, I could only hope for leniency. As I approached the checkpoint, I saw a stingy-looking metal frame into which my carry-on must fit in order not to be checked. A large, vigilant, and angry-looking woman opposite the metal frame brought to mind Cerberus, standing guard at the gate of Hades. Reflexively I crouched, to make myself and everything I carried look smaller. In this regard I failed. "It's too big!" she barked at me. "Check it!"

"What if I take some stuff out of there"—I pointed at the carry-on— "and put it in there?" I pointed at the personal item.

"That won't work either!"

I looked at her and saw someone obviously under stress, probably having to argue and fight with people all day long. I said, "Do you think there is some way that we can work this out together?"

She looked at me, astonished, and was quiet for a long moment. Then her face softened, and she said, "Sure, honey. We'll find a way." And we did. I thanked her and as I went on my way, I overheard her say to someone, "Did you hear that? It's the first kind word anybody has said to me in six months."

That's when I thought of Anna and how succinctly she had put her change of fortune: "People are nicer to me because I am nicer to them. I get more the luck of the draw." I know that I am a much nicer person since I have been meditating regularly—and people have indeed been nicer to me and I have felt luckier.

French writer Anaïs Nin is credited with first saying, "We don't see things as they are, we see them as we are." If we are stressed, depressed, or angry, others will often see us as rude, withholding, or threatening—and will treat us accordingly. If we are calm, happy, and open, others are more likely to feel good in our presence and well disposed toward us. There is no guarantee that they will, of course, but they are more likely to. As the American writer Damon Runyon said, riffing off Ecclesiastes, "The race is not always to the swift, nor the battle to the strong, but that's the way to bet."

I have treated many people with depression and anxiety, anger management problems, and other forms of distress. Generally, they experience their world as unfriendly or hostile, but invariably, once they feel better, they perceive others as being nicer—which they probably are. So there is a dynamic interplay between how we see the world and how the world sees us. After we have been meditating for a while and feel less stressed, after a stillness settles into our daily consciousness, we are more apt to view the world in a more kindly light and vice versa. When this happens over and over again, it truly feels as though there is a confederacy of people wishing us well and supporting us in various ways.

Another way in which support of nature may appear is in situations of conflict. Consider Anita, for example, a fledgling designer who secured a job with a Manhattan company. Within months of her arrival there, she was assigned to take the lead on a design project for New York City—a high-level job, considering her junior status. Luckily, Anita had recently started to meditate, and that made all the difference. The meditation helped her handle the stresses of the work, and somehow solutions to problems seemed to fall into place more easily. Instead of worrying about the whole project in all its detail,

Anita found it easy to take things one at a time. Here's how she describes her early TM experiences and their effects on her:

> On my fourth day of meditation, I spontaneously wept from a deep place within me. There was no particular subject related to it. What was most memorable was how safe I felt during the experience, and how relaxed I felt after. The world felt softer to me. It felt similar to the tenderness of a plant pushing its first sprouts through the ground. Beginning a new way of life.

Anita's project with the city was challenging, particularly because of several difficult people who stood in the path of progress. As she continued to meditate, the tender plant found that an unexpected tough side was developing as well. She became increasingly assertive both in meetings and in e-mails, though always in a very professional and courteous manner. This shift seemed to happen organically. She didn't *tell* herself to be more assertive; she just became so. And somehow people responded in a positive way. Nevertheless, the project eventually reached a stalemate because of one person who was preventing Anita from collecting the outstanding receivables (the city had been slow to pay). Success seemed impossible.

Anita kept meditating, however, taking things one at a time in a calm way. Then, to her surprise, without any specific intervention on her part, the difficult person was suddenly replaced and the new committee head was far easier to deal with. Anita could hardly believe her good fortune, as she felt a huge burden slip away—and after that things continued to fall into place. It reminded her of a video she had seen called *Creating Your Own Reality.* Through the process of meditation, Anita felt herself changing, and as she changed, the world around her seemed to change as well.

Anita reminds me of a friend of mine, Mirela Sula, a therapist originally from Albania, who is currently living in London, England. Although these countries are seventeen hundred miles apart, that distance hardly does justice to the vast chasm between these two worlds. Here is how Mirela describes her life in Albania in her book, *Don't Let Your Mind Go.*[2]

> At the age of twenty I lived in a remote village in the northern part of Albania. I was a bride in a big family with customs and traditions that

I had to abide by. It was expected that I bake the bread, clean the house—as well as the backyard—and wait for the goats to come in from the pasture. This was my life. I was isolated in the middle of the mountains where the nearest house was ten minutes away. . . . The one thing that sticks in my mind that I cannot forget is the requirement that a woman had to wash her father's and husband's feet. Yes, too many times I have washed my stepfather's feet. This was a necessary criterion for a female to be a good woman at that time. . . . This appeared to me to be my luck in life. However, I actually never accepted this as a part of my life and I knew that this would not be my future.

Somehow, as if by a miracle, Mirela managed to work her way from rural Albania to London. She attributes this in part to extensive reading, but particularly to learning TM. Despite her rural setting, Mirela succeeded in graduating as a psychotherapist and started a magazine. Nevertheless, she urgently wanted to change her life but couldn't see how. In her culture it was unacceptable to get a divorce "only because you want something better." To complicate matters, by then she had a thirteen-year-old son.

As you can imagine, Mirela encountered obstacle after obstacle, but over her husband's protestations, she left for London. She kept meditating, and in time her son joined her in London, at first for visits and later to stay. The divorce, however, was the final obstacle. According to Albanian law, her husband had to consent, which he declined to do. He told her, "No way, no chance. Don't even dream about it." They had a lot of arguments about it. Then one day, during meditation, she recalls, "A voice came to me that said, 'Why do you continue to argue with him? You don't need to focus your energy and attention on him. Focus on what you want.'"

From then on she focused on her desire to be free and choose those people she wanted as her friends and associates. She let her husband know that from her point of view the marriage was over. He could do what he wanted. And she kept meditating. Then one day he called and told her he would start the divorce proceedings from his end. She didn't believe him and wondered if this was some game he was playing—until the divorce papers arrived. Later he allowed her son to join her in London, where they now live together.

The story has a happy ending. Mirela and her ex-husband have been able to put aside their differences in order to co-parent their son, who speaks to his father daily. On one thing they agree: their son needs two parents. Presumably as Mirela became calmer but remained resolute, her husband settled down too and was able to shift his perspective—a reasonable explanation. But to Mirela it felt like she was being supported by unseen forces, thanks in part of TM.

I have linked Anita and Mirela together in this section because in both cases other people fell into line with what they wanted and thought was right. In both cases, however, it was only possible due to the moderating effects of TM, which allowed them to be clear in their vision and firm in their resolve. So we see another way in which the support of nature manifests itself.

GOOD PARKING SPOTS AND OTHER LUCKY BREAKS

Let us turn now to the CIQ, to see what it can tell us about the support of nature among TM practitioners. Of particular interest were the answers to the question, "Since starting to meditate, do you feel you have been luckier or that things have gone your way more than before without your having to put any extra effort into them?" Of all responders, about three-quarters answered yes, and of those, yet again three-quarters said this happened frequently or very frequently.

When I looked at the narrative responses, I was particularly interested by the number of people who commented on how much easier it was to find good parking spots since starting to meditate. Here are a few specific examples:

- I normally know exactly where my parking spot is going to be, even if the lot is crowded.
- I find parking places easily. Traffic opens up for me. Etc. and etc. Many etcs.

Responses such as these (and there were many) suggest that the responders believe that their luck has in fact changed—that the universe is being kinder—and often they provide other instances of "good luck."

Here is an especially impressive example:

- I used to always feel that I was a day late for everything. Whatever I wanted, it felt like I never got to it or thought of it in time. Someone else would beat me to it. But now it feels the opposite. Lately I have been in the right place at the right time. I have found the people I needed to connect with. I've been able to get things I wanted, not necessarily material things—but important ones.

Other TM practitioners, such as those quoted below, also recognize that life seems to go their way more often, but favor a more scientific explanation:

- I think I am simply more aware of how much good actually happens. So I don't know if things have changed or if my awareness has changed.
- Turns out "luck" is determined in large part by receptivity to change, circumstances, and unexpected happenings. I enjoy being open to new experiences, therefore everything offers some point of interest.
- Joy begets luck.
- I define luck as when preparation meets opportunity. I believe in continually preparing and honing my skills, so that when opportunity arrives, I can step into it without fear. You may call it luck, but I believe it's diligence and faith.

To be fair, there were a few contrarian responses, such as these:

- To be honest, I've always been pretty lucky (knock on wood),

and

- Things have gotten worse.

Bob Roth points out that the experience of being supported by nature does not come exclusively to those who meditate, and is often attributable to how a person feels on any given day. As he puts it:

These common experiences often have simple explanations (even if you are not a meditator). If you sleep poorly for a few days, you feel "off," and nothing seems to go your way. You miss a parking space, are late for a phone call, and lose things. You say you had a "bad" day. On the other hand, get a good night's sleep, exercise, eat well, feel strong, and you seem to be automatically in the "flow." Things go

your way more often than not. You say you had a "good" day. That is
similar to what happens when you meditate. Things just seem to go
your way more often than not. You have more good days than bad.

HOW MIGHT NATURE SUPPORT US? LET US COUNT THE WAYS

As I see it, here are some ways to categorize these support of nature experiences. (Perhaps you may have some additional explanations.)

1. You are nicer to others, so they become nicer to you.
2. You are more likely to see the good around you than you were
    before.
3. You are clearer in yourself and set firmer boundaries. You are
    therefore less likely to be mistreated and more likely to be taken
    seriously.
4. You take advantage of fortuitous happenstances. (As Louis Pas-
    teur famously remarked, "Chance favors the prepared mind.")
5. You read others and the world more accurately—much as a sailor
    who has a better feel for the winds and the currents can navigate
    more skillfully. You take ownership and responsibility for read-
    ing your environment correctly and responding appropriately.

Whatever the explanation, there is general agreement that after beginning to practice TM, as the Super Mind develops, life becomes easier and the
world seems like a more cooperative and embracing place. It feels as though
nature is supporting your efforts, dreams, and aspirations.

TO SUMMARIZE THE HIGHLIGHTS OF THIS CHAPTER:

•   After starting to meditate, many TM practitioners observe that
    things seem to go their way more frequently than before—as
    though the world is supporting their actions and well-being.
•   Several examples of such apparent good luck were presented, and
    a number of potential explanations were provided to explain this
    phenomenon.

14

TRANSCENDENCE AND MINDFULNESS

The most important time is now. The present
is the only time over which we have power.

Leo Tolstoy

We are all, all of us, pilgrims who struggle
along different paths toward the same
destination.

Antoine de Saint-Exupéry

It's surprising how often I find myself talking with strangers about meditation. It might be with a cabdriver who sees me with my eyes closed or the person next to me on the plane. One thing is clear to me: The fascination with meditation in the United States is on a growth curve. As we talk, however, it becomes apparent in most instances that people think all forms of meditation are the same. When I start explaining to them that different forms of meditation come from different traditions, ask different things of the meditator, and have different effects on the brain, their eyes begin to glaze over and they make generic statements that suggest that these are distinctions without a difference—abstruse matters that concern only the specialist. Meditation is good, and that's all they want to know.

This chapter is intended for those people who would like to understand, at least to some degree, the difference between two forms of meditation that arise from two great traditions: mindfulness from the Buddhist tradition, and Transcendental Meditation from the Vedic tradition. And there are indeed differences, as I hope to illuminate. Let me hasten to add, though, what this chapter is not. First, I am not attempting to review the extensive literature on mindfulness. An Amazon search for "mindfulness" (as of the day of this writing) reveals more than thirty-five thousand book titles, suggesting that yet one more book on the subject (especially from someone who is by no means an expert in the field) is the last thing the reader needs. There is also an extensive scientific literature, with hundreds of papers finding benefits of mindfulness for various physical and emotional conditions. If you wish to learn more about these, you'll find some review articles in the notes, along with one critical commentary.[1]

Second, this comparison is not a competition between two practices. In a nation where millions of devoted fans watch teams competing furiously against one another week after week, it may seem natural to ask, "So, which one is better? Which meditation team wins?" Although each school has millions of followers, many of whom fervently recommend one above the other, as of the time of this writing there is not to my knowledge even one published head-to-head comparison between the effects of mindfulness and TM, either with regard to physical or psychological measures. So any statement about the superiority of one versus the other is at this time without scientific basis. Nevertheless, the data in favor of one versus the other form of meditation may be stronger in certain areas than in others, which may simply reflect the focus of researchers working in these different fields. For example, the extensive data supporting cardiovascular benefits of TM (see chapter 8) are not to my knowledge available for studies of mindfulness. Thus, the American Heart Association has endorsed only the use of TM as a complementary treatment for high blood pressure—not meditation in general—as of the time of this writing.[2] Perhaps there are data supporting advantages for mindfulness, but not TM, of which I am unaware.

Although I strive here to present a balanced picture, I cannot claim to be a neutral observer. Although I seek to be mindful in my daily life, I don't practice mindfulness in a formal way, nor am I steeped in the subject. On the other hand, I practice TM twice a day without fail and have spent thousands of hours thinking, reading, and writing about the subject. Also, the anecdotal reports to which I have access come predominantly from TM practitioners. Aware of these disparities, I will do my best to present this important comparison in an evenhanded manner.

WHAT IS MINDFULNESS?

For a lovely description of eating an apple mindfully, take a look at the poem "Mystic" by D. H. Lawrence (see chapter 19). For a more professional description of mindfulness in everyday life, allow me to quote my friend and colleague Rezvan Ameli, a psychologist working at the National Institute of Mental Health and author of *25 Lessons in Mindfulness*,[3] who has been teaching mindfulness for ten years.

> You may ask yourself when was the last time you chewed very slowly and really tasted and sensed the fragrance of a single grape, a cherry, or a bite from an apple with your complete attention? How often have you taken the time to notice the sensation of the cloth from your clothing on your skin? Have you been conscious of the felt sensation of wool, cotton, or silk? Have you ever brought your full attention to a single breath and closely followed it from the beginning to the end? How do the bottoms of your feet feel? Have you noticed the way in which you balance your weight on the four corners of your feet? Do you pay attention to the components of a single step? How do you lift, move, and place your foot as you step forward? Do you ever bring your full attention, curiosity, and open attitude to a pain experience, or rather quickly and automatically decide to reach for the bottle of ibuprofen or some other remedy? Attention to and acceptance of these everyday experiences help to increase the awareness of the present moment. The idea is not to judge or evaluate these experiences, rather simply to notice them. By doing so, we will dwell less in the past or the future and adjust and relinquish our expectations about how things should be. Rather, we accept and allow what is. As such, we greatly diminish stress, unhappiness, and suffering.[4]

According to Ameli, "Mindfulness has three indispensible components. One piece is intention, one is attention, and one is compassion." She elaborates the definition by saying that "I would define mindfulness as paying attention in a focused way, with a certain attitude, which basically is defined as the attitude of openness, friendliness, acceptance, you know, of love. I mean love sums it up." Ameli points out that Thich Nhat Hanh, the Vietnamese Buddhist monk whom she regards as "the living embodiment of mindfulness," defines it as "being in touch with your felt experience in each moment."[5] Jon

Kabat-Zinn, emeritus professor of medicine at the University of Massachusetts Medical School and a pioneer in developing mindfulness as it is widely used, defines the practice as "paying attention, on purpose, in the present, and non-judgmentally, to the unfolding of experience moment by moment."[6]

Mindfulness encompasses two different types of meditation, according to the classification of Fred Travis and Jonathan Shear:[7] open monitoring, which includes being mindful of internal states, such as breathing, one's own sensations, thoughts, or feelings; and focused attention, in which attention is selectively directed toward an image, idea, feeling, or other specific target.

Although mindfulness can be applied to many different activities, such as breathing, walking, and eating, to name just a few, the practice requires training if it is to be done properly. Training in one popular form of mindfulness, Mindfulness Based Stress Reduction (MBSR), for example, typically requires eight sessions lasting 2.5 to 3 hours per session with a one-day retreat lasting 6 to 8 hours—for a total of about 30 hours on average.

Even the short synopsis that I have provided so far should make it clear that mindfulness and TM are very different practices. In mindfulness, the meditator is systematically trained to intentionally focus attention on something in particular, whereas in Transcendental Meditation emphasis is placed on the automatic ease with which a mantra is accessed. That accounts for its allocation to a third category in the Travis and Shear classification: "automatic self-transcending."

To refresh your understanding of some of the key differences between mindfulness and TM, I recommend you look again at figure 1 on page 19.

There is another important distinction between mindfulness as properly taught and TM: Mindfulness is difficult; TM is easy. The first statement is not my opinion alone, but that of no less an expert than Bhante Henepola Gunaratana, author of the classic work *Mindfulness in Plain English*, which Jon Kabat-Zinn has called a masterpiece. Here's what Gunaratana has to say on the matter at the beginning of chapter 1 of his book:

> Meditation is not easy. It takes time and it takes energy. It also takes grit, determination, and discipline. It requires a host of personal qualities that we often regard as unpleasant and like to avoid whenever possible. We can sum up all of these qualities in the American word *gumption*. Meditation takes gumption.[8]

I have to admire the honesty of these opening remarks. Anyone who goes on to read the rest of the book evidences tough-mindedness for not being deterred by this warning. Alas, I was not one of them. Perhaps I lack gumption. Or perhaps it was simply because I had personally found TM to be simple and easy, as advertised. Here, for example, is how the TM technique is described on the official TM website[9] in a statement attributed to the Mayo Clinic.

> Transcendental Meditation is a simple, natural technique.... This form of meditation allows your body to settle into a state of profound rest and relaxation and your mind to achieve a state of inner peace, without needing to use concentration or effort.

This description conforms entirely to my own experience with TM, and that of dozens of friends and patients whom I have referred for TM training and followed over years. For example, one of my patients, a young man, recently summed up his experience with TM as follows: "It's mind-bogglingly simple but unbelievably powerful."

CONSCIOUSNESS: STATE AND CONTENT

Early in this book I made a distinction between the state or quality of consciousness and its contents. When people practice TM, they experience a change in their state of consciousness, which is known as transcendence or, according to Vedic tradition, the fourth state of consciousness. After meditating for a while, people find this transcendent state entering their daily lives, an early sign of the Super Mind. In no way is any content introduced or encouraged as part of TM training. Nevertheless, the shifts in consciousness precede (and almost certainly induce) major changes in how the body and brain work, as well as in the contents of consciousness. For example, seasoned TM practitioners often feel more compassion for their fellow human beings, even though this shift in attitude has not been directly suggested.

In contrast, mindfulness practices do not claim or aspire to induce alterations in states of consciousness, whereas they do directly encourage alterations in the *contents of consciousness.* Thus, as Ameli puts it, "We cultivate our attention with an open, accepting, and friendly attitude. There are several specific compassion training practices such as loving kindness, giving and receiving, and forgiveness."

Chris Germer, a friend and colleague, and author of *The Mindful Path to*

Self-Compassion, practices loving-kindness compassion as his core form of meditation. When I interviewed him for this book, I asked him what kind of meditation he had done on that particular day. He said he had started with TM, then moved on to loving-kindness compassion. Here's how our conversation went:

> **NR: WHAT DID YOUR MINDFULNESS PRACTICE CONSIST OF TODAY?**
> CG: Whoever came to mind I reflected on and thought, "May he have peace. May he be free," or "May she have peace. May she be free."
>
> **NR: AND WHO CAME TO MIND, FOR EXAMPLE?**
> CG: It could be anyone—a friend, family member, or someone I met that day. Or even a dog or other animal.
>
> **NR: AND WHAT WOULD YOU THINK IF KIM JONG-UN CAME TO MIND? (THE NORTH KOREAN DICTATOR HAD BEEN PARTICULARLY BELLICOSE IN THE WEEKS LEADING UP TO MY INTERVIEW WITH CHRIS.)**
> CG: I would think, "May he have peace. May he be free." Which would be a very good thing. If he had peace and were free, a lot of people would be a lot happier.

I respect and admire such cultivation of positive thoughts and feelings, which are integral to mindfulness practices. In addition, it is self-evident that such practices would inculcate congruent states of mind in those who perform them on a regular basis. How could they but wish to make the world a better place? In a very different way, there is evidence that the regular practice of TM, which fosters transcendence and the development of consciousness, is also likely to promote kindness and harmony—and perhaps greater peace among people. In this regard, the two practices have elements in common.

WHY NOT DO BOTH?

If TM and mindfulness are both helpful in different ways (as I believe they are), why not simply do both? One obvious reason is time. It is hard enough to maintain even one regular meditation practice in the busy lives we lead, let alone two. Another is that different forms of meditation might suit different people. It would be interesting to research whether certain types of people prefer one form of meditation over another—and not surprising if this turns out to be the case. In this section, however, I would like to introduce to you two people who *do* practice both forms, and find that each yields its own particular benefits.

CHUCK BLIZIOTIS: THEY EACH SERVE UNIQUE PURPOSES

Entertainment marketing consultant Chuck Bliziotis writes:

I practice both TM and mindfulness meditation—they each serve unique purposes. I begin and end each day with TM. With it I'm able to still my mind, de-stress, and start the day open and relaxed. My profession is entertainment marketing—a remarkable aspect of TM is that some of my best ideas come right after practice, while sitting quiet and calm, allowing my mind to drift. It is in this drift that I'm able to see the connectivity of what I'm working on and possible solutions or outcomes—it's still exciting each time it happens. I end each day with TM practice: it helps to let the day wash out, letting go, drifting off to a deeper sleep and more rested morning. I believe that TM is directly responsible for sharpening my visual and intellectual memory, recall, and creativity. It is part of my foundation.

Mindfulness works to facilitate clarity, focus, compassion, and truth. As humans we have the tendency to create narratives (I more than most), and mindfulness allows me to examine clearly exactly what is going on, what is being said, and notice my reaction to it—all done by breathing slowly, rhythmically, and being aware of what is happening inside. This practice allows me to take a "step back," listen to what is being said, and respond with compassion that goes to the heart of the issue at hand. It is difficult at times not to get caught up in the heat of the moment, as well as to face what we truly fear. Mindfulness takes courage to look at the world as it is.

LAURA: TWO TOOLS WITH DIFFERENT PURPOSES

Laura is an artist, writer, and teacher whom I have been seeing in my practice for some time. She learned mindfulness in a multiweek formal training course taught at Johns Hopkins University about ten years before this interview. Six years later she learned TM in the hope that it would help her manage her winter depressions. She practices both regularly, and has this to say about what she has gained from the two techniques:

Mindfulness

The ongoing impact mindfulness training has had on me is in how to quiet the emotions and quiet the mind, and appreciate life as it's passing right in front of you. One of the things you learn to do is simply acknowledge how you're feeling in the present moment. And acknowledging that and saying to yourself, I am happy today and I'm enjoying the sun today. I'm feeling a lot of confused emotions today. Somehow it's very calming to the mind. I can't explain the mechanism, but in some ways you're not fighting your internal monologue.

You're acknowledging it, bringing it up into the light, and you're sort of letting it go. Other things I really enjoy are just seeing the present moment, a visual. One of the things I happen to do as a daily meditation is sweep the floor. I happened to get brand-new wooden floors in my house at the time this course took place. And sweeping the beautiful wood floor was an enormous pleasure. The new floor was so beautiful, and the old carpet so ugly, it was a great transformation of my house. But it kept me focused on my actions in the present moment—not going back and not going forward and projecting. And that was the biggest thing that I've taken from mindfulness.

I practice mindfulness every day as part of my daily orientation for life. A lot of the day and especially when I'm feeling sort of upset emotional states, I turn to mindfulness and acknowledge my feelings, and I try to listen and look, and be in the present moment.

I wish I could say it was transformational, but I haven't experienced that. But I would say it certainly increased my quality of life to a great degree. And it's certainly helped me manage my fluctuating mood swings every day.

Mindfulness is part of a tool kit that any person can take with them. Some people go on to insight meditation. They link the two. I have never had particular insights from mindfulness. I use it to regulate moods and manage daily life. I have just not practiced it in a way that has led to deeper insights.

Transcendental Meditation

TM has a different, I would have to say magical, impact only because I have no idea why it works (laughs). I cannot, I cannot figure it out. TM has the ability to remove pain, actually. It's some sort of miracle thing. I've gone through painful medical procedures, practiced TM during them, and not felt the discomfort one would expect. I cannot explain that, except that it happened for me. I find that when I practice TM, I have a greater flow of creative ideas that help me organize my day and be productive. I also find that I'm much less reactive. I'm an irritable person. I may hide it well, but I'm pretty irritable. And when I'm practicing TM, I'm much more able to step aside from whatever it is and be calm.

I asked Laura to tell me more about the effects of TM on her creativity. Here's how she replied:

Most recently I've had some losses in my family and I've had a lot of trouble getting back to my artwork. And recently, within the past two or three weeks, I have started to practice TM twice a day regularly (previously it had been once or twice a day). And as a result of that I have suddenly turned out a whole series of prints. I'm an artist and a printmaker. And I've created a whole series of prints that I'm continuing to produce right now. I suddenly was able to put aside the distractedness and loss of concentration and just get down to work. And I actually didn't use those words in my mind ("get back to work"). I said, well, let's just sit down and play with this and see what happens. And as a result of saying that in my mind, I turned out all these prints, which are just exploring the process of white line printing, and I'm continuing to do it right now. I seem to have gotten over a barrier that was standing in my way. So most recently that's an example.

TM somehow encourages productive risk taking. It has allowed me to sketch in public, and take on some public roles that I might not normally do. And I really can't explain why it would have that effect, but I just have started to do these more public things since I've started meditating twice a day.

I asked Laura if TM had helped her self-actualize—to be her best self (a topic I will discuss further in chapter 16). She replied:

Yes. I do, and I'm thinking not only about my prints, my paintings, and my writings, but even about how I've been a community activist over the past two years. I've done public speaking and interviews on television, and written speeches, and become a local community leader. And I'm really surprised by that role. It's not a role I would have picked for myself. And yet I've done it and enjoyed it, and maybe it's a role I will continue if the opportunity presents itself.

Also, in the past eight months, since starting to meditate regularly twice a day, I've written a book proposal, I've started to market it, and I hope to sell it. I'm going to pick up that process also. It's all ready to go; it's set out. And it's certainly not something I contemplated or produced before six to eight months ago. There were many years where—I'm an excellent writer but—I really hadn't produced anything that would be sold. I'm sure TM has a role in changing that. As you speak of self-actualizing, I'm sure that writing is part of that too, trying to break that block. I deliberately stepped away from writing, and I was lucky enough to be able to paint. So that's what I've done. I am a person who needs to take more risks and put myself out there more, and I haven't done so for a variety of reasons. And I can see that since I've started TM, these things have happened. I can't explain it but it's clear. I'm sitting here surrounded by the results.

It is difficult to make meaningful generalizations from just two people. Nevertheless, as we look at Chuck and Laura, certain themes emerge.

Mindfulness, as advertised, has helped both people to be present in the moment and experience it fully. In Chuck's case, the payoff for this has been "to take a 'step back,' listen to what is being said, and to respond with compassion that goes to the heart of the issue at hand . . . [to take the] courage to look at the world as it is." In Laura's case, mindfulness has been calming, has increased the quality of her life to a great degree, and helped her regulate her moods.

TM has helped both people to still their minds, a property that they carry forward into the day. In Chuck's case, this allows him to start his day open and relaxed. In Laura's case, the stillness has reduced her irritability. As she puts it, "On days, especially when I do TM twice, I have the ability to step away from situations. I feel the acceleration toward irritation, and then I just feel it fall away." It is this sort of stillness in the presence of activity that suggests the early stages of the Super Mind.

In Laura's case, she describes a powerful effect of TM in preventing pain during medical procedures. This type of effect on the body is commonly seen in people who practice TM and may also manifest as improved blood pressure and cardiovascular function, and in other ways. One example you may recall is the ballerina Megan Fairchild, whose fainting spells disappeared after she started TM.

One benefit of TM that both people described in detail is its effect on cognitive functioning, creativity, and, in Laura's case, creative risk taking. Such effects, which carry over from meditation into the active day, are commonly seen in those practicing TM. If you want to refresh your memory about them, look back to chapter 9, "Building a Better Brain." This is one of the prime reasons why TM—and the state of the Super Mind that it induces—is of particular interest to those seeking to perform at their highest potential.

One possible difference between the two techniques may relate to the ease with which TM practitioners enter "the zone"—a state that is important for athletes and artists, among others. Such people—like Megan Fairchild and Barry Zito, featured in this book—have particularly singled out TM as valuable in this regard. Being in the zone requires one's active thinking mind—such as the prefrontal cortex—to go off-line and allow long-practiced skills to proceed with automatic ease. In this regard, mindfulness, which stresses active attentiveness to specific aspects of awareness might be less useful—or even detrimental—though solid data on this point are currently lacking.

In Chuck and Laura, we have two people who practice both forms of meditation, each reporting sufficient benefit to keep doing both on a regular basis. The benefits are different and, for Chuck and Laura, complementary. As Laura puts it, "I use them as I'd use tools in the kitchen. They have different purposes. Both a spoon and a knife are useful but different."

Mario Orsatti, a longtime TM teacher, whom you will meet again in the next chapter, has experiences which support Chuck's and Laura's observations. He has taught TM to a group of New York therapists who work with teenagers and adults in recovery. All of these therapists had previously been formally trained in mindfulness meditation, which allowed them to compare their experiences of the two types of meditation. All concluded that each type led to two different sets of benefits. Most found that it worked better to do TM first (corroborating Chuck's experience) and felt that their mindfulness work was sharpened and enhanced when done in this way. In my experience, TM puts one in a better frame of mind for undertaking any activity, including work requiring focus and concentration, such as mindfulness.

IS THE "WANDERING MIND" AN UNHAPPY ONE?

Do you have a wandering mind? And if so, is it an unhappy one? In a celebrated study published in the prestigious journal *Science*, Matthew Killingsworth and Daniel Gilbert of Harvard University conclude, as the title of the article reflects, that "A Wandering Mind Is an Unhappy Mind."[10]

In this study, the authors developed a web application for the iPhone that allowed them to contact participants at random moments during their waking hours to assess what they were doing and how they were feeling at that very moment. The program further explored whether they were thinking about something other than what they were currently doing and, if so, whether the thoughts were pleasant, unpleasant, or neutral. The researchers reported results from 2,250 adults.

What they found was that mind wandering is common, occurring in almost half the samples and at least 30 percent of samples taken during every activity except lovemaking. It is a tribute to the participants' dedication that they would be willing to answer the call of the app while making love. I wonder, however, whether people might have been reluctant to acknowledge while making love that their minds were elsewhere . . . but I digress.

In any event, the researchers found that people were equally happy when their minds were on task or wandering to pleasant topics. On the other hand, they were less happy when their minds were wandering to neutral topics, and *least* happy when wandering to unpleasant topics. In addition, by means of time-sequence analysis, the researchers were able to show that their subjects' mind wandering preceded—rather than followed—their unhappiness.

This is indeed a fascinating finding, but what are its implications for our present exploration? Mindfulness is geared toward focusing the mind on the task at hand, and it appears to succeed in that regard. If the mind that doesn't wander is a happy mind, then mindfulness might be expected to make people happier. Transcendental Meditation, on the other hand, does not involve focusing on the present as part of its technique. The mantra is accessed in an automatic fashion, which allows the mind to transcend. Could transcendence be construed as a type of mind wandering? And if so, might it make people less happy?

The latter seems unlikely, as both surveys and anecdotal evidence suggest that TM helps people feel happier (as we will see in chapter 16). The former question, whether transcendence is a type of mental wandering, is perhaps more interesting. As transcendence enters the waking state and the

Super Mind starts to develop, does the waking mind start to wander and, if so, how does that affect the individual? When I go for a walk, as I often do, my mind wanders. I think about my writing and where I want to go next with it, friends, ideas—anything, really. I pass by familiar houses, trees, and plantings, which offer a pleasant backdrop to my musings. Then suddenly something grabs my attention, rivets my eyes, and delights my imagination. For example, tufts of grass pushing up through cracks in the asphalt, green as emeralds—and my mind is off and running. I remember Peppermint Crisp, a childhood candy in which strips of green, minted sugar were embedded in brown chocolate; Malvina Reynolds singing "God bless the grass that grows through the crack"; or, years earlier, Tolstoy in *Resurrection* noting that not even concrete could hold back the exuberance of spring.

On a more practical note perhaps, as I sit with my clients, I listen to what they say and how they say it. I try to understand it as best I can. I ask questions and listen to the answers. But then my mind goes darting like a grasshopper across a lily pond. I think of other people I have seen with similar problems, and what has been helpful to them; I dip into my basket of experience to try and pull out something useful that will offer a different angle, suggest a remedy, or assuage a pain. I would say I have a wandering mind, but not an unhappy one. Also it seems to me that the wandering is part of the creative process, which involves scanning the mind in different ways to help address an issue or solve the problem at hand.

The paper of Killingsworth and Gilbert is compelling. I can imagine that many people might be unhappy when their minds wander. I ask myself what prompts the mind to wander. Perhaps some unresolved matter pokes its head up into the conscious mind and exclaims, "Don't forget about me! You haven't solved me yet." So the mind noodles away on the unsolved problem and the ambiguity and lack of resolution may make a person unhappy—especially in those people who are uncomfortable with the uncertainty inherent in so much of life. I am reminded of the words of the German poet Rainer Maria Rilke, who wrote, "Be patient toward all that is unsolved in your heart and try to love the questions themselves." That seems like good advice to me because so much mind space is full of unanswered questions.

In their paper, Killingsworth and Gilbert acknowledge that "human beings spend a lot of time thinking about what is not going on around them, contemplating events that happened in the past, might happen in the future, or will never happen at all. Indeed, 'stimulus-independent thought' or 'mind wandering' appears to be the brain's default mode of operation."[11] The authors go on to point out that "although this ability is a remarkable evolutionary achievement that allows people to learn, reason, and plan, it may have an emotional cost." That cost, which the authors go on to illustrate in their study, is the unhappiness associated with a wandering mind.

Now, the evolutionary advantages of being able to access past and future, and integrate them with the present, should not be underestimated. Essentially, they can save your life and the lives of others. "Don't eat that fruit. The last person who did dropped dead," is just one of a myriad of examples. On the other hand, as a psychiatrist, I am all too familiar with people who spend too much time fretting about low-likelihood events. Somehow a healthy mind needs to integrate the indubitable benefits of being in the moment with the need to remember and plan. Eckhart Tolle has coined the terms "clock time," for when it is useful to think of past and future, and "psychological time," for when it is not because it takes you out of the present moment.[12]

Perhaps I can add to this excellent schema a new term, "cosmic time" (one aspect of the Super Mind), to denote a state in which past, present, and future all comfortably coexist. In "cosmic time" the mind moves to where it needs to be—present, past, or future—in an easy and seamless way. Ambiguity and unresolved problems are understood to be part of the way the world works, and a sense of security that comes from dipping repeatedly into transcendence imbues you increasingly with this steadiness as you move about your daily life. Perhaps it is this amalgam of mind wandering, waking transcendence, problem solving, and tolerance of ambiguity and even conflict that is responsible for the creative boost reported by many TM practitioners.

I should point out that reference to the "default mode" mentioned above is based in solid science. An extensive network of nerve circuits in the frontal and other portions of the brain—the so-called default mode network (DMN)—becomes *less* active when people undertake a variety of tasks, with greater decreases of activity occurring the more cognitive effort the tasks require. Conversely, the DMN becomes more active when the brain wanders to a person's own thoughts and memories, envisions the future, considers other people's points of view, or attends to stories containing either first- or third-person pronouns.[13]

Now it may come as no surprise to you, given what you already know about mindfulness and transcendence, that mindfulness (which is associated with focus and concentration) is accompanied by decreased DMN activity[14] whereas TM (which is not associated with focus and concentration) is accompanied by increased DMN activity.[15] These differences provide further evidence that mindfulness and transcendence work via different neural circuits—which is hardly surprising, considering the different effects reported by their respective practitioners. As our knowledge of neuroscience grows, these two different practices may provide valuable insights into the workings of the human brain and how best to develop its capacities.

DOES TM PRODUCE MINDFULNESS?

In discussing the relationship between mindfulness and TM with a friend who had been practicing TM for decades, he observed, "The longer I practice TM, the more mindful I become." Based on observations such as this one, I asked about this association in the Consciousness Integration Questionnaire. Specifically, the question asked: "Since starting to meditate, do you feel you have become more mindful of your own inner experiences or of the world around you?"

The vast majority (94 percent) responded that they had, and of these, 90 percent said that it occurred frequently or very frequently. Here are some of the narrative comments that accompanied their responses:

- I move from one thing to the next. I am more interactive with people, and life is what it is. Just happening, with me experiencing and interacting.
- I move much more in consciousness and awareness of myself, others, and my surroundings. I am more mindful of the blessings of the present and I find myself focusing on that without effort.
- There is an ever-increasing amount of calm alertness.
- I feel very in touch with my inner self, much more than ten to twenty years ago.
- Earlier in life, I had many occasions to feel bored. I am never bored anymore. Even if I am sitting doing nothing at all, I am content. Again, I feel the calm and soothing gap of transcendence between thoughts, and if I sit long enough the thoughts stop and the gap gets bigger and I realize that I am transcending even without intentionally meditating. I carry this feeling with me throughout the day, and it makes the experiences I have with the world around me so much better and there is a harmonious interaction with the environment instead of a dissonant one.

- As I've become more mindful of inner awareness I also have become more aware and appreciative of the outer world.
- I feel like I'm more balanced now between the two [inside versus outside]. I'm not constantly in my head like before, and I'm more perceptive of what's going on around me in the world.
- I can now pinpoint emotions without taking them personally. For example, recently while commuting from work, a driver cut me off in an aggressive and deliberate way, then smirked after almost crashing into me. In the past I would have been infuriated. This time, although I noticed anger flaring up, I saw it as separate from myself. It seemed as though the emotion was simply taking place. With this realization, the emotion actually dissolved within a few seconds. The whole incident felt quite impersonal.
- I feel less separate from the world around me and more mindful of the positive effect I can have on my environment. If painful or anxious thoughts arise, I can look at them objectively and choose how I want to respond to them.
- I find myself so completely aware of what is happening around me and to me that I can pass through experiences much more easily and quickly than before.
- Though my devotion to mindfulness has been with me for a long time, it has deepened tremendously with TM. I can now see through the surface of people, things, and actions to what is really going on behind them.
- I feel as though I am more aware of my thoughts. I am an observer at times. Being able to observe my thoughts has helped alleviate a great deal of anxiety. I think of it like someone hiding behind the door and waiting to jump out as I walk by—only I know that someone is there, so I am prepared and not frightened.

Whereas in earlier chapters, I have chosen quotes that are distinct from one another, here I have deliberately included quotes with overlapping features; my goal is to convey the sense of common elements in what respondents to the CIQ regard as mindfulness. Certainly some of these comments reflect mindfulness as the word is commonly used, but others refer to internal states that sound more like transcendence. In some instances—including the person with a long history of mindfulness practice, who now also practices TM—elements of mindfulness and transcendence intermingle. Given what we know about stimuli that activate the default mode network—such as introspection and comparison of your own thoughts with those around you—some of these comments would suggest that TM might be associated with activation of the DMN—as one study has indeed found.[16] Yet none of the comments by TM practitioners in our survey sounded unhappy. Such evidence reinforces my personal experience that a wandering mind is not necessarily an unhappy one.

A FEW FINAL THOUGHTS

What I have attempted to do here is to show that in mindfulness and TM we have two distinct types of meditation practices. Each has an enormous, worldwide following and is supported by substantial data to the effect that they benefit people both physically and emotionally. As I mentioned earlier, there are not at present any head-to-head studies that speak to the superiority of one technique over the other. That said, there are differences between the practices—in the tasks being set for the brain, stated goals, subjective experiences reported by their practitioners, and differential effects on the default mode network. Aside from time constraints, there is no reason why people should not practice both techniques, and I have described some who report an ongoing benefit from both. As with most activities, different people have distinct preferences—though, in some instances, prejudice may play a role in this regard. It is my hope that I have highlighted common elements, clarified differences, and helped people decide how to proceed with their meditative lives.

TO SUMMARIZE THE HIGHLIGHTS OF THIS CHAPTER:

- TM and mindfulness are two quite different forms of meditation that involve different techniques and goals, and produce markedly different outcomes.
- Mindfulness is generally more difficult to practice than TM.
- Other key differences are outlined.
- As of this time, there are no head-to-head studies comparing the efficacy of these two forms of meditation for any specific indication.

- Each form of meditation has extensive literature, which is not reviewed here.
- A few instances of people who have done both forms of meditation have been described and discussed.
- The relationship between the two types of meditation, the "wandering mind," and the default mode network were also discussed.

15

MEDITATE AND GROW RICH

Earning capacity is going to increase . . .
there's no doubt about it.

Maharishi Mahesh Yogi[1]

Who is rich?
The one who appreciates what he has.

Talmud, Avot 4:1

"Will meditating make you rich?"

That was the question posed to me by my friend Janet Attwood, as part of an interview that she and her coauthor, Chris Attwood, were conducting for their book *Your Hidden Riches.*[2] I could tell that she wanted me to say yes (she had already asked the question in other ways), but something in me balked.

Perhaps it triggered in me some ancient taboo against praying to become rich—as opposed to praying for sick people to become well or hungry people to be fed. I rationalized that I knew many meditators who did not appear to have much money, though they seemed happy anyway. As a counterpoint, I knew many people who were rich and miserable. And so my thinking cranked away, frustrating my poor friend in her quest to get a simple question answered.

Were Janet to ask me that same question today, I would have no trouble answering it. To reconcile my new position with my previous refusal to answer, I now realize that the wise person does not meditate, pray, or work exclusively for material gain. Many are the myths and stories that admonish us to be careful what we wish for. Remember poor old King Midas who wished that everything he touched would turn to gold? His wish was granted, but trouble ensued as he began to turn everything into gold—such as his food—and finally, to his horror, even his beloved daughter.

The truth embodied in the Midas myth is that people who draw their satisfaction exclusively from material things are bound to be disappointed. Increasingly, however, wealthy people who are intelligent and thoughtful understand this. They work hard to achieve balance so that material wealth is just one element in a happy life. They recognize the value of philanthropy, of warm relationships with others, of physical and emotional well-being, and of a spiritual dimension to their lives, which may include meditation. Often their resources make it easier to accomplish these other goals. And with growing frequency, we find people becoming rich by doing what they love to do anyway.

So with these thoughts in mind, let me finally answer Janet's question: Yes, TM can certainly help you grow rich. Let me count the ways.

And as I do, bear in mind what I shared with you in the chapters "Connecting Body and Mind" and "Building a Better Brain." Many of the ways in which TM can help you grow rich involve the growth and development of physical and emotional qualities conducive to success both financially and in other ways—such as having more energy and being less stressed, more resilient, more creative, and, in many respects, smarter.

MANAGING OTHER PEOPLE'S MONEY
KEN GUNSBERGER: REACHING OUT TO A FRIEND

I was impressed by the video, which showed a well-dressed, youthful-looking, middle-aged man talking about his business, his life, and how TM had helped him. The man spoke with such obvious candor that I knew I must talk with him in person, and happily he agreed to be interviewed. The setting for our conversation could hardly have been nicer—a terrace on Manhattan's Upper East Side, with a view of the East River, from which a gentle breeze added the finishing touch to a perfect spring day.

The first thing that impressed me about Ken Gunsberger was that he knew he had a problem; second, that he sought help for it—successfully. But most of all, I was impressed that he was willing to share his knowledge with others—on YouTube, no less. Here is how he told his story to me, nine months after starting to practice TM regularly:

I'm a financial advisor, I'm a husband, and I'm a father. I wasn't as moti-vated, efficient, or happy as I could be. If I were a machine, I would say I was working way below my potential in many facets of life. I was doing very high quality work, but the size of the business was not as big as it should have been. Now, why is that? Well, in life you have to make things happen sometimes—even most of the time. What's the difference between somebody who starts a business and makes it happen and somebody who wants to start a business and doesn't? One idea may be just as good as the other. You have to ask yourself why? What is it that will stop person A from making a phone call, while person B makes the call? I don't know what it is. You might know, because you're the doctor. But I will tell you that TM al-lowed me to conquer whatever that mental block is. Whatever that speed bump, whatever that hurdle might be, was removed.

When I asked Ken how TM had improved his performance, and how that had affected his business, here's what he answered:

No more procrastination. Highly efficient. Much better momentum. After meditating, I feel calm, like I'm ready to make decisions with-out anything holding me back. Maybe there are different things that hold different people back. I find that meditation removes psycholog-ical barriers.

My communication skills have gotten way better. They were good to begin with. But when you're interacting with people in life, it doesn't matter what something is; it matters what people think it is.

I feel like I was driving a Ferrari in first gear. And now I'm shifted up, and I will continue. I'm very confident that the longer I meditate, the higher the gear will be. TM has helped me size situa-tions up very quickly—like Malcolm Gladwell describes in *Blink*.[3] So I'm able to process things much quicker. Instead of just basing deci-sions on the first order of thought [by which Ken means the immedi-ate consequence of the action], I am able to base them on the second, third, fourth, and fifth in less time than it takes many people to make it only on the first.

I can see when I'm in a meeting with people who don't meditate how much better my decision making and the things that I say are by comparison. It's not arrogance. It's just a fact. My wife works at Gold-man Sachs, and what they tell her is if you really want to be successful you have to think strategic. You can tell when somebody's thinking strategic and when somebody's thinking small and getting bogged down. It's like Warren Buffett once told me, there are a lot of things to know about an investment—and most of them are irrelevant. Do you want to get bogged down in irrelevance? Or do you want to focus on the things that really matter? TM has helped me do the latter.

Here Is What Ken Says TM Has Done for Him and His Business:

As you read through the list, consider what we already know about the Super Mind and see if you can discern its elements at work.

- Improved his ability to separate things that matter from irrelevancies.
- Increased his efficiency in making decisions and acting.
- Helped him "work smarter, not just harder" and improved his creativity.
- Made him less emotionally reactive. This ability is important for everyone, but especially for people whose work involves investments that can swing widely up or down, leading to euphoria or panic, both of which can trigger bad judgments. The decreased reactivity that comes with TM buffers people against making such mistakes.
- Has given him more energy, leading to a better ability to make healthy choices (such as going to the gym and cooking healthy food for the family) that make him feel younger.
- Significantly increased his volume of business.

As a consequence, this past year has been the best Ken has had in his twenty-five years of practice.

"When Do You Get the Time to Meditate?"

I have highlighted this question, which I put to Ken because so many people tell me that they can't find time to meditate. Yet some of the busiest people I know seem to manage. In fact, they insist that they never miss a TM session if they can possibly help it (and I fall into that category). There's a running joke about a busy executive who said, "On a regular day, I meditate once, but on a really busy day, I meditate twice." Here's what Ken has to say on the matter.

Most people waste most of their time. When you look at the average day of an average person, they're wasting a lot of time. Anyone who says they don't have time to meditate, they don't have time to work out, they don't have time to do this or that—it's like trying to go out with a friend, or somebody, and they just don't seem to have time. People make time for the things that they want to do. There's always time! It just needs to be allocated properly. There's no conscious decision to allocate time properly after doing TM. It just happens. Certain things just happen when you meditate. I accomplish more now than I did before I meditated.

Bob Jones, formerly a portfolio manager for a top-tier financial services firm on Wall Street for twenty years, and a longtime TM practitioner, echoes Ken's observations:

The reason people get stressed is that they have too many things going on. Well, not all those things are important. I think meditation helps you sort it out—these are the things I need to do, while these are less important and I'll get to them if I have time. I actually end up with more free time than I would without meditation.

In the video, Ken had mentioned how his relationship with his twelve-year-old daughter had improved since he started to meditate. Now he told me:

She's seen a material change in me. Rather than being too quick about things or answering right away, no! How many parents out there, when the kids want to do something, immediately say no? Most of the time. Well, I don't say no anymore. [What do you say instead? I asked.] I say, we want to find a way to say yes. We don't want to tell you no. What we want to do is figure out a way to say yes. And we need you to help us figure that way out, because if we can't find a way to say yes, then the answer is going to be no. How about that? And it doesn't need to take forever.

While this conversation was going on, Ken's cell phone rang—it was his daughter. After establishing that there was no urgent matter at hand (she was calling to tell him she'd just been to her first softball practice), he proceeded to explain to her in a kind voice that he was busy but was looking forward to talking to her as soon as he had a break in his schedule.

*   *   *

I asked Ken what it was about the particular friend he had mentioned in the video that prompted Ken to seek his advice. He told me that he had seen his friend's business flourishing in recent years, adding: "He was able to multitask in many aspects of his life—work, home, extracurricular activities—and all that with energy. And I was working hard but below my potential. So I said, 'What are you doing that's made such a difference?' And he told me it was TM."

His friend Mark had put Ken on notice that with TM, "like anything else, you're only going to get out of it what you put into it." Ken turned to me and said, "You can tell me that better than anyone. You started and stopped." Ken had read my book *Transcendence*, in which I shared with the reader that I had started TM in medical school and let it drop, then picked it up much later. Whenever my patients report to me in a guilty tone that their TM practice has lapsed, I tell them that I can relate. I let mine lapse for thirty-five years. That invariably helps them feel better and (I hope) sometimes helps them start meditating again. Ken quoted his friend—with whom he now clearly agrees that when it comes to TM: "If you're all in, it'll work. You can't afford not to be all in. You can waste a lot of time if you don't do something like this properly."

I like the story. A guy sees he's in trouble, realizes he needs help, then looks around to see who best might provide it. He spots a friend who's turned things around in his life, reaches out, gets the help he needs, and turns his own life around. Now he's sharing the secret of his success with me—and I am sharing it with you.

MARK AXELOWITZ: A FRIEND IN NEED

When Mark Axelowitz heard that I was interviewing his friend Ken, to my delight he volunteered to let me interview him as well. We met at his club on the top of Rockefeller Center, which boasts commanding views of Manhattan on all sides. It was April 15, our taxes were in, and there was nothing to complain about.

After we meditated together and had breakfast, Mark went on to tell me about his experiences with TM. At the time Mark had been meditating for three years and four months. Even though he had been satisfied with his life before starting to meditate, he has always been the sort of person who "wants to do more and better, and experience different things." He adds, "I don't think that's ever going to change with me—hopefully. I just want to always go to the next level and do different things, so meditation was something that I thought would be different."

Mark, a high-energy person, describes himself as follows:

I look at myself as a father of three, as a philanthropist (I'm involved in a lot of different not-for-profits), as a financial advisor, and a husband. So I weave all that into eighteen hours a day, and I enjoy it all. Also, I act and I have an entertainment company.

I asked him how he could fit his TM practice into such a packed schedule. He smiled and said:

My initial concern was that the only way I'm going to get the morning session is to get up earlier. And I was concerned because I only sleep six hours a night. But what I was taught, and what actually happened, is that even if I have to get up twenty minutes earlier, those twenty minutes of meditation are better than twenty minutes of sleep. It's sort of a deeper relaxation; it's better for me. So the lost sleep hasn't affected me at all.

I asked Mark whether the twenty minutes twice a day repays itself. "Absolutely!" he said.

"How?" I wondered.

"Because it's not really the twenty minutes of meditation twice a day that makes the difference (much as I enjoy it). Rather, its effects linger all day long. It gives you energy."

Mark went on to describe the value of his twice-daily practice:

It has totally paid off. I think the past three years have been the best professional years of my life—and personally also. In the past three years I've had the most success of my entire career. I'm a financial advisor for very wealthy individuals, and I have to come up with investment ideas that have made the returns to my clients the best they ever have been. And they've been the best for me personally because I eat my own cooking. So whatever I recommend for my clients, those are the investments I do for myself and my family.

I asked Mark for an example of the increased creativity that TM had inspired in him, and he was kind enough to give me one. It was complicated, involving understanding markets in different countries, sifting out a few genuine nuggets from a heap of fool's gold, and coming up with an innovative investment that carries a high risk-reward ratio.

When I asked Mark whether he thought TM could help someone make more money, he replied:

> I think it will because I think TM helps in general, no matter what you want to do, whether it's manage money, teach, be a doctor. If you think clearer in life, you're going to make better decisions. When you're stressed out and emotional, you're not going to make the proper decisions. In fact, one of the greatest money managers of all time, working in the eighties and nineties, was Peter Lynch from Fidelity. He had a saying: To master investing you need to master your emotions. You cannot get emotional in making investment decisions. And the same applies in life every day, with regard to all kinds of decisions: Should I cross the street right now? Should I run across the street because I'm late for an appointment? If you make an emotional decision because you're late and you run across the street when the light is red, you can get killed. So I think TM helps you think and see clearer, and certainly with investments.

I asked Mark whether he thought that a person's improved demeanor after starting TM might also influence that person's success. His reply was appropriately numerical, given his profession.

> A hundred percent! You know, they say in business the clients reflect you. So if I'm calmer, if I'm more thoughtful, I'm going to attract people like that, the sort of people I want as my clients. I wouldn't take on a client who is very stressed out. In fact, people ask what's my minimum—and I do have a dollar minimum—but my real minimum is working with good people. And I have great clients, but I've also recommended meditation to my clients. In fact, some of them already meditate.

As a hobby, Mark has been acting for the past ten years, appearing in a Three Stooges movie and on TV. His goals, he says, are to "work hard, play hard, give hard." He credits that maxim to a colleague Paul Tudor Jones, who founded the Robin Hood Foundation.

Mark is an upbeat person, who summarizes his worldview as follows:

My personal view is that if nothing bad happens to me in a day, I've had a good day, and if something good happens to me in a day, then I've had a great day. So I've always been. I live that way, but I'd say my meditation has made me appreciate things much more.

Well, I certainly appreciated the time both Mark and Ken had given me, and the candor of their responses. I left Rockefeller Center with much to reflect on—and one final impression: how kind Mark had been to the waitstaff at his club and everyone who had helped us make the visit memorable. I thought again of how kind Ken had been on the phone with his daughter. And I realized that these two men were successful, not only financially, but as people as well—and that TM had helped them in all aspects of their lives.

MARCIA LORENTE: NOT ONE OF THE BOYS

After interviewing several high-level men in the corporate world, a fairly obvious question crossed my mind: where are the women? And indeed, it was difficult to find female counterparts to the men I had interviewed. To my delight, however, I was referred to Marcia Lorente, a director of the creative department in an advertising agency in New York City.

Many of you might be familiar with the world of such ad agencies (as I am) from the blockbuster TV series *Mad Men*. According to Marcia, the re-creation of that world in *Mad Men* is accurate in many ways. She reports that the New York City business world is "a very tough, aggressive type of culture, and advertising is even worse. Madison Avenue is particularly aggressive, very cutthroat." It was one year after she arrived in New York City that Marcia recognized she needed "some sort of practice that would center me. That's when I found TM, and it was fantastic. It's totally changed my life." At the time of our conversation, she had been meditating for about two years.

Marcia was born in Madrid to a Spanish father and an American mother. She began her career in Madrid before moving to Chicago, where she was transferred to a big agency. Later, she worked in San Francisco and found the atmosphere on the West Coast more relaxed. She was unprepared for the *Mad Men* atmosphere of New York City. In telling me how TM had helped her in so many ways, Marcia sorted its benefits into the following categories:

Relief of Stress

This was Marcia's primary goal in seeking out TM, and it has worked. Here's how she describes her daily practice:

> The first thing I do when I get up is I meditate; I do a run. And then I go to work. And I can feel the tremendous difference that TM has made in the morning. I also meditate when I get home from work. It helps me shed, forget about the day. Not forget, rather acknowledge the day—and let it go. If it's a particularly rough day, I will sometimes sneak out at lunchtime, go to a park or a church, meditate, and then go back to work. But normally it's morning and early evening.
>
> And it's just helped tremendously in terms of forgetting about the bad things or the tensions and conflicts. There's a lot of conflict in my job. It's how the creative process happens. It's about confronting, and people can get pretty aggressive. So it's been really great to be able to acknowledge that conflict—to let go of that, not take it personally. I guess it's especially helpful for me—I'm sure it's different for everybody else—but I'm a very sensitive person. And now I feel like I'm not taking things personally, which is great.

Being a Woman in a Man's World

Reflecting on my difficulty in finding a suitable high-level businesswoman to interview for this chapter, I asked Marcia about the male-female ratio in the upper ranks in her organization. She responded:

> There's a bit of an equal distribution, but when it comes to the creative department, which I'm technically part of, and when it comes to upper management, it's mostly male. This is a topic dear to my heart because I'm actually quite good at what I do, and during my career I hit that glass ceiling, as they call it, and I found myself in a room with just men—I was in my early thirties (I'm forty-four now)—and I had to make a decision as to whether I was going to try to be one of the boys and blend in, or if I was just going to be me. And I chose to be me. And I've done okay careerwise, so I'm really glad I made that choice.

For Marcia, one aspect of being herself, and a woman, is being comfortable looking and behaving in a traditionally feminine way—wearing lipstick and a dress and feeling good about it. As she puts it, "Perhaps because I was born and raised in Spain, I've really held on to my feminine traits. Early on in my career, I saw a lot of successful women who became very manly and aggressive—and that's just not me. I don't think it's feminine, but I think there's a lot of power in the feminine too."

In talking about feminine and masculine traits, Marcia also observes the differences in emotional style and behavior between men and women, and how these differences affect one another. In discussing these themes, as Marcia does below, references to *Mad Men* prove irresistible.

If you've seen *Mad Men*, you have witnessed the conflict. I work with "creative," so when *Mad Men* came out it was great because I could just explain to my parents what it is that I did. I'm Peggy, basically. I'm a woman but I'm in the creative department, which consists mostly of men. I actually have a role in between the creative department and outside of it, but I basically give direction to creative, and in that sense tell creative what we have to do. And the way creative people work—and the way I work—is by trial and error. So a lot of times I'm wrong. And I will encounter people who are just unhappy or insecure, or are trying to find ways to sort out a problem, and they will just blow up on me.

I'm not very good at dealing with verbal or physical aggression, and that's happened to me. I think there was a scene in *Mad Men* where Donald Draper throws some papers at Peggy and tells her to leave the office. That's the type of aggression I've encountered with coworkers. Men may say, "I can't talk to you right now. Get out of here!" And it's behavior that in other industries might be considered unprofessional. In advertising it's allowed because it's part of how we work. There's some chaos in the creative process. I was reading about how in the creative process you think about something. You come up with ideas and at some point you think it's all bad. It's all awful. And I'm worthless; I'm useless; I'm never going to be able to crack this. And then at another point you hit bottom. You come out of that and realize that some of the thoughts you had were good. TM has helped me deal with my own emotions regarding this process.

But we're still dependent on one another's opinion. I may think something is a great idea, and this is what we should do, and this is what we should say. But how do I know if it's any good? I'm really dependent on feedback from my colleagues because we work in a very collaborative fashion—or that's how it should be when things are working properly. At some point, we need to hold hands and say this is the way, but there's a stress in feeling judged all the time. And it doesn't matter how many awards and how many titles you've won. It doesn't matter. There's a lot of stories of creatives in the industry having washed up and lost their magic. We're always fearful of that, and you can sense that fear. So I guess that TM has really helped me navigate that.

I think women react differently from men when it comes to con-flict. We don't throw our arms in the air and yell or have outbursts. We have been trained to not do that. We've been trained to hold emotion back. When men experience frustrations, they just let them out like a flash in the pan. It's like thunder strikes and then it's gone. And it's *truly* gone. *And* it's okay. Whereas for women, I find that's not allowed. When a woman loses it, men freak out. They just look at you like, what the hell happened? And because we also don't do it as often, I feel there's some sort of muscle that we haven't exercised, which makes it hard to use then go back to neutral. So when women lose it, we actually do lose it. And that's not good.

I think TM has really helped me claim my power at work—it's helped me to "dust it off." When things don't go right or I make a mistake, big or small, I don't get stuck anymore. I can move on. It's like when you meditate and you acknowledge a thought and let it go.

I think men have it easier in that regard. They're taught to over-ride emotion when they fail. To acknowledge it. Do whatever. Crack a joke. Kick a wall. Have a full-blown explosion of fury. Let it out. Learn something. Or not. And move on. It is also somewhat manly to say "whoops." Mess up. Break stuff. I grew up with boys. They broke a lot of my toys.

Women are expected to be perfect. Take care of others. Be gentle. Ironically, the "weaker" sex is expected to be stronger. Also, as women we are taught to feel. It's harder for us to change gears. Feelings are important. We must dwell in them, understand them, talk about them, even though sometimes that's a perfect waste of time, especially at work. But even when strong feelings are appropriate, don't you dare show emotion. Don't you dare shed a tear. That's unprofessional.

Since I started meditating, I'm showing my true colors at work more. If I'm having a bad day, I'll say it. If I screwed up, I'll admit it. If you give me great news, I'll ask if I can hug you. Sorry, I'm a hugger. Yes, it was a bit scary at first, but it's great now. I'm one with the boys but in the right way. They know I'm different. I'm still a girl. But I'm in control of my on-off emotional switch.

Improved Creativity and Success at Work

Marcia has little doubt that since starting TM, she has been more creative and successful. People have responded more favorably both to her and to her work, and she has received promotions more rapidly than before she began to meditate. She has no doubt that TM has boosted the trajectory of her career. Here are a few of her thoughts on the matter.

> Creativity is what I do for a living. I basically sell what comes out of my head. I work in a fear-ridden environment—and there is a fear inside of me—and TM has helped me grapple with that fear. Once you've let go of the fear, you can actually let creativity happen. Fear is the opposite of creativity. Creativity is having no fear of failure, just trying things out, just having fun. It comes from an almost childish place. You have to be able to go there and not worry about the outcome, not worry about the consequences. And the moment the fear level in my life came down—after I started TM, it plummeted—all of a sudden my creativity bloomed. And I'm also having a lot of fun at work. It becomes a virtuous cycle, because I'm better at my job too, which leads to less conflict.
>
> People have noticed that I'm relaxed and happy. Again, in a very competitive environment like the one I work in people don't open up and say, "Oh, you're awesome. You're great. I love you." But they do notice that something has shifted. They'll be, like, "Oh, wow! That's great. Where did that come from?"
>
> Particularly for women in the workplace, I think TM could make a crucial difference. I think we're much more driven by emotion, and TM helps you settle that down and understand it. In my industry at least—and this is being heavily publicized—in the creative and upper ranks it's mostly men. So I think it's crucial for women to have this vital tool. I just honestly don't know how I'd be functioning without it.

How Do You Find the Time?

I had asked the guys this question, and was curious to see how Marcia's response resembled or differed from theirs. How did she find the time and justify taking twenty minutes twice a day out of her busy schedule?

Marcia identified an important distinction between the early phase during which she was establishing a regular meditation routine and a later phase, when the benefits kicked in. Here she explains the distinction:

I think in the beginning, the first couple months, you're still trying to find a routine. You're still trying to figure it out; you still haven't quite gotten the full benefits of the meditation in your life. In my case I started to feel better immediately. And just feeling physically better is fantastic. But I think in the beginning it's true—you're looking for time. What I did, honestly, I just stole it from my sleep. I thought, I'll just sleep twenty minutes less. I actually sleep a lot. I get up at seven. I go to sleep at ten. I was going to sleep at eleven, and I was getting up at six thirty in order to put in that meditation. And the reality is if you shave a little off here and there—it's not that big of a deal. And how I rationalized it—because I'm sure you know by now I'm a very rational person—I actually thought, well, when I meditate I was told this is like restful sleep but better. I'm awake; I'm alert; I'm mindful. But my body and my head, my brain, are resting. So I'd gladly give up a little bit of my time of sleep, during which, by the way, I may not be sleeping (I may be tossing and turning and trying to fall asleep or sort of waking up). I'll give that up for another form of sleeping, is what I told myself.

And I didn't feel any consequences from the loss of sleep, which was very surprising to me. I think that's because immediately I did get—and I know everyone is different—the physical benefits of TM, which were very evident to me right away. So my body immediately felt better and more rested, and although technically I was getting a little less sleep, the net result was I was just fine.

Now that my TM practice is established, I have extra time. I may want to sign up for dance lessons. Nowadays I'm trying to think what to do with this free time.

And What About the Emotional Benefits?

I asked Marcia, "Do you feel different within yourself?" Her response:

Oh yes! Oh yes! I just feel calmer, happier. I'm a hypersensitive person, an introvert. TM has calmed me down and allowed me to be more open to strangers and to people in general. My senses are heightened: the colors are brighter, the smells richer, everything around me is more vivid. But not louder, just brighter and calmer. I'm just having a lot of fun. Life has become a much more pleasant place to be in. Whereas before everything seemed to be loud and aggressive, and I had to always find time to be on my own. Now I don't have to run away from the world, because the world's become a much better place.

TM IN CORPORATE AMERICA

When you think of the effects TM has had on the lives of Ken, Mark, and Marcia, just three among the multitude of corporate professionals in the United States alone, can you imagine the impact of teaching hundreds or thousands times that number? Well, that uncontrolled experiment is currently being conducted by the David Lynch Foundation in conjunction with the "TM Business" outreach of the nonprofit TM organization, with veteran TM teachers Mario Orsatti and Linda Mainquist, a husband-and-wife team spearheading the New York part of the endeavor. So far they have taught approximately a thousand executives in the New York City financial world to meditate.

Linda, who has given special focus to bringing TM to women executives, endorses many of Marcia's observations, and finds that TM helps these women in several ways: First, it empowers women to stand up for themselves in a male-dominated arena. Second, it helps them move outside their comfort zones and take risks, perhaps because they feel that they always have transcendent consciousness to come home to. Third, it helps with work-life balance, which is often harder for women because they are expected to shoulder more responsibilities at home. Finally, TM helps people to be their authentic selves *and* be successful—to feel as though they don't have to choose. In other words, with development of consciousness, women feel they can operate on different levels. They can retain their femininity and at the same time do what is necessary to succeed in the business setting.

Mario summarizes the value that he and Linda find when business executives—regardless of gender—practice TM regularly. The sections below represent a summary of his thoughts:

LISTENING

To a psychiatrist, the power of listening should come as no surprise. Yet sometimes it does. Not long ago a friend called me, distressed about something going on in her personal life. I know her to be an intelligent and thoughtful person, and it was clear that she had considered many aspects of the problem—what the other person had done, her feelings about it, and her options as to what she could do next. She was not asking my opinions on the subject, nor did I offer them. An hour passed, she sounded better, and we said good-bye. I was glad to be there for a friend, but didn't come away with the impression that I had done much good.

Apparently I was mistaken. A week later, she called me and thanked me for my help. I asked what I had done that she had found helpful. "You were very wise," she said. "You just listened. In the past you would have been 'the expert,' giving me suggestions, pointing me in different directions. By just listening you were much more helpful."

Mario echoes the value of listening in the business world:

The *capacity* to listen is vital in business. We can take a hundred courses that are so commonly offered in business programs, which help us understand that listening is an essential part of communication. We know that. So why is it an issue? Because we often lack the *capacity* to listen—which is painfully difficult when our minds are noisy. And so many people find meetings increasingly rough because of their internal stress level. They find themselves easily distracted. I often ask people, "How many of you are in meetings regularly?" Almost everyone says yes. I ask them, "How many of you feel that most of the people in the meetings are having a constant impulse to check their e-mails or text messages rather than listen to what's going on?" Everyone laughs and says, "Yeah. Sure."

Then I ask, "Don't you think it diminishes the capacity of the meeting to accomplish its goals? I mean, why have a meeting if someone's not really interested or capable of listening? Or maybe they're interested but just not capable. And they all say yes. I tell them, "You're all inevitably going to notice that as a result of practicing TM, you're going to be more present in your conversations, and in meetings, in one-to-one or in group settings. Your mind's going to be quieter, simpler, and more able to hear what people are saying and why they're saying it. You won't be just hearing words but really listening. And people inevitably say during our follow-up meetings that that's one of the big changes they notice. This is really one of the major factors that helps to develop leadership: that quality that when you're communicating with someone, you are really present and listening.

Leaders need to be engaged, fully, with whomever they're speaking to, not distracted. So becoming a better listener is one of the rewards of TM that many of our students report.

SETTING PRIORITIES

Another very common benefit that people report after starting to practice TM is that priorities just seem to fall into place while you are meditating. I notice this personally all the time. It is very strange to sit down with no conscious agenda to sort out some problem, then have it somehow get organized during the session. Often we are confronted with the question of where to begin, what to do first. With regular TM practice, answers tend to come more readily. Here are Mario's thoughts about how this development helps businesspeople:

In today's business world, the ability to deal with priorities is more important than ever. For most people there aren't enough hours in the day. You could work twenty-four straight hours and you'd *still* have things to do. So the question to ask is not, "How do I do more?" Instead, we should be asking, "How do I focus on first things first?"

This isn't just my opinion. In Stephen Covey's book *The 7 Habits of Highly Effective People,*[4] which was rated by *Forbes* as one of the top twenty management books ever,[5] Covey mentions seven strategies, of which doing first things first is the most important. How do you maintain focus when you're constantly dealing with multiple inputs, constant e-mails, text messages, and phone calls? And what about everyone else's emergencies that come to you? How do you maintain the vision to stick with doing important things first, not making everybody else's emergency necessarily your emergency?

Prioritizing is a quality that comes with the development of what you're writing about—super consciousness. It results from an inner stability that comes from the brain having a regular experience of that least excited state of consciousness.

MANAGERIAL AWARENESS

Mario brought to my attention a business term that has some striking similarities to super consciousness (an aspect of the Super Mind). It's called "managerial awareness." Here's how Mario explains the similarity between these two ideas:

Managerial awareness means the capacity to maintain awareness of many things, even while focusing sharply on one thing. It's the essence of knowing what to do next, while also understanding the larger picture. If you have people in your organization who do not have managerial awareness, you give them a task and let them just work on that task. But you as the manager have to maintain broad comprehension of *all* the different tasks—what the priorities are, who needs to implement them, and in what sequence.

As you can see, the two-channel aspect of the Super Mind has its analog in managerial awareness. According to Mario, as people meditate regularly and develop expanded consciousness, managerial awareness becomes one of the many ways in which it manifests, thus improving their effectiveness and performance.

DECREASED REACTIVITY: DEVELOPING INTERNAL SPACE

A common benefit of regular TM practice is reduced reactivity (see chapter 8), which pays off in many situations, and business is no exception. Lose your temper with your employees and guess what? They won't work as well. Instead, they'll spend time gossiping about you and speculating about the problems that cause you to lose it so often. Worse yet, they may actually sabotage your goals. Lose your temper with your boss and . . . It's not hard to guess how that can come back to bite you.

Reactivity comes in many forms besides hotheadedness—none of them good: hasty decision making, frequently changing one's mind with every shift of perspective, moods that yo-yo up and down depending on the moment. The list goes on and on. As you develop the Super Mind, however, things change in a way that may seem small but is actually huge—in business as in life. Time and space enter the psyche. The mind seems to slow down and expand at the same time. Things that seemed urgent before seem less so.

As entrepreneur Josh Zabar puts it:

TM has enabled me to create a space between my thoughts and my actions. . . . It's wild. So before I started meditating, I may have been in a situation where I reacted harshly and abruptly due to something that I felt was affecting me negatively. Now, if that same situation happens, there is a calm space, a serene environment that lasts maybe a few milliseconds but feels like an eternity before I act where I can actually "choose" the reaction that I want to have. Now that's true power.[6]

Zabar's comment reminds me of the famous quote by neurologist, Holocaust survivor, and the author of the classic work *Man's Search for Meaning*, Viktor Frankl:

Between stimulus and response there is a space. In that space is our power to choose our response. In our response lies our growth and our freedom.[7]

The Super Mind enables us to grow that space.

Developing such a space has several advantages. First, it acts as a buffer against impulsive words or actions. The prefrontal cortex can use those extra few seconds to decide how best to respond rather than to react reflexively. Second, it feels good to be calmer, to feel as though you can deal with whatever comes your way. Third, that shift has a soothing effect on other people. When we are nervous, we make others nervous. Finally, developing a space enables empathy to enter one's consciousness. How is the other person feeling? How is my response going to affect the other person? And what downstream consequences (the second-order effect) might those responses cause? Many people reported feeling greater empathy and concern for others since starting to meditate. Such altered responses may be mediated by so-called mirror neurons, which reside in the cerebral cortex of many animals studied to date.

Mirror neurons are so named because they appear to be responsible for the commonly observed propensity of many animals to mimic actions.[8] For example, when macaque monkeys copy the manipulation of an object (washing potatoes, for instance), certain specific neurons can be observed to fire. It is a speculative leap—though in my opinion a plausible one—to hypothesize that mirror neurons may also operate when it comes to emotions, such as empathy. In primates, mirror neurons are located in the prefrontal cortex (as well as other cortical areas)—and insofar as TM is believed to strengthen PFC functioning, it is tempting to wonder whether the reported effects of TM on empathy might be mediated by mirror neurons.

Such speculation aside, the contagious nature of emotions is a commonplace observation. A calm demeanor reassures both clients and colleagues, whereas a reactive, impulsive, or edgy manner is bound to have the reverse effect.

OPENNESS AND NONATTACHMENT

In chapter 12 I discussed the value of being able to detach from some things while remaining engaged with others—a combination of traits that are part of the Super Mind. It is self-evident that success in business is more likely to occur when people are passionately engaged in what they are doing. But where does nonattachment fit in? I will quote Josh Zabar's blog once again:

> I've gained acceptance of others whom I've often begrudged, and I've become far more likeable to a number of people who were irritated by the "my way or the highway" attitude I once held dear and was proud of. My ego has died a little, which is probably the best thing that's ever happened to me, because the more the ego dies, the more one really begins to live.

In business, as in life, it pays to be open to the best ideas out there—even if those ideas happen not to be yours. Ray Dalio (whom we have already encountered here, and will meet again soon) writes in his famous "Principles":

> I learned that there is nothing to fear from truth. While some truths can be scary—for example, finding out that you have a deadly disease—knowing them allows us to deal with them better. Being truthful, and letting others be completely truthful, allows me and others to fully explore our thoughts and exposes us to the feedback that is essential for our learning.[9]

Sometimes truth can be scary because it hits us on a sensitive spot—like dealing a blow to the ego or challenging a dearly held belief. Being open to the truth requires not being overattached to your opinions. In that state, you can allow other peoples' ideas to enter your mind and mix with yours, to promote the most successful outcome. You can let go attachment to "being right," valuing instead the successful outcome of the project at hand.

In Zabar's words quoted above, TM has allowed him to be open to other people's opinions. By becoming less attached to his ego, his life has expanded. Certainly many people in leadership positions have hefty egos, but I would argue that those who are most successful listen to data and to the opinions of others. Not being able to do so can be costly. Besides missing out on potentially important ideas and opinions, not listening to others squashes creativity. As Mario Orsatti puts it, "Ultimately that is a huge stumbling block for many leaders, in both their professional and family lives, because if you're that way with your children (biological or professional), you're not going to get that far. In the twenty-first century—unlike centuries past—you can't be a dictator and succeed. You have to allow people to enjoy their work, express their ideas—and actually listen to them. The development of consciousness, by providing inner security, helps people become less attached to their ideas and their egos."

COMPOUND INTEREST

Several of the businesspeople I interviewed pointed out the relationship between the development of consciousness and compound interest: both grow geometrically over time. Growth of the Super Mind begets more growth. And this is not an idle impression. When we surveyed over six hundred meditators and asked them, "Since starting to meditate, if you have noticed positive changes in yourself or your life, have these changes continued to grow over time?" we found that 82 percent said yes.

RAY DALIO: LIKE A NINJA

It was a fine evening in late summer, and I was traveling from Manhattan to Connecticut to visit my friends Ray and Barbara Dalio. When I arrived, Barbara greeted me; Ray was still working. She and I chatted as she arranged the flowers I had brought and presently Ray arrived, talking animatedly into his cell phone. He looked like he had been going strong since dawn, and when he turned the cell phone off, after greeting me, said, "Have you guys meditated yet?" We both said we had. When I saw his look of disappointment, I suggested that maybe we could meditate again—which we did. I had never meditated twice in a row before, but I felt wonderful when I emerged—a sense of renewal—and the joyful quality of the evening suggested that the others perhaps felt that way too.

As I have alluded to Ray Dalio several times already, it seems like a good time to tell you something of his story, particularly as it intersects with TM and the Super Mind. When I interviewed him for this book, he simplified matters for me by saying that he endorses everything he had told me previously, which I wrote about in *Transcendence*. I have reproduced the earlier description here with minor changes. Since that time, Ray's status as a legendary entrepreneur and advisor to world leaders has grown, and I will pick up Ray's story later to bridge the gap between the earlier book and this one.

"Meditation Has Been the Biggest Single Influence on My Life"

Ray Dalio is the founder and president of Bridgewater Associates, a hedge fund that he started in 1975 in the spare bedroom of a two-bedroom apartment. Bridgewater currently has more than fourteen hundred employees, is widely praised for its innovative investment strategies, and is one of the largest hedge funds in the world.

Now in his midsixties, Ray has been practicing Transcendental Meditation for forty-six years, since he was a college student. He has thought long and hard about meditation, and he and Barbara have contributed generously to helping huge numbers of disadvantaged people to meditate, such as schoolchildren, veterans with PTSD, and the homeless.

As you can imagine, he has a great deal to say about TM. First, he emphasizes the importance of persevering, especially in the early phases:

Originally when you start meditating, a lot of ideas go through your mind at the same time as the mantra—that was true for me—so you don't transcend. You just go back and forth between the mantra and your ideas. So it took me a while, probably months, to get to the point where I was able to clear my mind of thoughts and start transcending. When I did that, it was great.

Here's how Ray describes transcendence:

It is a combination of relaxation and a very blissful experience. That sounds more like an orgasm than it really is, but it is blissful in the sense that I just feel really good and relaxed and in good shape. You go into a different state—neither conscious nor unconscious. When you're meditating, you're just not aware. Everything disappears, in a sense. But unlike when you're sleeping, if a pin drops all of a sudden, it can reverberate through you; it's shocking.

Here is how meditation has helped him:

It produced a great deal of relaxation, so that a little bit of meditation would go a long way, even making up for sleep. Then I discovered that it changed the way I was thinking, in two ways: It made me more centered, and also more creative. With a more centered, more open state of mind, everything got better. My grades went up. Everything became easier.

Meditation helped my creativity. I find that creativity is not one of those things you sort of muscle in on in your conscious state. Instead, it's like when you're very relaxed, like when you take a hot shower, and really cool ideas pass through your brain and you just want to grab them. That's very much like a meditative state. One of the challenges for me is that as meditation got better and better, so did these thoughts. I didn't want to put them away! I wanted to have a pad and pen next to me to write them down. (But if I stopped to write them down, I'd stop meditating.) It was almost like the way it's hard to hold on to a dream. So TM had a beneficial effect on my creativity, and everything got easier as I became more settled and centered—and it was easy to continue meditating despite having to allocate time for it.

I asked Ray what he meant by being "centered," a word he used several times.

It means when things come at you—challenges, stresses, disruptive events—you can be calm and analytical and approach them almost, I imagine, like a ninja sees things coming at him in slow motion, so that he's obviously in control. Being "centered" is that state in which your emotions are not hijacking you. The ability to think clearly, put things in their right place, and have perspective: That's what I mean by "centered."

Well read in the area of popular neuroscience, Ray talks freely of the amygdala, the brain center that generates powerful alarm signals, and the prefrontal cortex, which governs executive functions. In becoming centered, he believes that "the balance of power shifts from the amygdala to the prefrontal cortex, so that you govern your emotions rather than the other way around." I agree!

Asked whether he could think of any specific creative ideas that came to him during meditation and that went on to become winners, Ray demurred. He hadn't meant single blockbuster ideas, it turns out:

> I think that every single day there are many decisions that people make, and they all have consequences. And your life essentially depends on the cumulative quality of the decisions you make. I've made a whole bunch of decisions, and they have generally speaking worked out for me. I love markets; that's my thing, but the way I've made my business is totally different from most other investment management firms. It's totally unique but, on the other hand, totally right, meaning that other firms are now starting to build their businesses in the same way. I think [our success] was the result of clarity of thought in various ways that have had a cumulative effect.
>
> When I look back at my life, I am happy to have had what most people would consider a successful life, not only in terms of business, but in my relationships and in lots of ways. More than anything else, I attribute it to meditation—partially because of the creativity, partly because of the centeredness. TM has given me an ability to put things in perspective, which has helped a lot. I think meditation has been the single biggest influence on my life.

Ray's description of feeling like a ninja during his negotiations offers an excellent representation of the Super Mind—a sense of being at the same time calm ("centered" as Ray puts it), acutely aware of one's surroundings, and ready at a moment's notice to respond with laser focus to whatever might come at you.

Transcendental Meditation relaxes him, improves his clarity and creativity, helps keep his emotions in perspective, and, through his sense of "centeredness," contributes to the quality of his day-to-day decisions. Despite his hectic schedule, Ray has weighed the costs and benefits of twice-daily meditation sessions and has concluded that the time commitment more than pays for itself.

SUBSIDIZING TM FOR EMPLOYEES

Practicing TM is becoming increasingly popular in the US business world. In some instances, CEOs who have learned and enjoyed their TM practice become aware of its potential benefits to their employees. Many choose to subsidize (in part or in full) the learning of TM both as a perk and as a method for improving well-being, productivity, and morale. The stories below illustrate how this has worked for some US companies, both large and small.

Ray Dalio was an early adopter in bringing TM to Bridgewater Associates. He subsidizes any employee who wants to learn, and when I last checked, about 40 percent of the staff had taken him up on the offer. Several other corporations have now followed suit.

Small businesses have also been enthusiastic about TM for their workers, usually after the CEO learns and realizes how much value there is to the practice. Lindsey Adelman, whom you met earlier in the book, is a case in point. As you may recall, Adelman is the CEO of a Manhattan business that manufactures and sells designer lighting fixtures—a description that doesn't do justice to the works of art that her company produces. When I asked her whether she thought that subsidizing her employees to learn TM had played any part in her business success, she responded:

> Probably 100 percent. It has made a difference with the success for big-picture reasons that are quite specific, like employee retention—which is very high. I think that has a lot to do with our success as a company, because there's nobody coming in and starting fresh, which makes the whole thing stop, nor do we have to replace people and train them. I think a lot of our success stems from this continuity, plus the fact that everyone's skills are evolving every year. Everyone's taking on different responsibilities; everyone's redefining their jobs; everyone has a deeper understanding of my vision for the future. I think that has so much to do with TM. And I'm really proud of our interpersonal relationships. I think that also has a lot to do with people practicing TM.

It also helps when the CEO meditates, as Adelman points out:

> When it was time for my employees to evaluate me, they said that I have a consistent positive energy and positive manner of communi-

cating. TM has definitely helped with that. And it is genuine. I don't ever feel like I just have to put on a happy face. I think when things are rough, I can be pretty honest about it. TM has also helped me really listen and acknowledge what they're doing well. I spend a lot of energy and time on that.

I would say that maybe the most important thing TM has taught me is how to enjoy life, to really have fun with it—to follow the fun, not to be afraid of feeling too good. It sounds strange but I think there's a lot of fear about feeling amazing and making someone else feel amazing. Perhaps it's not the most natural human endeavor. But TM has helped me enormously not to be afraid of passing along a compliment or reinforcing that someone's doing an awesome job.

Temple St. Clair, the CEO of a designer jewelry company in New York City, shares Adelman's enthusiasm for TM both for herself and her staff. As she puts it:

I find that where this world is going, we're juggling and multitasking so much. And TM keeps me steady, and it helps me to think before I speak, makes me less reactive. I'm passionate about my work, a perfectionist, and have high expectations for the people working with and around me. I find that TM keeps the boat steady and helps me be more compassionate. It helps me understand people's strengths and weaknesses more, and be patient about bringing them along.

St. Clair has been so pleased with the benefits she has seen that she too has offered to subsidize her staff, and is already appreciating the benefits she sees in the relationships between staff members.

Jeffrey Abramson, a managing partner of the Maryland-based real estate development business Tower Companies, is a longtime TM practitioner who has been offering TM to his employees since 1999. "People need tools to stay young, vibrant, and competitive," he observes. "When I looked at my staff over time, I realized that I needed a tool to invest in their excellence and keep them the way they were when we hired them. Time wears people out—and businesses pay the price for having them lose their brilliance, youth, and vibrancy. But after they've started to meditate, people tell me, 'I am who I was.'"

Abramson offers yet another reason for providing TM to personnel.

Besides its other advantages, TM is a technique for prevention [see chapter 8]. Businesses inherit people's vulnerabilities—for example, to stroke or heart attack—but if the illness doesn't happen, you never know what you prevented. Yet everyone benefits from preventing these illnesses.

Abramson has also seen his workers become more flexible and interested in changing, working as a group and accomplishing things. Here's how one of his workers expressed his gratitude for having TM training subsidized.

All day long I work for other people, such as our clients and my family. You have given me twenty minutes for myself.

Abramson has a special meditation room in his offices, as do some other companies that promote the practice. Elsewhere in corporate America, there is often no place to hide. Floor plans are open, walls are transparent, phones ring constantly, and people are inclined to barge in. So how does one meditate in such an environment, especially when the activity has not been generally accepted, let alone endorsed? One of my corporate clients finds refuge in the chapel. A few less fortunate ones without such a facility have sought refuge in a bathroom stall—apparently the one place in the building where you can be reasonably confident that nobody will bother you.

Stephen Covey called the last of his seven habits "sharpening the saw,"[10] referring to the way a saw gets blunt and less effective with use until you sharpen it. That's not a bad analogy for how we feel when we've been working too hard and need renewal. My hope is that the potential value of TM will become more widely recognized as helpful, not only to business leaders, but also to their employees, who are likely to feel better about their work and therefore to perform better. I personally find the renewal I experience from my twice-daily meditation to be crucial for my continued creativity and productivity. As you can read from the small sample of people listed here, others agree.

EXECUTIVE FUNCTIONING AND THE EXECUTIVE

You now have encountered references to the prefrontal cortex of the brain—that region just behind the forehead—several times in this book (and very likely elsewhere too). The PFC has been called the CEO of the brain, for good reason. It is that part of the brain responsible for weighing pros and cons, assessing situations, making decisions, and issuing instructions to the rest of the brain. People who sustain injuries to that part of the brain may suffer impaired executive functions and become intemperate, exercise poor judgment, and make bad decisions.

There is evidence that the practice of TM involves physical changes in the PFC, including increased blood flow,[11] greater concentration of soothing alpha waves, and greater alpha-wave coherence (a state in which the wavelengths in different regions are more closely correlated).[12] We know that regular practice of TM, which involves repeated transcendence, leads to the mind settling down throughout the day and even the night—so these physical changes in the prefrontal lobe may become more established even outside of meditation.[13]

The decreased reactivity that accompanies the stillness seen in regular meditators is consistent with their improved judgment and demeanor. They are less likely to react reflexively and more likely to respond thoughtfully to stimuli both good and bad—and therefore less likely to make that impulse purchase, blurt out an inappropriate remark, or lose their temper. In this way the regular practice of TM influences the quality of our daily consciousness and makes us more successful in our executive functioning.

It is often useful to consider the amygdala—a deep-seated brain structure that serves an alarm function—in conjunction with, and as a counterpoint to, the PFC. In response to a dangerous signal—like a tiger in the grass—the amygdala shouts out to the rest of the brain to get out of the way. Over the course of evolution, we have learned to listen to the amygdala in such circumstances, and those who have failed to do so may not live long enough to pass along their genes.

Extending the metaphor of the brain as a corporation, if the PFC is the CEO, the amygdala is surely the fire marshal. When there is a fire, the fire marshal is in charge. He sounds the alarm and bangs on doors and everybody has to listen—including the CEO. But when there is no fire, the fire marshal needs to stay out of the way and let the CEO run the show. A person with an anxiety disorder is like a corporation where the fire marshal is in charge. Whether or not there is a fire, he keeps banging on the door, and the poor CEO has a hard time getting any work done or knowing when the warning signal is appropriate and when it is a false alarm. There is extensive evidence that regular TM helps people feel less anxious—that is part of the Super

Mind—providing further evidence that the practice settles down the brain's alarm systems and strengthens the PFC.

CONCLUDING THOUGHTS

When I asked Mark—the multitalented wealth manager who introduced Ken to TM—whether TM can help you become rich, he answered: "I think it will because I think TM helps in general, no matter what you want to do, whether it's manage money, teach, be a doctor." That sums up my view as well. With creativity, energy, clarity of thought, and ability to sustain focus over time—all benefits of the Super Mind—you are more likely to accomplish anything you set out to do.

Napoleon Hill in his classic bestseller *Think and Grow Rich*[14] set out thirteen principles for attaining wealth. The very first principle is "desire." If you wish to become rich, you are most likely to succeed by being clear in your desire for that goal. With that in mind, let me refine my answer to the question posed at the beginning of this chapter: "Will meditating make you rich?" My answer: yes, you will be more likely to become rich *if* that is your desire *and* you meditate.

To close, let us consider another definition of being rich, the one encapsulated in the quote from the Talmud mentioned at the head of the chapter: "Who is rich? The one who appreciates what he has." In the next chapter we will consider another type of wealth, one that consists in being happy and grateful for what you have.

TO SUMMARIZE SOME OF THE KEY POINTS IN THIS CHAPTER:

- If you desire to become wealthy, TM is likely to help you because it enhances many of the skills this goal (and many other goals) requires. These include health and energy, interpersonal skills, a multitude of cognitive functions, creativity, openness, and field independence—to offer just a partial list.
- Several anecdotes, buttressed by the experience of TM teachers who have taught TM to hundreds of men and women in business, support the above contention.
- The point has also been made that a feeling of being rich involves a sense of satisfaction as much as any hard number—and evidence shows that TM enhances happiness and well-being (see next chapter).

16

MEDITATE AND BE HAPPY

Happiness is the meaning and purpose of life,
the whole aim and end of human existence.

Aristotle

I believe that the very purpose of our life is to
seek happiness.

Dalai Lama

The person who got me meditating again was Paul, a writer and film-maker, who had consulted me for treatment of his bipolar disorder. One day, after his vertiginous manias and thunderous depressions had been stabilized, Paul explained to me that although my medicines had helped level out his moods, he did not believe they were the source of his happiness.

He went on to tell me about another bipolar man whom he had met in San Francisco. That man had been practicing TM for twenty years, and he said that it had made him feel *really* happy 90 percent of the time. The encounter had inspired Paul, who had learned TM a few years before, to meditate more regularly, as the other man had done—with highly favorable results. Here's how he described them:

Ever since then, things got better over time. The positive effects took a couple of months to set in noticeably. When they did , they came gradually, progressively, stronger, and more profound as time passed. It is now four years since I have been meditating regularly and I'm

better than I've ever been. Just like the man I met that day in San
Francisco, I'm not just happy—I'm *really* happy 90 percent of the
time.

I told Paul that I had learned to meditate in South Africa but had let it
slip off my agenda thirty-five years before. He urged me to pick up the practice again, introduced me to Bob Roth, nagged me, and checked up on me
regularly (as I had surely done in urging him to keep taking his medicines)—
and the rest of the story fills the pages of this book.

One thing that struck me about what Paul said was his emphasis that he
had been *"really* happy." Of course, I have seen many people in the foothills
of mania say that they are *"really* happy"—many of whom are actually *too*
happy—but Paul was not in the least manic when he said it. He was dead
calm. It was clearly important for him to communicate the message to me
seriously. It is not common for me to hear a patient tell me in such a measured
way that he has been *really* happy—let alone 90 percent of the time. I had to
wonder—might TM have a similar effect on other people as well? We will
consider that question in this chapter, but first let's look at happiness a little
more closely.

WHAT MAKES PEOPLE HAPPY?

Studies of twins have been reported to show that about 50 percent of
happiness is genetic,[1] though more recent estimates suggest that it is closer to
36 percent.[2] It follows that as far as what we can *do* to become happier, we're
playing with the other 50–64 percent—which is really quite a lot, when you
come to think of it.

Although William James wrote about the importance of happiness at the
beginning of the twentieth century, and a handful of scientists have worked in
the field since then, it is only in the last decade or two that the science of "positive psychology" has taken off. Until then, most psychological research
focused on negative emotional states, such as anxiety and depression. Nevertheless, there is already some scientific evidence that certain attitudes and
actions can, in fact, increase your happiness—and they are listed in table 6
(below), as summarized by happiness expert David, professor of psychology
at Hope College.[3]

Table 6: Research-Based Suggestions for Improving Mood and Increasing Satisfaction with Life

1. Understand that having more money may not lead to lasting happiness.
2. Take control of your time.
3. Smile. Evidence shows that acting happy can make you so.
4. Find work and activities that you're good at and that are meaningful to you.
5. Invest in shared experiences (such as vacations) rather than things.
6. Stay active. Exercise boosts mood.
7. Get enough sleep.
8. Cultivate and nurture close relationships.
9. Do good. It makes you feel good.
10. Embrace gratitude—both in your thoughts and actions. Keep a gratitude journal and express gratitude when you feel it.
11. Nurture the spiritual side of yourself.

As you can see, meditation would fit into the last category, which also includes people who observe their faith or religion on a regular basis. One problem with pinpointing what is responsible for making people of any faith or spiritual practice happy is that they also tend to have other assets and habits that often lift the spirits—such as strong community bonds, friends with whom they share their tradition, and better self-care practices.

In order to determine if meditation itself leads to happiness, one would have to conduct a controlled study with all the necessary elements, such as random assignment. Several controlled studies of TM have been done, but because positive psychology has come into focus only recently, these studies did not include measures of happiness.

Perhaps the TM study that comes closest to looking at the happiness question is that of the freshman recruits (also known as rooks) at Norwich University, which I described in chapter 9. In that study, sixty freshman officer trainees were randomly assigned to TM versus controls on a waiting list, and a variety of personality measures were taken at baseline and after two and six months.

At the two-month mark, the young meditators showed a significant increase in resilience, as measured by the Dispositional Resilience Scale

(DRS-15),[4] an increase that remained significant at the six-month testing. In addition, overall constructive thinking as well as behavioral and emotional coping, all measured by the Constructive Thinking Inventory,[5] increased significantly as well. Global constructive thinking increased at both two and six months (compared to baseline) as did behavioral coping.[6]

All these findings were replicated in a similar study of rooks conducted the following year.

I include the study results here because qualities such as resilience, constructive thinking, and good behavioral coping might be expected to go along with happiness, but this is admittedly an indirect measure. I anticipate that future studies will include measures that speak more directly to the question of happiness.

WHAT DOES THE CIQ TELL US ABOUT TM, WELL-BEING, AND CONTENTMENT?

Although surveys are not as definitive as controlled studies—which speak to causation as opposed to mere correlation—it is legitimate to mine survey data in the quest for insight. In this regard the Consciousness Integration Questionnaire appears to be something of a gold mine, as two items inquire into states of mind that bear directly on happiness: well-being and contentment (items 11 and 19 in the CIQ—see chapter 7 and appendix 2).

We analyzed these two items with regard to the background variables obtained as part of the survey: first, according to whether people responded yes or no; and, second, according to how often those who responded yes actually had the experience.

When asked whether levels of well-being and contentment had increased since they started to meditate, 94 percent and 90 percent of the TM practitioners said yes, respectively.

When we analyzed the data according to how frequently people experienced well-being, three background variables emerged as significant correlates of well-being: (1) duration and (2) frequency of practice (those practicing for more than four years—the median duration—and at least twice a day) reported higher levels of well-being; and (3) country of residence (Americans expressed higher levels of well-being than South Africans). Results were similar with regard to contentment.

*   *   *

Absent controlled studies and aside from our questionnaire data, in seeking a causal link between TM and happiness, we must resort to anecdotes—but compelling anecdotes are a useful starting point.

Before I go on to share some of these, however, I should address one point that you might think is incorrect in table 6 (Research-Based Suggestions for Improving Mood and Increasing Satisfaction with Life): money. Doesn't more money mean more happiness? Certainly, if you ask people what they *think* will make them happier, most say more money (73 percent in a 2006 Gallup poll and 82 percent of students entering US colleges).[7] Yet the idea is not borne out, at least in more affluent countries. In poor countries, where many people are unable to afford basic needs such as food, shelter, and medical care, an income increase of a thousand dollars can make a significant difference in overall happiness. Not so in more affluent parts of the world.

One human trait that prevents a sudden windfall from bringing enduring happiness is something called the "happiness set point."[8] For example, winning the lottery or getting tenure at a university (to give just a few examples) may make you happier for a short while, but in time your level of happiness will drift back down to where it was before—that is, to your happiness set point. The good news about the set point, however, is that it works just as well in reverse. When bad things happen, people feel less happy, but this reaction tends to pass more quickly than expected. Despite deficits that might result—physical, personal, or financial—you can generally depend upon your set point to hoist you back up to your usual level of cheer.

ABSOLUTELY! 100 PERCENT!

In my interviews for this book my last question was usually: "Have you been happier since starting to practice TM?" Even though I have generally interviewed people I believe have responded well to TM, their answers to this last question were qualitatively different from their other answers—more wholehearted, less ambivalent. Often in a louder voice, and higher in pitch, their initial responses were ringingly simple—"Absolutely!" or "100 percent!" Here are responses from some of the people you have already met to the question, "Has TM made you happier?"

KATIE FINNERAN, ACTRESS

Oh, a hundred percent, yes. So much happier. My number one priority is living a happy, positive life. And I consider TM part of my education at becoming a happier person.

When I asked Katie whether TM had helped her become a better actress, she responded: "I think that I've really been preparing and studying for this since I was a child. I don't think it's because of TM that I'm successful."

I specifically include the second set of responses to illustrate that discriminating people (such as Katie) do not reflexively attribute every positive experience to TM—and in the interest of obtaining accurate information, I have sought out discriminating people. With regard to happiness, most TM practitioners give substantial credit to their meditation practice.

SHARON ISBIN, CLASSICAL GUITARIST

Here is a qualified answer to my question from this longtime meditator:

After looking at your book again, I realized, yes, TM has played a role in helping me feel happier. Now, to be honest, of course, part of my happiness as a person is the fact that I have managed to accomplish most everything I've ever wanted to. And I look forward to accomplishing many more things, to constantly staying active and bringing new works to light, and to nurturing new creative projects. There is a sense of fulfillment that all the things that were dearest to me, that I most believed in, I have succeeded in doing. So part of my sense of happiness comes from that fulfillment.

But there is also a sense of appreciating what I've done, and not feeling that I won't be happy unless I also do this or that. And that is wonderful and beautiful, and it gives me the freedom to enjoy all the other things in life that I also believe in, that don't have anything to do with my career—and that is where TM has played a significant role.

HUGH JACKMAN, ACTOR

Hugh's comments on happiness were complex but, in all fairness, I approached the question indirectly. Here they are:

Prior to learning TM, my life was a series of activities, which could be anything from personal relationships, to the job, to learning—whatever. And because each of those activities felt like the center of my life, my happiness was predicated on how they turned out. So it could have been a relationship, a job, an interview, a party next Saturday—whatever. I was living this roller-coaster ride of a life that depended on something going well. But okay, even if it did, then there's the next event. Or say it didn't go well, then I'm down. I've got to pick myself up for the *next* event, etc.

Since starting to meditate, I have the freedom of finding what Rumi called "the field beyond." And what I think he meant by it—that I totally relate to—is a duality: on the one hand, there are health, disease, poverty—all those things we measure our life with—but there is actually a field beyond that. That field is far richer, happier, more blissful, and effective in every way, and I would say only meditation can get you to that field beyond. You can have a great relationship—and Deb and I have an incredible marriage—and we meditate together. But falling in love or this or that—whatever it is—that doesn't keep you in the field beyond. What keeps you there is this ability to tap into this deeper sense of who we are, this deeper existence. To me the key to that field beyond is meditation. And it has completely changed my life.

LINDSEY ADELMAN, LIGHTING DESIGNER

Before TM, I felt extreme variations in mood—from very, very low to very, very high. Since practicing TM every day, I love normal. I'm so enthusiastic about the most normal day in the world! I feel like my general mood level is between medium and high all the time. I get this feeling of optimism and hope, and belief, and trust, and my mind always gravitates toward those areas. And in general, TM brings a happier life.

TEMPLE ST. CLAIR, JEWELRY DESIGNER

I definitely feel happier since starting TM. There's sort of a lightness of being that comes along with it. But not in a silly or frivolous way. I just feel lighter.

MEGAN FAIRCHILD, DANCER

I said to Megan that she seemed happier since starting to meditate, and asked if I was correct. Here is her response:

You are super correct.

When I practice TM, I find a calmness and peacefulness that bring me back to my most neutral self, and when I get there I discover joy. I'm not sure why or how it works, but if I am struggling, I can meditate, and get out of a depression or frustrating time. And the feeling isn't forced joy or happiness—it comes in a completely subtle and easy way. It just appears, like something I lost beneath a pile of papers or clothes, and I unveiled it. That is something I really benefit from.

HAPPINESS IN UNEXPECTED PLACES: ONE PERSON'S STORY

Before closing off the anecdotes about happiness, let me anticipate and address the legitimate observation that I have chosen a group of highly successful people. I can almost hear some readers asking, "Why shouldn't they be happy?"

Well, the fact is that not all successful people are happy—and studies have shown that money and fame do not in and of themselves bring happiness. In addition, as the above responses indicate, all these people have found greater happiness since meditating. In the past, I have interviewed people who had been drug addicts, prisoners, or homeless, and even *they* have reported greater happiness after learning to meditate. You can read some of their stories in *Transcendence*, a book dedicated more to people with problems they were seeking to solve, as opposed to people who are already highly functional but are looking to turn up their game a notch. Let me close, however, with the story of one man who was not included in *Transcendence*, but who exemplifies TM's ability to help even those reduced to life's most pitiful circumstances.

John had spent years in a penitentiary, for dealing drugs, and had been addicted himself. After being released, he was homeless for a long time, until he was lucky enough to land up in a shelter that gave its residents work to do, paid them a small wage, and had TM as one of its programs. Here he describes the effects of TM on his daily life:

> There's times when my lunch break winds up being close to Central Park, and I've gone there and meditated up on the slopes. And I sit down and I listen—I hear the birds in the background, the wind in the trees, you know, while I'm sitting there. And I meditate. It actually makes me feel great. And it helps me through my day at work. I'm always telling people, "Good afternoon," "Good morning." It feels so good to get feedback from people on the street.

HAPPINESS IN THE MIDST OF SORROW

Debbie decided to learn TM when an ad for the program popped up on her computer screen. It featured the picture of a "beautiful tree in blue and white—a sign of hope," or so it felt to Debbie. And hope was what she sorely needed. Two months before, her nineteen-year-old son, a recreational drug user, had died of an overdose. A new and very powerful opiate had arrived on the street and, perhaps not realizing its potency, many young people had succumbed to it.

After this devastating shock, Debbie was left grieving, along with her husband and daughter. Observing some of the symptoms of her grief—insomnia, flashbacks (to hearing the terrible news), and a sense of unreality (this really can't be happening)—Debbie likened her grief to post-traumatic stress disorder. She decided she had to do something, take some special steps to feel better. Her son had been about to take a course of study, and the college was good enough to return his fee. It would cover her TM training, Debbie thought. What better way to use it?

When Debbie arrived at the TM center, she was wearing a necklace bearing her son's name—a gift from a friend. According to her TM teacher, her face and posture were heavy with grief. Yet she learned TM, practiced regularly, and went about her life. Over the next few months, Debbie's teacher noticed that her step seemed lighter, her grief less overwhelming—and she stopped wearing the necklace. After one of the evening sessions, Debbie's teacher told the gathering that I was looking for any experiences that related TM to happiness. Debbie was good enough to respond. Here's what she wrote:

Many would say the loss of a child is the complete opposite of being "happy." However, through my learning TM two months after the loss of my son, I feel that practicing is keeping me balanced and helping me find new and different types of "happiness." Nothing will make up for the loss of my child. I am still grieving and life will never be the same. But TM has truly helped me cope with these crazy emotions, helped me find an inner calmness and peace so that I can appreciate being "happy" again. Happiness for me now is the gratitude I have when experiencing unexpected serenity and moments of joy in day-to-day living. Taking nothing for granted, living in the moment, and trying to appreciate everything: that is my new "happy."

Debbie's observation is echoed by several CIQ responders, who noticed that TM helped them retain a sense of equilibrium and even find joy in the midst of adversity. Here are a few of their responses:

Even if something is upsetting, I have this feeling of well-being underneath the frustration. It's almost as if this underlying well-being gives me the freedom to experience ups and downs without any lasting negative effects.

I feel "on top" of everything, even though there are myriad challenges in my home life right now . . . new house, aged husband with memory loss and confusion. I seem able to roll with it and enjoy all that life has to offer.

Even after surgeries I feel unexpected well-being. I went to a fiftieth high school reunion and many classmates remarked on how happy I appeared and asked how I maintained my feelings of well-being after my health issues.

Of course, happiness flows more readily without serious adversity. A great majority of CIQ responders (94 percent) reported increased well-being since starting TM. I will leave you with just one of their quotes:

Nothing has changed, yet everything has changed. It's the power of perspective. Better life choices go hand in hand with a better perspective, leading to a personal environment where anything is beginning to seem possible—though without pressure of any kind.

SELF-ACTUALIZATION: BEING YOUR BEST SELF

The term "self-actualization" was coined by psychologist Abraham Maslow, famous for describing what he called a "hierarchy of needs." This important concept is often diagramed as a horizontally striped equilateral triangle, with its base below and its apex above. To represent Maslow's schema, the lowest stripe of the triangle represents basic needs such as food and shelter, next highest comes love, and higher yet the esteem of others. Right at the apex, once all other needs are met, sits Maslow's final need—self-actualization.[9] Maslow wrote, "Musicians must make music, artists must paint, poets must write if they are to be ultimately at peace with themselves. What human beings can be, they must be. They must be true to their own nature. This need we may call self-actualization."

Maslow was eloquent on the subject, but the diagram is often drawn with only a small area for self-actualization—a tiny triangle right at the top of a vast maw of needs. To me, that seems inadequate to depict the importance of this final need. I am reminded of a diagram we had to memorize in medical school, indicating the surface area of the limbs and other body parts. We needed to know it in order to calculate the percentage of skin involved in burns: 36 percent for the back, 18 percent for each leg, and so on, all the way down to just 1 percent for the pubic region. "One percent!" I would think, smiling to myself. "One percent! Yet consider the amount of thought devoted to it—the novels, movies, tabloids, and reality shows that 1 percent has spawned—not to mention all the trouble it causes!"

So it is with that little triangle of self-actualization. Why can't we be happy if the rest of the triangle is full? you may ask. But the fact is, we just aren't. Milton, in his famous sonnet on his blindness, grieved for "that one Talent which is death to hide"—his ability to write, which his blindness impeded. The world is full of people who feel it would be a sort of death not to be able to express their full potential. And this feeling may apply not only to a person's career but also to his or her personal life.

In Milton's case, the impediment to full self-actualization was physical, but for many people, the obstacles are less apparent. Emotional suffering and learning disabilities are examples of obstacles that are invisible yet all too real. In addition, many people who have already accomplished a great deal but continue to strive may cause others to wonder: "Why do they struggle so? Aren't they self-actualized enough?" Yet these strivers know deep down that they have more to give—perhaps their most important contribution. To feel blocked, unable to achieve this ultimate goal, can be disheartening and stifling; to release and express it, a great source of joy. Consider, for example, Sharon Isbin's comments on her delight at having been able to accomplish so many of her dreams, along with happy anticipation of other dreams yet to be fulfilled.

In my thirty-six years as a psychiatrist, I have seen few if any techniques so powerful at helping people free up their desire to self-actualize as Transcendental Meditation. If you are wondering how such a transformation is possible, just flip back to chapter 9 on building a better brain. You will read once again about the improved creativity, memory, independent thinking, intelligence, resilience, and positive attitude associated with TM. Or look back at chapter 10 on being in the zone to see how TM enables people to be fully present in the moment, letting them execute long-practiced skills with spontaneous virtuosity. Or try chapter 11 on internal growth, which tells how TM helps people become comfortable with who they really are—and who they wish to become.

When you think back to the many talented and distinguished people profiled in this book, the role of TM in their self-actualization is evident. For example, recall the crucial National League Championship Series game in which pitcher Barry Zito held off the Cardinals from beating his team, the Giants. He credits TM as having had a pivotal role in helping him make his astonishing comeback.

Ray Dalio and Hugh Jackman credit TM with much of their legendary success. In both instances, their drive to self-actualize continues to flourish.

In the world of asset management, consider Ken Gunsberger and Mark Axelowitz, both of whom have had their best years ever since starting to meditate. Yet both also continue to strive to be their best selves in other ways as well. Ken, for example, is enjoying growing his relationship with his daughter in new and exciting ways. Mark is excited about his work as an actor and philanthropist, where his goal is to give away a billion dollars.

Although I have cited as examples of self-actualization people with outstanding talents, it's important to realize that the need to self-actualize is universal—to be all that you can be, as the slogan goes. If you just think of yourself and your own aspirations, I'll wager there is something for which you are striving, maybe something you haven't told anybody or even admitted to yourself. If so, I hope that you will consider the importance of addressing Maslow's uppermost need—to fulfill all your potential. Perhaps TM could help you realize that goal.

RESEARCH ON SELF-ACTUALIZATION

Anecdotes aside, there is also solid research indicating that TM can promote self-actualization. Researchers have developed a variety of scales to measure self-actualization, the most widely and best validated of which is the Personal Orientation Inventory (POI).[10]

The POI was developed with the help of psychotherapists, who weighed in as to what they considered mentally healthy. Their opinions were used to create 150 two-choice statements, which present opposite points of view on a particular issue. For example: do you feel obligated to do—or free not to do—what others expect of you? Or: do you think it is a good idea—or conceited—to think about your greatest abilities?

The POI has been used in fourteen (out of eighteen) studies evaluating the effects of TM on self-actualization, which distinguished TM researcher Charles Alexander and colleagues[11] used in a meta-analysis (an overview achieved by pooling data from several well-conducted separate pieces of research). Overall they found a highly significant effect of TM on self-actualization—a beneficial effect that increases over time.

Alexander's team then went on to compare the effects of TM (in eighteen studies) to other forms of meditation (eighteen studies) and various relaxation techniques (six studies). Overall, the effect size for TM was on average about 0.8 (considered large), whereas for other methods the effect size was about 0.2 (considered small). In other words, TM's effect on self-actualization, as measured by pencil-and-paper tests, was about four times as great as that for other meditation and relaxation techniques compared so far.

FROM STRESS RELIEF TO SUPER MIND IN DANCE AND SONG

I have shared with you many stories of people who credit TM with helping them self-actualize in various ways, as well as a body of research on the subject. Let me conclude this section with one last story, which illustrates

TM in action as it exercises its effects on this ultimate human need, about which Abraham Maslow wrote, "What human beings can be, they must be." You have already met the person in question—principal ballerina for the New York Ballet, Megan Fairchild.

As you may recall, Megan learned TM to forestall the fainting spells that were bedeviling her and threatening her career. The strategy was successful, and she has had no fainting spells in the eighteen months since starting to meditate. Megan also reports that TM helps her stay in the zone and "out of my head" while she dances, so that her many hours of practice can take over and free her up to dance with the fluid brilliance expected from a prima ballerina.

If all TM had provided for Megan were relief of stress and stabilization of her physiology, that would have been huge. But there were more good things to come. As we have now seen, it is the nature of the Super Mind, as long as you continue to meditate regularly, to develop and expand in the direction of self-actualization. And so it was for Megan.

Word got around that a new Broadway revival of *On the Town* was looking for a ballerina who could also act and sing well enough to handle a lead role. Others in the New York City Ballet had already auditioned for the part when, at the last minute, Megan was asked to audition as well. Although flattered, Megan knew that she was afraid of speaking in public, not to mention singing. In fact, on a previous occasion, when she had been required to talk about a small piece she was about to dance, she describes it as "my worst nightmare—to talk and be human, then dance." In earlier times, given such powerful fears, auditioning for Broadway would have been unthinkable. But here she was, planning to audition—"jumping off a cliff." She credits TM with enabling her to do so. How might TM have made such a plunge possible?

All her life Megan had been a perfectionist. Even as a child, she would plan out her day in minute detail. On a sheet of Hello Kitty paper, which her mother has saved from her childhood, the young Megan had written: "8 o'clock wake up, 8:15 go downstairs eat breakfast, 8:20 read a book." Her mother recalls her throwing a jack-in-the-box across the room if it didn't pop up when she thought it would. Her world had to be, above all, predictable. If she colored outside the lines, she would throw the whole paper away and say she wanted to start her whole life over. Although Megan's perfectionism was ideal for a career in ballet, it was not conducive to taking risks or experimenting with new art forms.

*   *   *

TM changed all that. Things no longer needed to be perfect. Risks were opportunities—as were the inevitable small "failures" that occur along the way. Here's how she puts it:

> TM made me aware that the opportunity to audition was a once-in-a-lifetime thing. Instead of thinking, "Oh I can't do that," and just missing it—which I know I would have done before TM—I seized the day in a way that I had never done before. And it led to an unbelievable experience.
>
> I approached auditioning for Broadway as an exercise in being out of my comfort zone. It takes guts to do that. You have to be in an open place—and not afraid, even though it felt like I was jumping off the edge of a cliff. I worked with an acting coach to put the scene together and with a Broadway actress who's a great singer to help me with the song. I did the audition and got the part right there in the room, which is not at all common. It was pretty cool.

When I asked Megan how she felt about the risk of venturing into such a different career direction, she replied:

> I have never thought of myself as a risk taker. And I don't even see what I've done as having taken a risk. TM has completely changed the way I look at these things. And because I don't see them as risks—I only see them as amazing opportunities, like "what have you got to lose?" opportunities—I can easily think of them without much anxiety. So if they don't go well, the exercise of trying that new thing was worth it in and of itself.
>
> I really believe that people who succeed in anything are those who are okay with not always being perfect—those who have failures along the way, then pick themselves up and try again. And TM is perfect for that because every day you're practicing just accepting yourself. You go back into your meditation—and back to your core. Whatever happened is past, and you feel fresh to start again.
>
> And it's been crazy being in this Broadway world and having a party every night. I look at my Broadway year as the time of my life. It's been like dessert, like the cherry on top.

As I write this, Megan is rehearsing for her enthusiastic return to the ballet. Her great talent was acknowledged by one Broadway reviewer, who wrote that when she danced, she looked like a goddess. Not only were the show and her performance a success, but they also expanded Megan's world, introducing her to a new art form and a new set of friends. What other opportunities lie ahead for Megan? Who can say what this amazingly talented young woman will do? Self-actualization and the Super Mind just keep on growing in unpredictable ways, and I know of no better method than TM to foster this growth.

CLOSING THOUGHTS

Aristotle, as quoted at the head of this chapter, regarded happiness as the ultimate goal. After all, he reasoned, people strive for all other goals—such as money, power, or status—in the hope of becoming happy. But nobody strives for happiness as a means to any other end: it is an end in itself.

As I think back over the diverse people featured in this chapter, as well as the data from the Consciousness Integration Questionnaire, it seems to me that TM can clearly help people become happier. Paul, the young man who challenged me to return to TM, was correct in that regard. And even if one-third to half of our happiness is genetically determined, as research suggests, perhaps TM will prove to be a good way to grow the other half to two-thirds.

And as for me, when I ask myself whether I have been happier since learning to meditate, the answer is an unequivocal yes—not perhaps "*really* happy 90 percent of the time," as Paul reports—but moving slowly in that direction.

TO SUMMARIZE THE ESSENTIAL POINTS OF THIS CHAPTER:

- Twin studies suggest that approximately one-third to half of our happiness is hereditary, so to boost happiness, we need to look to how we can grow the other half to two-thirds.
- Numerous anecdotes, supported by questionnaire responses, strongly suggest that TM is a valuable method for enhancing happiness and a sense of well-being.
- One key to happiness is self-actualization. Several controlled studies, using a standardized scale for self-actualization, suggest that TM is superior to a variety of control conditions for achieving this goal.

PART III

BEYOND THE SUPER MIND

17

THE SUPER MIND IN ACTION

In my belief that a large acquaintance with particulars often makes us wiser than the possession of abstract formulas, however deep, I have loaded the lectures with concrete examples.

William James[1]

The unfoldment of Cosmic Consciousness starts from the beginning.

Maharishi Mahesh Yogi[2]

We know from the Consciousness Integration Questionnaire that there is a significant correlation between length of practice in years and favorable outcomes. I emphasize these facts up front so that when I describe the rapid and dramatic transformations that *some* people experience, you realize that these are the exceptions, not the rule. Regardless of which group best describes you, I have found that the rewards of TM practice are dependable and cumulative. But you can't force the rate of change—so simply enjoy the ride.

In this chapter, we will encounter some people who exhibit early dramatic evidence of Super Mind development and others whose development in this regard is more subtle but often just as profound over time. I hope you enjoy meeting them.

EARLY SIGNS OF THE SUPER MIND: TWO EXPERIENCED TM TEACHERS TALK

I sat down with David and Rhoda Orme-Johnson, two highly experienced TM scholars and teachers, after lunch on the campus of Maharishi University of Management. I asked them how consciousness grows and, to my surprise, they began by telling me how soon after the first TM session you can see signs of shifts in consciousness and improvement in the quality of life.

Here David relates a short vignette about a common malady—resentment of housework:

One lady we taught couldn't bring herself to unload the dishwasher. And then, about the second day after learning TM, it was no longer a problem for her. She just started doing it—and singing while she did it.

David explains such changes as follows:

One of the qualities of expanding consciousness is freedom from the effects of your conditioning, from a behaviorist point of view. You're not being jerked around.

The feeling of emotional attachment—"I can't do that"—that sort of thing starts falling away immediately. We realize that before starting to meditate, people often spin their wheels unnecessarily, or get into arguments that could be avoided. These behaviors may result from fears that cause them to run away from things that may be beneficial, or pursue attractions to things that may be bad for them (like a bad relationship). After they start meditating, these aversions or attractions become less powerful. Life moves more smoothly and people feel more in control of their destiny.

Rhoda offers a different example of early change after learning TM:

Years ago, one of our TM students had fought in Vietnam, where he had lost a leg and consequently became very angry and bitter. When he returned to have his meditation checked, he told me that as he was driving up the hill to his home, he burst out laughing, then kept on laughing. I said, "Oh well, that's good," to which he replied, "No, you don't get it—I haven't laughed in *several years.*"

Rhoda pointed out that the changes that come with meditation are not always apparent to the person who is changing—though the shift may be glaringly obvious to a spouse or partner.

> I once taught a couple where the husband seemed to be enjoying his meditation. The wife had only complaints, such as: "It's not working." "I'm not getting anything out of it." "I don't feel it." "There's nothing happening for me." When I met with the husband, however, he thanked me for the dramatic changes he'd seen in his wife.
>
> "Why haven't you said anything about that in the group?" I asked.
>
> "I couldn't figure out a nice way to say that she was less of a bitch," he responded. I gave him some alternative wording that did the job.

OH MY GOD! THIS IS A DIFFERENT PERSON

The most dramatic story David and Rhoda had to tell—and their most personal one—they left for last. Here's how David recounts the event:

> I would say, as a general statement, what happens during TM depends on the condition of your physiology at the time you learn. Quite a common finding is that people who are highly stressed often find a big, dramatic change with TM right away. And people who are very mellow may really like TM but not feel such a big contrast.
>
> *Moi* was a highly stressed person. And part of that stress was a paranoia that came on when I was a teenager. If I was walking in New York—or wherever I was—I would visualize a sniper aiming at me through some window. It was an irrational fear. If pressed, I would have said that I didn't really think that anyone was there, but I always felt uncomfortable in public places. I was also very shy to talk to people.
>
> I decided to learn TM after my best friend from high school learned and I saw a fundamental change in him. He was less pretentious, more himself, and more productive—more like his authentic self than ever before.
>
> On my first day of learning, we went to the park with our son, and so we were standing in an open area—and I'm feeling completely

in the moment. I'm not the least worried about someone in one of the windows over there, aiming a rifle at me. Rhoda said, "Oh my God, this is a different person!"

That day when David first felt comfortable in an open space was so dramatic that Rhoda remembers it clearly forty-four years later. There was a radical difference in how he felt. This shift was to continue as David became increasingly at ease around other people in open spaces—and everywhere. He went on to become a foremost TM researcher and continues to be a leading figure in the field.

Although in the unusual instance, impressive changes may occur early during meditation, profound changes more often happen gradually and by small degrees, and may feel so natural that people don't even notice—for a while. Here's a good example from David's own experience:

> After I'd been meditating for a few months I was looking in my medicine cabinet and noticed at the back—it had drifted to the back—a large bottle of aspirins, covered in dust. Then it hit me: "Oh my God! I haven't had a headache in three months, since starting TM." The pain had just gone away and I didn't even notice.

SLOW BUT PROFOUND GROWTH OF THE SUPER MIND

Let us examine now the subtle but powerful ways in which developing consciousness perfuses people's lives over time in such a way as to transform how they experience and deal with the world. Although I could have chosen many examples, I have selected just two, largely because both people are especially articulate. I specifically chose relatively new TM practitioners (each had been meditating for less than three years) to illustrate how even when change is not overnight, it often occurs quite soon and progresses steadily in ways that can be powerful and ultimately transformational. These two individuals are representative of many people I might have chosen. I tell their stories in some detail to illustrate how the development of consciousness interacts with other things that are going on in a person's life.

Meet Elaine and Roger.

ELAINE: TUNING IN TO THE NOISE OF THE UNIVERSE

Elaine is a childhood friend of mine, dating all the way back to second grade in Johannesburg. Like me, she immigrated to the United States with her family. She now works as a university psychologist in a large US city. We have stayed in touch over the years, and we always call to wish each other happy birthday. After reading *Transcendence*, Elaine decided to learn to meditate.

When I interviewed her, Elaine was sixty-four years old and had been meditating for two years and eight months, about ten times a week for twenty-five minutes per session. Here is how she describes her experience of meditation:

> When I sit down to meditate, I start to hear the silence underneath the sounds of everyday life. It's almost like hearing static—but not annoying static—rather, it's like what astronomers talk about when they describe picking up the background noise of the universe. There have been times when I have been so upset that I haven't been able to hear it and have been unable to start meditating, ending up just sitting there, thinking. Usually, however, I am able to "tune in" to this background silence. Then I seem to melt into it, using my mantra to gently come back when I start having thoughts—which was fairly often at first. Then, after a few iterations of coming back voluntarily, I start to experience an energy running through me, almost like a cell phone being charged.
>
> While I'm aware of what is going on around me, I feel calm and detached, which was a new and liberating experience when I started meditating. I become aware of bodily sensations of pain or discomfort, knowing that they will melt away, and by the end of the meditation they have mostly gone. There is quite often time that I "lose," becoming aware of returning to myself, refreshed and calm, yet feeling the energy pulsing through me. Not wanting the experience to end, I'll sometimes go back in for a few minutes before opening my eyes. When this happens, I'm surprised that it is time to stop and even more surprised that I've come back, usually within the space of time I had intended to meditate.

I asked Elaine how long it took before she felt as though some transcendent experiences were entering her daily life. Here's what she had to say:

I was surprised at how quickly there was an effect. After two or three days, while I was still learning the technique, I had an amazing experience. At some point on the third day, I was just working when I felt a very strange sensation in my stomach. You know how it is when they've turned the water main off, then turn it back on. There's a gush of air bubbles before it resumes a full flow. Well, I felt something like that. All of a sudden my body was suffused with this very warm energy that took me totally by surprise. I had been feeling very empty and unhappy for a number of months, which is why I looked into meditation. And then I had this wonderful experience—it surprised me that it happened so quickly. And it has not abated over all this time. Obviously for a few days it was wonderful because it was very new, different, and powerful. Now it's not that unusual for me. But TM certainly unblocked some kind of energy in me, and it remains unblocked.

Incidentally, I have frequently encountered such reports of pleasant physical sensations, accompanied by infusions of energy. Here Elaine describes these experiences further:

The key area involved is below my ribs—I would say in my stomach—an area that I feel tensing up when I am unhappy. It's clearly an area associated with emotion. The pleasant sensation feels like warm water flowing through me, with a definite current to it, and I experience it as being golden.

At the time I was under a lot of stress and had been for a long while—very drained of energy. Life felt like drudgery and I was often on the verge of tears. After I got this energy back, nothing much changed in my external circumstances, but now I had the energy to not be drained by them. That surge of energy doesn't make me want to go out and climb mountains or do other amazing things. It just makes me feel so much better.

Elaine has noticed other surprising changes in her life—for example, a growing detachment: the last thing that this devoted wife and mother and diligent professional would once have seen as a virtue. Here's how she describes it:

I'm not a person to be detached. In the past, I found it hard to let go of certain thoughts that were holding me back—and that continued during my sessions. So I went back to my TM teacher, who reviewed elements of my technique and gave me several pointers that turned out to be just what I needed. These pointers allowed me to just let go of whatever I was thinking about. A sense of detachment is something that I have been able to get from meditation that I never had before. I have found it to be incredibly liberating.

As you may recall, I discussed the delicate balance between engagement and detachment in chapter 12. I discussed the fear of dying, where detachment can offer a welcome reprieve. It turns out that this has been an important issue for Elaine. Here's how she describes it:

I hadn't thought about any changes that might have occurred with regard to my fear of death, but when you asked me the question directly, I thought, yes, my feelings have changed—surprisingly so. I have always been terrified by death, having had extreme phobic responses to dead animals, and being very easily disturbed by thinking of losing loved ones to death. My own death has now become more imaginable and less like being ripped savagely from life. Experiencing detachment during meditating has been a huge new experience for me, who previously couldn't ignore a ringing phone or a boiling teakettle. Now I can, and it's not a matter of white-knuckling it, just an inner calm or disconnection. It's like getting information without feeling compelled to respond. In a similar way, I can now understand "leaving life," like melting into my meditation, rather than being ripped from it. There are some previous fun things that I have lost interest in, and I see people aging and becoming disconnected from things that were once very important for them—and that doesn't seem so terrible anymore. So I can now envision taking leave of life, although I'm not in any hurry. But I'm definitely less afraid of death.

Although Elaine has experienced the ability to detach more easily as a relief, paradoxically she values an opposite effect even more highly.

The thing that meditation has done for me that I appreciate the most is having a sense of being fully engaged again. As I said, I had felt drained, so everything felt like a burden. Even nice things felt like a duty. Now things feel more real, more solid, like "this is my life—

everything about it." It feels as though my spirit and the physical world are more connected. I always felt that way as a child. So it was distressing to me as an adult to feel tired, stressed, empty, and drained—like there was no juice. Now the juice is back and I feel connected.

In a way, it sounds like I'm saying two opposite things, but when I meditate and I'm detached, that's pleasant. And the rest of the time, when I'm not meditating, I feel very present in the world.

Elaine experiences many other benefits from TM, both when she transcends and in her daily life, on a regular basis. Some of these have been quite momentous. For example, she was turned down for a promotion in favor of another candidate, but she handled the matter so well that she not only received a substantial raise but also the person who was hired became a close collaborator. She has clearly scored points for accepting the new status quo so graciously and applying herself to her work with such renewed energy that she has been rewarded professionally on all fronts.

Other changes are more subtle, but meaningful nonetheless. She reports feeling periods of inner stillness even during activity and "a deep sense of the world unfolding as it should." As she puts it:

Those moments happen unbidden, usually when I've been particularly engaged in something, usually with someone to whom I feel a real connection. One time, I remember I was just at home, sitting next to the fire, when I was overcome by this wonderful certainty that everything was just the way it was supposed to be, and that I need never worry. Since then, even when I don't like how things are turning out, I remind myself of having experienced that sense of things unfolding exactly as they should. And even if I don't feel it at that moment, I trust it. Then, at some other time I sense that feeling again, often when I am moved by something—like the fire. It may be when I'm outside looking at the stars or just going for a walk, seeing the backlit trees—anything that stirs some part of me. And there is that sense of certainty and calmness—sort of like your mom saying something will be okay. She's not just saying it. It *will* be okay.

As Elaine talked, it was clear that she is engaged in an evolving process. As the Super Mind develops, many people, Elaine included, often experience the world as more vivid. Down the road, the growing changes in oneself, along with experiencing the world in more fine-grained detail and vibrancy, may be accompanied by a sense of perceiving a greater unity. Here is Elaine on that subject:

> I regularly (although not continuously) feel a sense of meaningfulness pervade my everyday life, and I'll perceive connections among details that briefly reveal a bigger picture at work. I'm not able to examine or hold on to that bigger picture for long, but it feels okay.

How wondrous and intriguing it is for me to witness my childhood friend on her rich spiritual journey—and to think of all the changes in her life that have unfolded in less than three years. Cosmic indeed!

ROGER: DEVELOPING CONSCIOUSNESS AS AN AGENT OF TRANSFORMATION

Roger is a seventy-three-year-old physicist and former CEO, a man whose distinguished and successful career in both government and the private sector enabled him to retire in his midfifties and spend his time traveling with his wife and enjoying his life. He has always been a seeker, and at the time I first met him had been practicing TM for almost two years. Roger's experiences of transcending during TM sessions are quite unusual. Here's how he describes them:

> In the first few weeks and months of my meditation, when I felt I was transcending it would feel as though I was going down a tunnel— deeper and deeper and deeper. My mind was quieting. Thoughts didn't capture my attention or my awareness. They would just pass by. Ultimately, after a few months, I had one experience, which I'm having frequently now, where I felt like I was going down a tunnel that was conical in shape, when all of a sudden I burst out the other side into another conical-shaped tunnel that was vast and huge.
>
> Typically, when I feel like I'm in a state of higher consciousness, it is a peaceful thing where I feel like I'm floating in infinite space and my mind is very quiet. That is my more common form of meditation, which I'll call "personal meditation." It is usually related to replenishing my energy, or a thought or insight will bubble out that I end up working on.

The second kind of meditation, which occurred about 20 percent of the time during my first year of meditating, I will call "high energy." During this form of meditation, it felt as though this energy flow was entering my head, flowing through my body and over its surface. It felt very peaceful and good. When I meditated at Machu Picchu last summer, the energy entering my head did not feel like a faucet with a slow trickle—which is how it usually feels—but like a huge fire hose pouring energy through my body and out the soles of my feet. I had never felt so grounded, so connected to the earth, as I did there. But it wasn't a very personal meditation, by which I mean it didn't result in an insight that I needed to *think* about or *work* on.

Roger believes that his personal meditation has led to important insights and changes in both his perception of the world and his reactions. Here are some examples:

I noticed in driving that when people cut me off, I didn't get as angry about it, so I felt there was a change going on. I was becoming more peaceful and not as upset about things happening in a normal, everyday situation. I didn't understand what was happening until a very simple little incident occurred that clarified the entire thing. My wife and I like to walk, so one morning I suggested we go for an hour's walk. And she said, "No, I don't want to walk." And I took that to mean she was upset with me for some reason and didn't want to walk with me. Then I realized, Wow! There's an example of leaping to a conclusion!

Well, I didn't know why she didn't want to walk, so I asked her. She said, "My knee's been bothering me since yesterday, so I don't want to walk for a couple of days." And there I had been in the process of concluding that she was upset with me and so on, all the baggage that goes along with that kind of thinking.

This was a new way of thinking for me, which occurred directly as a result of my meditation. In the weeks that followed, I realized that almost everyone at times leaps to conclusions that are probably wrong in 80 percent of cases. That realization has modified my interactions with people, because now I realize that communicating and understanding clearly what's going on in a situation is very, very important. It allows you to live in a harmonious manner without carrying a lot of dumb baggage.

Roger recognizes the infusion of transcendence into his daily life:

As I meditated more and more, I realized the transcendence really doesn't end. It's there all the time. I'm just not always aware that my consciousness is still expanded when I'm in the real world. But when I sit down and close my eyes, I realize that my consciousness is still expanded. I feel very clearheaded and peaceful, in complete concert with the laws of nature, if you will—with the way the universe operates. It feels like my insights are sharper and clearer, so that I'm more aware of what's going on in the real world.

Roger believes that when he transcends—whether during meditation or during a waking state—important insights arise.

During these states of transcendence, your mind is so quiet and you're very, very open to any thought that bubbles up. And so if there's something in your belief system, your makeup, or your interactions with other people that's not in complete harmony with the laws of nature, then at some point it will bubble up and you will have the choice of dealing with it or not.

Here's a significant example from my own life. My seventeen-year-old grandson ended up being addicted to ecstasy—a bad situation. We got him into a rehab program that did not allow him to communicate with the outside world, except by e-mail if he had some urgent question that required an answer. My wife and I received an e-mail from our grandson, the gist of which was: "I think I'm gay and how do you feel about that?" And oh, by the way, we had twenty-four hours to answer it. Now, here's a kid who grew up in Brooklyn (me), seventy-three years old, not homophobic, but always with an attitude of standoffishness toward gays—you don't bother me; I don't bother you. I didn't want gay friends, didn't have gay friends.

Now, my grandson knew my attitude toward gays. He felt it, so it was important for him to know how I was going to react to this news. And I didn't know how I was going to react. It really hit me hard in the beginning. After receiving the e-mail, I did my afternoon meditation—a very good, deep meditation. And within seconds of going into a state of transcendence, the answer came like a bolt of lightning. It didn't matter whether he was gay or not, because I loved him. He was my grandson. And I love him today as much as I did yesterday or last year. So I sent him an e-mail and I said, here's how I feel about it: it doesn't matter.

Over the next two meditations I realized how I'd been carrying this baggage around about gay people for seventy-three years and all of a sudden I realized I needed to resolve that too. And I knew the answer—to deal with gays as with anybody else, according to whether they were good people, how they treated others, and whether they contributed to society. I realized that gay people were no threat to me, that it was okay to have gay friends. So as a result of a set of meditations over two or three days, I resolved an issue that had been buried deep in my mind all my life. And as a result, my attitude toward gay people changed entirely. And that's just one example of how I have become more tolerant and willing to accept another's point of view—more open-minded.

Roger went on to talk about personality changes he had noticed in himself since starting to meditate.

I was this aggressive, hyper, type A, but I am much more patient these days. I've become more creative and am finding that when others talk to me about their problems or issues, I'm often able to contribute an idea that results in a creative solution. I have often thought, I wish I'd picked up this technique years ago, because I could have solved problems at work so much better, quicker, easier, and more insightfully.

As a clinician, I was intrigued by Roger's discovery that he was jumping to conclusions when he took it personally that his wife refused to join him on a walk. Now he was able to ask her the reason, and the answer comforted him. Likewise, deeper problems began to be resolved—like how to deal with his grandson's announcement or, in a larger picture, his need to reassess his attitude toward gays. I have certainly seen these types of changes occurring as a result of hard work in therapy, but to see them unfolding so quickly and simply as a result of meditation, especially in the eighth decade of a person's life, was amazing.

That concluded my first visit with Roger, and as a token of my appreciation, I gave him a copy of my previous book, *The Gift of Adversity*.[3]

*   *   *

I next met with Roger about two months later, just before the second anniversary of his learning to meditate. He said that his consciousness had continued to expand, now into the nighttime. Whereas previously his periods of transcendence had always been bracketed by wakefulness, now this was changing. It was not unusual for him to move into a transcendent state before falling asleep, and then again during the night itself—expanded consciousness interspersed, as it were, with sleep—and finally between sleep and wakefulness at the end of the night. Roger experienced transcendence as staying with him in one form or another alongside both waking and sleeping. In other words, he had begun to experience "witnessing," which I discussed in chapter 7 and which we will revisit in the next chapter.

As Roger's consciousness expanded, he started to probe his difficult childhood, which he had not previously mentioned to me. Here's how he describes it:

> When I was a kid my father had TB. He probably contracted it when I was about two or three years old, and he lived in a sanitarium for all but about a week that I remember when I was young. He died when I was eight, leaving my mother a single parent. My mother worked at a bakery for long hours, five days a week, including always on weekends. So when I got out of school, she'd be working three days out of five. I'd walk ten blocks from grammar school to my grandmother's house and she'd take care of me. Sometimes I'd stay the night at my grandmother's house—and almost always on weekends—because my mother worked from 6:00 a.m. to 6:00 p.m. My mother had a lot of behavioral issues, and would often be very upset with me when I was young, and I had no clue why.
>
> One Friday when I was six years old, in second grade, I went to my grandmother's house after school. It was maybe 8:00 p.m. when my mother came by after work, and she started screaming and carrying on. She yelled at me to get into bed and out of her sight. So I ran into the bedroom, jumped into bed, and tried to cover myself up. Pretty soon she came running in, ripped the covers off me, and shrieked, "I hate you! I wish I'd never had you! You ruined my whole goddamn life! I hate you! Do you understand me?" shaking me as she screamed. This went on over and over again for about an hour, until finally my grandmother came in and got her out.

But she returned and said, "I'm going to send you to an orphanage—I'm so fed up with you." At that point my grandmother made her go home. I was sobbing uncontrollably, and didn't know what was going on. My grandmother came back in—she was the best thing that ever happened to me, apart from my wife and family. She calmed me down as I kept begging her, "Please don't let her send me to an orphanage. Please don't let her send me to an orphanage." She said, "You can live with me," which I did. She basically raised me, most of the time. My mother remarried when I was about ten years old, and I went to live with her and her second husband at that time.

Anyway, lots of times in my early life and my teenage years I would play this movie over and over in my head, and it was very terrifying, until I grew up. By the time I was fifteen, I was six foot, two hundred pounds, and strong. I worked out with weights and threw the shot put and discus in high school. So I got physically fit and mentally confident, but the stuff with my mother never went away. There were times when I hated her. Although I finally forgave her, I kept trying to find ways to deal with it. As an adult I thought I had handled it well, but all I was doing was burying it and covering it over. Thank God for TM because it just kept pulling that memory up over the last month, letting me know that something was not resolved. I'd tried to rebury it but it kept popping up.

Finally, I decided—okay, I'm not burying it anymore. I was reading your book at the same time, *The Gift of Adversity*. I got to the chapter about Manet's boat [Roger was referring here to using an imaging technique to help let go of painful memories],[4] and I said, okay, I'm going to put this memory in the boat and send it down the river. And as I was walking down to the dock to put it in the boat, I thought, no, that's not it. This is not going to work. I need something else. But I didn't know what.

Well, I kept meditating over the next three or four days, and kept experiencing nice transcendent feelings at night. Then finally I got to the chapter that mentions the "silver lining" exercise [a technique for helping people extract some benefit from past adversity that they can then use going forward].[5] That was a bolt of lightning, man. All that pain? Could it have a silver lining? Well, it did. It came to me right away that my mother had planted a seed in this six-year-old mind, which grew as I became an adult: That memory would never let me treat anybody else like that. It made me want always to love my family—my wife and children—in a way that would allow them to feel secure in that love, so they would never feel threatened that I wouldn't be there for them. And I said, Wow! Sixty-seven years and there was a silver lining I didn't know about. Wow! Within minutes I said, let me try the boat deal again. So I rewound the film—you remember, in the old days we had film in canisters—and after rewinding it, I put the canister in its can, put the top on, and screwed it tight. I walked down to the dock, threw it in the boat, undid the anchor, and shoved the boat hard. It went out on the water, and the current took the boat down the river, through the estuary, and out to the ocean. The currents and wind took it over the horizon. It's gone. It's gone. Wow.

And you'll never believe what's happened. This is now six days and I've been so happy. I've had this deep happiness, all day, all night, for six days. It's unbelievable. So this meditation is spilling over into my life.

In addition to this remarkable development, Roger's life was continuing to unfold in all sorts of ways. He was beginning to understand that his mother probably suffered from a mental illness. (The week after the incident described above, she had behaved as though nothing had happened.) To his wife's amazement, Roger was becoming more spontaneous. Although he had always been a highly programmed person, now he was willing to embrace novel opportunities and experiences. For example, he pulled some unconventional shirts that his wife had given him years before out of their plastic bags and started wearing them around the house. He was having fun. He remained engaged with his grandson, who continued to battle in his recovery from drugs. Roger began to see gays everywhere—really *see* them—and felt very positively toward them (whereas previously he might have thought something like, "Oh damn, we got a gay waiter").

I have presented Roger's story in great detail because it provides a vivid example of how the Super Mind expands—and keeps expanding. And how it enables people to use tools and resources that were formerly inaccessible to them (like a self-help book). Had I left him after the first interview, I would never have learned about his terrible childhood trauma and how he had resolved it. I hesitated to interview him yet again, however, suspecting that his continued growth would run over my word count limits! Nevertheless, we have stayed in touch, and his brief e-mails confirm my suspicions to be correct. Although Roger was seventy-five years old when we last communicated, his consciousness was continuing to expand, and his personality to grow and ripen.

All the stories in this chapter bear out the quote by Maharishi shown above, "The unfoldment of Cosmic Consciousness starts from the beginning." It starts with the first meditation and grows from there. At times the change is sudden, at times gradual. Often, however, as we will see in the next chapter, changes are gradual—almost imperceptible at first—then dramatic.

I think it is likely that this form of growth is common to other life transformations as well—as when a chick hatches from an egg—but also in the realm of psychology and behavior. I believe that William James would agree. In his classic work *The Varieties of Religious Experience*, he expresses this general phenomenon beautifully, describing it in connection with religious conversion. James quotes the following observation from Edwin Diller Starbuck's *The Psychology of Religion*.[6] As Starbuck put it:

> An athlete . . . sometimes awakens suddenly to an understanding of the fine points of the game and to a real enjoyment of it, just as the convert awakens to an appreciation of religion. If he keeps on engaging in the sport, there may come a day when all at once the game plays itself through him—when he loses himself in some great contest. In the same way, a musician may suddenly reach a point at which pleasure in the technique of the art entirely falls away, and in some moment of inspiration he becomes the instrument through which music flows. The writer has chanced to hear two different married persons, both of whose wedded lives had been beautiful from the beginning, relate that not until a year or more after marriage did they awake to the full blessedness of married life. So it is with these religious persons we are studying.

And so it is, I might add, when it comes to Cosmic Consciousness, the fully realized stage of Super Mind development. In the next chapter we will consider two people who have reached this stage of full-blown Cosmic Consciousness.

TO SUMMARIZE THE CENTRAL POINTS IN THIS CHAPTER:

- Some people experience dramatic aspects of the Super Mind soon after learning TM, and for most there is some evidence of Super Mind activity early on.
- For others, the development of the Super Mind is slow and incremental but, as Elaine and Roger described in this chapter, over time it can be transformative. This is important to realize so as not to be disappointed if change does not occur right away.
- Even those who experience early changes will need to keep meditating if they wish to enjoy continued development of the Super Mind.

18

COSMIC CONSCIOUSNESS: SUPER MIND ROUND THE CLOCK

As is the human mind, so is the cosmic mind.

Ayurveda

"How does Cosmic Consciousness evolve?" I asked Fred Travis.

"Someone once asked Maharishi that question," Travis answered. "'Is its appearance gradual or sudden?' the man asked. Maharishi responded, 'It's gradual, gradual, gradual, gradual—and then it's sudden.'"

"And that's what we see in the EEG," Travis said. "There's a continuous change in the integration of brain patterns during TM, a process that takes place over days, weeks, and months. But it's only when this integration reaches a certain level of complexity that the full experience of Cosmic Consciousness dawns. So this is what people will probably notice—not an all-or-none thing, but a gradual, continuous change after they start meditating. And then there will be some instance when they can maintain inner transcendence in the midst of whatever else is going on. They may experience that as a sudden shift, but it's not. The subjective experience of Cosmic Consciousness is like a shape that is being formed by a series of gray dots, and it's only when the number of dots crosses a certain threshold that the person perceives the image."

As you can see from Travis's description, Cosmic Consciousness represents a benchmark in the growth of the Super Mind—a point at which transcendence is experienced continuously alongside both waking and sleeping states. A few points worth noting about this fifth state of consciousness (as classified in the Vedic tradition) are that (1) it is not common even among experienced meditators, and (2) it is possible to enjoy many benefits of developing Cosmic Consciousness (the Super Mind) even at much earlier stages of consciousness development.

Such benefits come about when the expanded consciousness from your meditation sessions begins to infuse your daily activities. It is as if instead of operating on one channel, you now have two: one that handles whatever you need to do, while the other fills you with a calm awareness that feeds back into channel one—thus making your daily activities go smoothly. To me, it seems as if the events of the day are backlit in a way that imbues them with a particular charm and radiance. It is the coexistence of these two channels that I am calling the Super Mind.

As we have seen, the development of consciousness is a process of *unfolding*, and as consciousness expands, life seems to broaden in important ways. Consider Roger, the retired physicist who in just a few years of meditation shed a long-standing prejudice, became more flexible and spontaneous, and came to terms with serious early rejection by his mother—all without any type of therapy. He e-mails me from time to time and, not surprisingly, he experiences continued development of consciousness and its attendant rewards. Amazing as his story is to me, it would be less so to more experienced TM practitioners. It turns out that consciousness can just keep on growing. Nobody has clearly defined an end point to the process.

When I think of Cosmic Consciousness, I'm reminded of a giant cactus that grew in my grandmother's garden when I was a child. This cactus would bloom only once a year, and to a little boy it looked ten feet tall. From a distance you could see its bud, right at the top, above all the prickles. It would be tightly coiled at first, then gradually loosen as it yielded to the temptations of the South African sun. Finally, the great day came and the gardener would rush in and tell my grandmother to hurry up and come! The cactus flower was in full bloom!—a glowing white trumpet atop its prickly green trunk. That's how Cosmic Consciousness arrives for some, as a flower that bursts full blown upon the scene. Only in retrospect does the long, slow, progressive growth that supported this glorious event become apparent.

Others have used different images to describe this threshold event—such as Fred Travis's description of accumulating gray dots. In the most famous image, however, Maharishi compares the development of consciousness to the dyeing of cloth. Initially when cloth is dyed and left out in the sun, it loses some of its color. So the process is repeated, and each time the sunlight bleaches the color until finally the color holds fast. But whatever image you use to describe the process, the final dawning of Cosmic Consciousness (the fully realized Super Mind)—though undetectable to the outsider—is unmistakable to the individual undergoing this experience.

WITNESSING

One feature that Maharishi flagged as the sine qua non of Cosmic Consciousness is the presence of "witnessing," in which expanded consciousness persists even while a person is asleep and dreaming.

We know a fair amount about sleep itself. It can be measured via EEG electrodes applied to the scalp. Sleep generally progresses through a cycle of stages, moving from stages 1 and 2 (the more shallow levels) to 3 and 4, the deeper levels. These different stages are identified by different wavelengths on the EEG. Then there is usually a period of REM (rapid eye movement) sleep, during which the eyes dart from side to side. That is when dreams generally occur.

In trying to understand what witnessing is, I have found it useful to recognize what it is not. Witnessing does not mean shallow sleep, during which we can register outside events. For example, we may suddenly become aware of a warm furry creature in our bed, even before we wake up to find that the dog or cat is blissfully snoozing beside us, basking in the warmth of our bodies. Or maybe our attention is roused by a new sound (as a child's footstep outside the door) or the absence of one, as when a partner quietly leaves the bedroom in the middle of the night. We didn't hear him or her get up and leave, yet the absence of the other person's regular breathing is registered and wakes us. These familiar examples indicate a level of external awareness that can occur during shallow sleep—*yet none of the above is an example of witnessing.*

Instead, here is a classic example of how one meditator described witnessing:

> The flurry of waking activity comes and goes; the inertia of sleep comes and goes. Yet throughout these changing values of waking and sleeping, there is a silent unbounded continuum of awareness that is me; I am never lost to myself.[1]

Note how this experience of the Super Mind persists throughout the twenty-four-hour day. The "silent unbounded continuum of awareness" abides throughout both sleeping and waking. In other words, the two-channel analogy applies not only during the day but also during sleep.

Perhaps the best way to understand Cosmic Consciousness, including witnessing, is to listen to the words of two people who have experienced these states firsthand. You'll notice here that Cosmic Consciousness—like all forms of consciousness—contains elements unique to the individual, along with others common to all humanity.

JOANNE: THE END OF OBLIVION

Joanne is a TM teacher living on the west coast of Canada. She was sixty-five when I interviewed her and had been meditating for forty-two years. She enjoyed her practice from the start, and she is convinced that it helped her university studies and her grades by enhancing the clarity of her thinking.

Besides learning the basic TM technique, Joanne also studied various courses and advanced techniques, which helped deepen her state of consciousness. These advanced techniques are discussed later in this chapter and also in appendix 1, in which I interview leading TM teacher Bob Roth.

The pivotal change—the opening of the cactus flower, if you like—happened for Joanne only four years before our interview (thirty-eight years into her meditation practice). At that point, the cumulative effects of her gradually shifting consciousness became apparent not only to her but also to her husband. One day she started complaining to him, "I didn't sleep a wink all night." He replied, "You must have, because you snored all night." Joanne, however, felt as though she could account for every minute of the night. How could she reconcile that with her husband's observations? Here is how she describes what she discovered:

> That piqued my interest, and I began to notice that my feeling of being aware never went away. It was not specifically an awareness of anything in particular but rather an inner awareness, a sense of not being dead to myself. It simply never went away. It didn't change in dreaming, during the day, or during sleep. I had had this experience before—of being aware even during sleep—but it had never lasted. Now it was here to stay.

When I asked Joanne to describe the experience of witnessing, she gently corrected me.

> Well, in a way it's not an experience. An experience means that there is an experiencer and an object of the experience, whereas this is a

way of being that has no experiencer. It's just being—knowing itself. There is no Joanne as a witness or an experiencer. It is more like a night-light that's on all night—there's awareness, but not awareness of the fact that I'm aware, nor awareness of anything in particular.

Had I heard Joanne's words as a young man—say a medical student or young doctor—I would have been closed to this line of thinking. I am ashamed to say it, but I likely would have thought, "This sounds like mumbo jumbo. Of *course* every experience must involve the experiencer and the object of experience!—even if that object is some aspect of the self." Such was the arrogance of my young self that I could not accept as potentially valid something so far outside my own experience. The concept of nonduality in which the experiencer, the object of the experience, and the experience itself merge into unity would have been foreign to my Western upbringing. What's more, even had someone persuaded me that such a thing was possible, I still would have questioned what value, if any, it might confer. I might have denigrated (smugly and to my private self) the niceties of the distinctions involved in this type of thinking as "debating how many angels can dance on the head of a pin."

Since returning to TM, however, experience has taught me that transcendence is in fact a state of nonduality in which thinker, thought, and object of the thought lose their boundaries and merge into pure awareness. This state is not only highly pleasurable but does indeed confer benefits—most immediately, a sense of calm alertness in which your viewpoint shifts, enabling you to acquire a new perspective of both the world and yourself. It opens up new creative possibilities. And as the state of transcendence has begun to infuse my everyday activities—though not, as yet, the night—it is now clear to me how nonduality carried through into sleep might well extend these benefits. Years of practicing TM have opened my mind, not only to new forms of awareness that are by now familiar to me, but also to the possibility and potential importance of further states that I have not yet personally enjoyed.

As I probed Joanne about her witnessing, further insights came tumbling out.

I do have a sort of light in my head sometimes—like an actual physical light. But this is more a feeling that I'm not asleep, I'm not dead, I'm not unconscious. For a while when I had it—you're going to laugh—I didn't like it because I was used to oblivion for part of the night, and I missed it. So I thought maybe some rum—a hot rum toddy—would do it. But it didn't. Nothing would do it—so I just let it be.

Here's another interesting thing. I broke my wrist about two years ago and had to have surgery to have a plate put in. So I thought, "Well, this is going to be interesting to see what happens when I'm knocked out with an anesthetic." But once again, it didn't feel like oblivion—as though I had lost myself, or gone dead or into blackness or non-me. It felt the same as it does during deep sleep. There was still awareness of awareness, though no awareness of the doctor or the operation. And just as it is for anybody to wake up—including me—I saw myself coming up into awareness, almost like surfacing from the bottom of the ocean. I was aware of different levels of wakefulness. Then I heard noises and I was back in my room again, in a wakeful state. What was interesting to me was that in many ways emerging from the anesthetic felt no different than emerging from sleep.

I asked Joanne what other changes, if any, had kicked in more fully along with witnessing. She pinpointed a few.

A SENSE OF BEING PRESENT OR IN THE NOW

Life has become simple, very simple. Often I have no thoughts about what is going on, whereas before I was always analyzing things: Should I do this? Should I do that? It was very exhausting! And that's just gone. Life is what it is, and I don't think about it. Thoughts may come and go, but they don't seem like my thoughts. Someone once asked Maharishi what it was like to be enlightened. He said, "It's very relaxing." He also said, "Enlightenment is being fully awake within the self. No shadows."

Joanne's description brings to mind Eckhart Tolle's *The Power of Now*,[2] a hugely successful book, in which he emphasizes the value of living in the present in a way that sounds very much like Cosmic Consciousness. Joanne actually mentioned Tolle's book, which she regards highly, but pointed out that Tolle's own transformation occurred spontaneously. After a long depression, he awoke one night and began to think in an entirely new way, one that focused on the here and now. That shift, according to Tolle, was the pivotal moment at which he moved from living in a state of long-standing anxiety and depression into an exploration that has permanently changed his consciousness—and has also inspired millions (we will revisit Tolle in chapter 19). Joanne doubts, however, whether such a spontaneous transformation is possible for most people. Most of us need a specific method, and as a long-time TM practitioner and TM teacher, she sees TM as one viable, well-developed, widely available way to do so—and I agree with her.

OVERALL CONTENTMENT WITH LIFE

In the last four years, since she first entered Cosmic Consciousness, Joanne has also felt a deeper overall sense of contentment with her life. When I asked about specifics, she mentioned that she is writing a book about her happy childhood, growing up in Canada. She is particularly delighted to have thrown off the yoke of being raised as a girl in the 1950s.

In the last four years I feel like I've come home. What fell away at that time was remorse and guilt. What liberation! It was huge, because being a woman in this world, I was acculturated to be a pleaser—like so many other women, I thought it was my responsibility to keep everybody happy, no matter what. I would always say to myself, oh, I should have done this, or why didn't I do that? And now he's mad, and something didn't happen that should have happened. I should have been there to make sure that it did.

Gosh, just that change alone is huge. But then, about four years ago, I began to notice that something would happen that I normally would feel guilty about—but I didn't. And since then, the guilt just seems to have disappeared. I still say all the right things: so sorry I didn't show up, or this didn't happen, or I forgot your book, or whatever. I say these things because it is the polite thing to do and I don't want to hurt anyone's feelings. But basically (*laughing*) I just don't feel it, and after a while I realized that the horrible guilty feeling is never going to come back. Never, ever. What a huge gift that has been!

DAVE: LIKE GRADUALLY TURNING ON A LIGHT

Dave is a retired sales executive who now has a second career, teaching middle school in Fairfield, Iowa, home to Maharishi University of Management (MUM). He learned TM at age twenty-eight and immediately enjoyed the experience, both of transcending itself and the typical psychological benefits that flow from it. Over the years he became aware of "an expansion of the heart." As he put it:

> I noticed that my whole experience of love changed—and I don't just mean love in relationships but love in general. I became much more attuned to the level of the heart and much more appreciative of everything. There was more tenderness, more softness, patience, and balance in me. Everything became more precious to me. It was a great joy.

For years, life continued this way for Dave, who would meditate with several hundred MUM students, faculty, and staff in the morning and evening, in a spacious, dome-like structure. One morning after finishing his meditation, a new development occurred. Here's how he describes it:

> I realized that something very subtle but powerful had changed. Even as I walked out of the dome, I continued to experience that transcendent pure consciousness that usually happened only when I sat down to meditate. That unbounded awareness was still with me! I thought it would fade—as it had before—but it didn't. No matter what I do or where I go, it hasn't left!
>
> I have to say that I didn't see it coming. There was no real precursor—nothing that said, "Wow! A breakthrough is about to happen." Nothing prepared me for it. It just happened. It was a very subtle thing and my physiology was ready to experience it, so there it was. And in a sense it changed everything—the whole ball game.

Once again we see the phenomenon: gradually, gradually, gradually—then suddenly the cactus flower. Here is Dave's own analogy to describe the new development.

> It's like you're in a room that's darkened and little by little someone starts increasing the brightness of the light, so gradually that you

don't even notice at first because you're living in the room, and the change is subtle. But then one day you say, "I never noticed that before. I didn't see that feature." And you don't think it's because your light is brighter, that you have more awareness. You think, "Oh well, that's interesting." It's not until the changes become *compelling*, which is what happens in Cosmic Consciousness, that you can't help but notice it.

"Has anybody else noticed the change in you?" I asked. He responded:

Nobody notices—in a way because there is nothing to notice. I am the same person. I have the same sense of humor and the same relationships with my family that I've always had. On the level of the individual persona, which is Dave, I look the same. But behind that level, the operating feature of that persona has changed completely, so it would be like you're watching a movie and they change projectors to a newer and more powerful one. As the audience, you see the same movie. But if you were the *projector*, the internal experience would be entirely different.

What, then, were the changes that Dave perceived? Besides changes in his perception, which I will discuss presently, Dave describes what we now know as Cosmic Consciousness—a sense of round-the-clock unbounded awareness. You will notice that the word "unbounded" comes up repeatedly as people describe these advanced states of consciousness, and how they feel unlike ordinary awareness, which generally feels more limited in scope.

Here is how Dave describes Cosmic Consciousness:

It's never overshadowed. It never goes away. In fact, it grows stronger and more powerful, more dominant. Sleeping, waking, dreaming, as I used to live and encounter them, are gone. What's left is a constant storehouse of pure awareness that goes with me wherever I am. And everyone and everything I see has become imbued and saturated with that same pure awareness. And all other things, all the hard edges of reality have become softened.

Dave struggles to find words to describe how "pure awareness" fills his mind. "It's pure being. It's is-ness, pure am-ness. It is the essential nature of existence, the very principle of awareness. I could not have imagined it or known I would ever go there. It never occurred to me that my mind could be without thoughts, that I would become a thought-free person."

I asked Dave how he could concentrate on the demands of teaching middle school if his mind was bathed in awareness. But I already knew the answer. To use my previous analogy, people in a state of Cosmic Consciousness operate on two channels simultaneously—one that handles ordinary daily functions, and one that is suffused with "pure unbounded awareness."

THE SCIENCE OF COSMIC CONSCIOUSNESS

So far we have considered only the subjective aspects of Cosmic Consciousness. What then can be said about the physiology associated with this state?

As with the science of transcendence, much of what we know comes from EEGs. Since Cosmic Consciousness usually develops over a period of years, however, unlike transcendence, which can be measured in minutes, it is far more difficult to study—especially using a prospective longitudinal approach. Nevertheless, by using cross-sectional comparisons (that is, comparing people who have been meditating for different lengths of time), a few ingenious EEG studies have addressed both Cosmic Consciousness and witnessing.

THE BRAIN DURING COSMIC CONSCIOUSNESS

Let us return for a moment to Fred Travis's laboratory, where his assistant took EEG readouts while I performed a medley of tasks (resting with eyes closed for five minutes, a TM session for ten minutes, and a computer-administered task that assesses reaction time) and analyzed the data. Well, Travis and colleagues have used similar methods to study the EEG patterns associated with Cosmic Consciousness.

Just to recap, we have already considered the EEG patterns associated with transcendence (see chapter 5), which occurs while people are actually meditating, and recognized two EEG signatures associated with this state. Both of these findings are seen predominantly in the frontal part of the brain, the so-called CEO of the brain, which is responsible for executive functioning. The readouts show: (1) increased alpha power (the density of alpha waves), and (2) increased alpha frontal coherence (correlations between alpha wavelengths across different regions of the frontal lobe). By definition, these measures were taken while subjects were meditating with their eyes closed—as in the second phase of Fred Travis's research protocol mentioned earlier.

What happens, however, in the EEG when longtime meditators move beyond their meditating states and into their active lives? Specifically, what are the EEG hallmarks of Cosmic Consciousness, and do these physical changes shed light on the subjective experiences described by experienced meditators, such as Joanne and Dave?

Before we address that question directly, let us look at a study that deals with EEG changes observed in people over their first year of meditation. Even though none of these short-term meditators attained Cosmic Consciousness, this study is of particular interest because it addresses the underlying brain physiology that corresponds to the developing Super Mind. The study examines the EEGs of people during meditation, eyes-closed rest, *and* while taking part in active tasks—like me when I visited Travis's laboratory. In this study, Travis and Alarik Arenander, director of the Brain Research Institute in Iowa City, measured the EEGs of fourteen people (nine men and five women, the average age being twenty-seven years), first at baseline (before starting TM), and then at three further time points over the course of a year.[3] After baseline measurements were taken, the subjects were taught TM and then meditated regularly twice a day for the next year. EEG measurements were repeated after two months, six months, and a year. At each point, subjects underwent EEG measurements during the same three conditions (resting, TM, and doing tasks with eyes open).

The researchers found a significant increase in frontal broadband coherence during all three of these conditions. Interestingly, however, during the meditation condition, broadband frontal coherence increased from baseline to two months, but thereafter no further increase occurred. In other words, beyond two months, there is no evidence of further change in the EEGs of people practicing TM. That is surprising, since you might expect brain changes to improve or become more marked with practice. To explain it, Travis points out that transcendence—like sleep—is a natural function of the brain. Once you get the hang of it, therefore, your EEG during TM is likely to look the same regardless of whether you have been meditating for three months or thirty years.

A different picture emerged for the other two conditions (eyes-closed rest and eyes-open tasks). A yearlong steady increase in broadband frontal coherence was seen in both these two conditions, suggesting that people who meditate regularly do gradually develop EEG changes consistent with gradually expanding consciousness—early evidence of the emerging Super Mind. So we see that from the very beginning of TM practice, expanded levels of consciousness begin to unfold—just as Maharishi said.

Travis and colleagues then went on to investigate the EEG underpinnings of Cosmic Consciousness during both wakefulness and sleep. In the latter study, Lynn Mason (then associated with Maharishi University of Management) was the lead author.

In the daytime study, Travis and colleagues recruited seventeen long-term meditators (average duration of meditation was 24.5 years), who reported having frequent transcendent experiences during the day as well as witnessing, which was a necessary criterion for their inclusion. The researchers elicited this information by means of an interview, the semistructured Peak Experiences Questionnaire, and two standardized scales.[*]

The researchers then recruited two control groups of seventeen people each, matched for age and gender. The first control group consisted of TM practitioners with a history of few, if any, transcendent experiences during waking or sleeping states. A second group consisted of people who intended to learn TM but had not yet done so. All three groups were put through a one-time protocol similar to the one I did when I visited Fred's lab (resting, TM, and doing tasks with eyes open).

As you might expect, the group with more transcendent experiences had been meditating for longer (on average 24.5 years versus 7.8 years). Of the control groups, those who had not yet been taught TM, when asked to describe themselves, reported mostly their quotidian thoughts, feelings, and actions. In contrast, the long-term meditators who had experienced witnessing reported having a continuous sense of self that was separate from the ups and downs of their daily lives. Although these longtime TM practitioners were aware of time constraints in organizing their daily activities, when it came to thinking about themselves, their predominant sense was that they had a continuous existence outside time constraints such as schedules, clocks, or deadlines. As you might expect, the intermediate group (who had meditated for fewer years than the advanced group) had responses that fell somewhere between the groups at the two extremes. All reported differences were statistically significant.

The researchers ran the data from the EEGs through an appropriate statistical battery, and the following three elements emerged as significant discriminators among the three groups in the expected direction.

- EEG coherence in the frontal parts of the brain, seen across a broad band of wavelengths—not only alpha, but also beta and gamma. That makes sense, since the subjects were doing tasks that are generally accompanied by higher frequency wavelengths, particularly beta and gamma (see table 3, in chapter 5).
- An increase in alpha power despite the fact that people were doing tasks, suggesting internal stillness in the presence of dynamic activity, which is an essential element of higher states of consciousness.
- A better match between computer task requirements and brain response, which has been called contingent negative variation.

All these findings are consistent with the mental state changes described in Cosmic Consciousness, as well as the benefits that accrue from this development. Greater broadband coherence (that is, not just in the alpha range while subjects were at rest) would predict greater effectiveness as different brain areas collaborate more efficiently, even during tasks. The association between broadband coherence and effectiveness is supported by Norwegian studies of athletes and businessmen and businesswomen. In these studies, higher levels of brain coherence have been significantly associated with higher levels of performance and accomplishment.[5] Increased stillness in the presence of activity enables a person to operate as if on two parallel channels (as mentioned above), one intensely engaged with the task at hand, the other deeply grounded in an abiding sense of self. Finally, it is self-evident that improved brain response to demands, as evidenced by EEG responses, would be conducive to better performance.

Statistical analyses were performed on various traits as measured by standardized personality tests administered to the three groups of subjects: inner/outer orientation,[6] moral reasoning (Gibbs Sociomoral Reflection Measure—Short Form),[7] anxiety level (STAI),[8] and personality (International Personality Item Pool).[9] Significant results emerged in the predicted direction (longest-term meditators performed better than shorter-term meditators, who performed better than nonmeditators) for inner/outer orientation, moral reasoning, state and trait anxiety, and emotional stability.[10] Many of these personality features overlap with descriptions of expanded states of consciousness that you have already read.

To date, the EEG data summarized above are the strongest "signatures of Cosmic Consciousness" found during wakefulness. Surprisingly, however, there also appear to be signatures of Cosmic Consciousness during sleep, as I will describe in the next section.

BRAIN SIGNATURES OF COSMIC CONSCIOUSNESS DURING SLEEP

As previously discussed, one hallmark of Cosmic Consciousness is witnessing—transcending during sleep. This phenomenon is also detectable in brain-wave studies.

In 1996, Lynn Mason and colleagues at Maharishi University of Management ran sleep studies on three groups, matched for certain variables such as gender and left or right handedness, but with different TM histories:[11] a long-term group (eleven people whose average duration of meditation was eighteen years), a short-term group (eleven people whose average duration of meditation was 1.4 years), and a nonmeditating control group of eleven people. Mason and her colleagues found that the long-term meditators revealed a highly distinct and unusual EEG pattern during deep sleep (stages 3 and 4). Besides showing the slow-wave (delta) rhythms that typically occur in deep sleep, the long-term meditators simultaneously exhibited two other rhythms—theta 2 (6–8 Hz) and alpha 1 (8–10 Hz), a pattern not seen at all in the nonmeditating controls. An intermediate trend in these measures was seen in the short-term controls.[12]

The coexistence of alpha 1 rhythms (associated with the transcendent state) and delta rhythms (associated with deep sleep) is consistent with the subjective reports of witnessing—namely that transcendence and the pure awareness it involves, which is associated with alpha waves during TM sessions, persists throughout the night. The normal EEG shows no alpha rhythms in deep sleep. This finding supports a physiological basis for what Joanne, Dave, and others say—that their awareness never goes away, asleep or awake. While alpha waves have been reported superimposed on delta waves in certain pathological conditions, notably fibromyalgia (in which sleep is typically disturbed), the subjects in the study were all healthy.

Fred Travis, a coauthor on Mason's sleep study, found the results inspiring: "Dr. Mason's findings set me thinking about how enlightenment grows—that it's really day by day. And it grows on all levels of the individual. We look at brain waves because EEGs are the best tool we have, but I'm sure that enlightenment is also growing in other ways—in biochemistry and the autonomic system. Of course, it's also growing in subjective experience. So far we have found no EEG event that corresponds to the sudden subjective change that heralds Cosmic Consciousness—[that cactus flower experience]—such as we see in witnessing."

Since expanded states of consciousness are so clearly important (at least in my opinion) and the science on the topic so promising (such as specific sleep changes, and transcendent-type EEG changes during activity), it occurs to me that if some young researcher out there is eager to make a contribution, the development of consciousness is a field ripe for harvesting.

TO SUMMARIZE SOME OF THE KEY POINTS IN THIS CHAPTER:

- In certain TM practitioners—usually only after many years of practice—the Super Mind grows to the extent that it is present throughout the day and even at night.
- This state has been called Cosmic Consciousness, and the nighttime component of awareness has been called "witnessing."
- In the chapter we heard from two people who report reaching this stage.
- A daytime EEG study of TM practitioners at different levels of consciousness, and who had been meditating for different durations, were compared, along with a nonmeditating control. Key differences were found, which were summarized in the chapter.
- A similar EEG sleep study also revealed differences between groups: long-term meditators showed a highly distinct and unusual EEG pattern during deep sleep, whereby the EEG rhythm associated with deep sleep (delta) was overlaid with the EEG rhythm typical of transcendent states (alpha 1).

19

TRANSCENDENT SURPRISES AND THE GROWTH OF CONSCIOUSNESS

Mystical states, strictly so-called, are never merely interruptive. Some memory of their content always remains, and a profound sense of their importance.

William James[1]

So far we have considered the growth of consciousness as a more or less orderly incremental series of developments that in some people may lead to a stable, established state. This was certainly the case for Joanne and Dave, profiled in chapter 18.

When I showed an early draft of the Consciousness Integration Questionnaire to Vicki Broome, the TM teacher who first taught me the technique in Johannesburg and has remained a friend, her response, which follows, took me by surprise:

Most of your questions are about pervasive states that are gradually becoming more established—which is great—so that as Cosmic Consciousness grows, we have more and more of these experiences. You might like to add a question about a flashy full-blown Cosmic Consciousness experience, which may not necessarily last but you can't miss because it can blow you away.

THE POINTS I WOULD MAKE ABOUT SUCH EXPERIENCES ARE:

1. Once you have this glimpse of full-blown enlightenment, you are never the same again. Just one glimpse is enough.

2. It can come at any moment—not only in a peaceful or relaxed or meditative environment. It is completely unexpected.

Vicki agrees with other TM experts that the incremental progression of consciousness, fostered by repeated experiences of transcendence during meditation, is essential to expanding consciousness—like the cloth in Maharishi's image that gradually takes on permanent color by being dipped repeatedly into dye. Nevertheless, it is her opinion that "peak experiences," such as she has observed both in herself and in others, need to be understood as another way in which consciousness can progress—in quantum leaps. As she puts it:

> I would not swap these types of experiences for anything. They have been the best moments of my life, and they make sense of everything else! They are like God's grace: just to experience this—without drugs, which damage—and know the truth of things. What a blessing!

MYSTICAL EXPERIENCES

> They call all experiences of the senses mystic, when the experience
>   is considered.
> So an apple becomes mystic when I taste in it
> the summer and the snows, the wild welter of earth
> and the insistence of the sun.
>
> All of which things I can surely taste in a good apple.
> Though some apples taste preponderantly of water,
> wet and sour
> and some of too much sun, brackish, sweet
> like lagoon water, that has been too much sunned
>
> if I say I taste these things in an apple, I am called
> mystic, which means a liar.
>
> D. H. Lawrence[2]

I have started this section with D. H. Lawrence's poem "Mystic," not only for its gorgeous sensory imagery, but also for the important point that he is making. How can we believe the sensory experiences of another person—or rather, why should we disbelieve them? In this section, I have chosen three famous examples of fantastical experiences of transcendence reported by people outside the context of meditation. According to Vicki Broome, however, who has taught TM to thousands of people, she has encountered transcendent experiences that arise "out of the blue" in meditators as well.

FAMOUS EXAMPLES OF TRANSCENDENT FLASHES AND THE GROWTH OF CONSCIOUSNESS

Let us turn now to a few well-documented stories of what I am calling "transcendent flashes." My chief interest here—aside from the inherent fascination of the stories themselves—is how such experiences contribute to the growth of consciousness. From a multitude of possibilities, I have chosen just a few examples.

RICHARD BUCKE

Richard Bucke was a prominent Canadian psychiatrist in the latter part of the nineteenth century. He is best known for his book *Cosmic Consciousness*, published originally in 1901. The book is the fruit of Bucke's decades-long quest to understand how consciousness develops among certain gifted people. The long quest and resulting book demonstrate, as Vicki Broome might say, "How a single transcendent event can come out of nowhere and blow your mind."

Here is Bucke's description of his experience:

I had spent the evening in a great city, with two friends, reading and discussing poetry and philosophy. We parted at midnight. I had a long drive in a hansom to my lodging. My mind, deeply under the influence of the ideas, images, and emotions called up by the reading and the talk, was calm and peaceful. I was in a state of quiet, almost passive enjoyment, not actually thinking, but letting ideas, images, and emotions flow of themselves, as it were through my mind. All at once, without warning of any kind, I found myself wrapped in a flame-colored cloud. For an instant I thought of fire, an immense conflagration somewhere close by in that great city; the next, I knew that the fire was within myself. Directly afterward there came upon me a sense of exultation, of immense joyousness, accompanied or immediately followed by an intellectual illumination impossible to describe. Among other things, I did not merely come to believe, but I saw that the universe is not composed of dead matter, but is, on the contrary, a living Presence; I became conscious in myself of eternal life. It was not a conviction that I would have eternal life, but a consciousness that I possessed eternal life then; I saw that all men are immortal; that the cosmic order is such that without any per adventure all things work together for the good of each and all; that the foundation principle of the world, of all the worlds, is what we call love, and that the happiness of each and all is in the long run absolutely certain. The vision lasted a few seconds and was gone but the memory of it and the sense of reality of what it taught has remained during the quarter of a century that has since elapsed. I knew that what the vision showed was true. I had attained to a point-of-view from which I saw that it must be true. That view, that conviction, I may say that consciousness, has never, even during periods of the deepest depression, been lost.[3]

As we see from Dr. Bucke's account of his pivotal experience, his subsequent fascination with consciousness, and resulting book[4]—which is still in print over a century after its publication—a single powerful transcendent event influenced him for the rest of his life.

EDGAR MITCHELL

Edgar Mitchell was one of the three men on the Apollo 14 space mission, which landed on the moon in 1971. He spent nine hours on the surface of the moon and was the sixth person to walk on it. On the way home, he gave the following account to my friend and colleague Jules Evans, author of *Philosophy for Life and Other Dangerous Situations*:[5]

Every two minutes, a picture of the earth, moon, and sun and a 360 degree panorama of the heavens appeared in the spacecraft window as I looked. . . . I realized that the matter in our universe was created in star systems, and thus molecules in my body, and in the spacecraft, and in my partners' bodies, were prototyped or manufactured in some ancient generation of stars. And I had the recognition that we're all part of the same stuff, we're all one. . . . And it was accompanied by a deep ecstatic experience, which continued every time I looked out of the window, all the way home. It was a whole body experience.

Mitchell was so fascinated by the experience that he went on to research similar experiences in other cultures, virtually all of which gave descriptions of what he called "The Big Picture Effect." He reached a conclusion similar to that of William James: that mystical (and very likely transcendent) experiences are the beginning of all religions. He went on to establish the Institute of Noetic Sciences to explore and promote the expansion of human consciousness.

He also discussed his mystical and intellectual journey with other astronauts, who had had similar experiences derived from seeing the earth as part of a larger system. These conversations led in turn to a book by Frank White called *The Overview Effect*.[6]

Reflecting on himself and his fellow astronauts, Mitchell remarked: "If we could get our political leaders to have a summit meeting in space, life on earth would be markedly different, because you can't continue living that way once you have seen the bigger picture." Once again we see the power of a single mystical or transcendent experience to influence the development of a person's consciousness and the trajectory of that person's life.

ECKHART TOLLE

Eckhart Tolle is an author and contemporary spiritual teacher whom we have already met. In *The Power of Now*, he describes how, after decades of anxiety and suicidal depression, he woke up one night with a feeling of dread. He thought, "I cannot live with myself any longer." He became intrigued with the duality implied by that realization—of an "I" and a "self"—two separate entities. When he woke up, he saw the first light of dawn and knew that "there is infinitely more to light than we realize."[7]

For the next five months he lived in a state of continuous peace and bliss, characterized by a form of awareness that focused on the present moment. This new type of awareness became the inspiration for, and the substance of, his famous book. Many elements of the type of awareness he describes in his book resemble the Super Mind as we understand it. Yet, the "now" awareness did not grow incrementally, as occurs in those who practice TM over time. Rather, at least as described in the book, it appears to have emerged suddenly, mysteriously, and fully formed like Athena from the head of Zeus.

WILLIAM JAMES ON MYSTICAL EXPERIENCES

With regard to how best to view mystical experiences, my chief mentor is William James, who set out with exemplary objectivity the mystical experiences that came his way. Open-minded as to what their causes might be, he approached them as a scientist but never overlooked the people behind the phenomena. Finally, he regarded the information inherent in these "religious experiences" as potentially important to our understanding of the mind. An exemplary mentor, if ever there was one!

James points out four elements that he regards as key to mystical experiences:[8]

- Ineffability: "No adequate report of its contents can be given in words. . . . In this peculiarity mystical states are more like states of feeling than like states of intellect."
- Noetic quality: "Mystical states seem to those who experience them to be also states of knowledge. They are states of insight into depths of truth . . . illuminations, revelations, full of significance and importance."
- Transiency: "Except in rare instances, half an hour, or at most an hour or two, seems to be the limit beyond which they fade into the light of common day."
- Passivity: It feels as though the experience is happening to you, not as though you are the initiator or architect of the experience.

To these he added a fifth quality—that such experiences were never merely "interruptive" but that "some memory of their content always remains and a profound sense of their importance."

As best as I can tell, James's observations—and these five criteria—are as relevant today as they were when he penned them over a century ago.

WHO GETS TRANSCENDENT FLASHES?

Over dinner with a dear friend, I shared with her that I had had in my life just two episodes that might be called flashes of transcendence, along with vivid sensory experiences, when not meditating—"mystical states" as defined by James. You may recall one experience that I described in an earlier chapter, which involved my coming home after meditating in the late afternoon and walking up the front path through two columns of tall flowers (see chapter 7). The second experience, which I reported in *Transcendence*, occurred at the same time of day—at the end of a summer afternoon—once again after meditating. As I sat down to dinner and gazed at a place mat that featured Monet's water lilies—a commonplace souvenir from a museum in Paris—I felt as if I'd been transported into Monet's gardens at Giverny, where I stood before his iconic bridge, watching flecks of light glint off the surface of the dappled pond and lingering in the beauty of his willow trees and water lilies.

My friend, who is an expert in bipolar disorder, pointed out to me that the sort of experience I was describing, which had happened to me twice in my whole life, were the kinds of experiences that people with bipolar disorder might have lots of times in a single year. She reminded me that ecstatic experiences are a classic part of hypomania, and suggested that no discussion of them would be complete without drawing that connection. Her point is well taken. It is possible that transcendent experiences that arise apparently out of the blue might in some instances be fueled by hypomania. This condition, which is less prominent than mania but shares some of its tendencies, often involves elation or irritability, a flight of ideas and rapid speech, increased energy, less need for sleep, and greater creativity. Hypomania can be intensified by prolonged exposure to bright light (such as at the end of a long summer afternoon), sleep disruption, and jet lag.

As someone who has spent many years researching the relationship between light and mood, I am intrigued that so many transcendent experiences involve alterations in perceived light. Richard Bucke found himself "wrapped in a flame-colored cloud," and immediately afterward felt "a sense of exultation, of immense joyousness." Many people I interviewed have seen light of different types—a golden pearl on the horizon, light around the heart area, or a vision of a bright angel. Tolle commented on the amazing quality of the light following his radical change in consciousness. Edgar Mitchell felt a deep ecstasy that continued every time he looked out the spacecraft window.

A SOBER CONCLUSION

Surprising transcendent flashes, which may be accompanied by heightened or unusual sensory experiences, are fascinating to contemplate, but they are not necessary to benefit from TM, and the steady growth of consciousness is the surest pathway to the Super Mind.

As we listen to dramatic stories of visions and mystical experiences, it is easy to feel inadequate or envious as we contemplate our own less dramatic experiences of transcendence and expanded consciousness. It is natural to wonder what is to become of those of us who have ecstatic mystical experiences rarely or never. That applies to most people (myself included). I am happy to say that in practicing TM regularly over time, we have as smooth and reliable a path to expanded states of consciousness—and the development of the Super Mind—as those who experience four-star special effects.

Each time you dive into the waters of transcendence, your consciousness develops. We know that both from personal accounts and EEG studies. And as you transcend repeatedly, so your consciousness expands. That expanded consciousness is the basis of all the fruits described in the previous sections of this book. Now, when you sample them—as I hope you do—you will have a better understanding of how they arise and ripen.

In the next, and last, chapter of this book, I will briefly describe how as consciousness develops it expands to encompass our fellow human beings and other aspects of our universe.

TO SUMMARIZE SOME OF THE KEY POINTS IN THIS CHAPTER:

- Although Super Mind development usually proceeds slowly and incrementally, occasionally it is influenced by transcendent experiences that arise unbidden either during meditation or in waking states.
- A few examples of this well-described phenomenon were presented.
- Such transcendent flashes appear to be an unusual but well-documented way by which the Super Mind can develop.

20

TOWARD A CONNECTED UNIVERSE

Out beyond ideas of wrongdoing and
rightdoing, there is a field. I'll meet you there.
When the soul lies down in that grass,
the world is too full to talk about.
Ideas, language, even the phrase *each other*
doesn't make any sense.

Rumi[1]

Our journey through the stages of consciousness has taken us beyond waking, sleeping, and dreaming, on through transcendence. Now, as the Super Mind rises within us and grows, so does our capacity as human beings. We often become more successful in our personal and professional lives. But even as we grow within ourselves, a new desire begins to unfold within our consciousness—a desire to reach out to people we know—or even to strangers: a desire to share our growing abundance with those around us. It is this aspect of growing consciousness that will occupy our attention in this last chapter.

I have long enjoyed the words of Rumi quoted above, moved by the idea that there may be a place where we can put aside all our differences and be together in harmony. It is a dream shared by people of all persuasions that there will be a time, as it is written in Isaiah, when nation will no longer wage war against nation, when "they shall beat our swords into plowshares and our arrows into pruning hooks."[2] How then might meditation and the growth of consciousness contribute to such a dream?

On a personal level, as I have continued to meditate over the years, I have felt more part of a fabric that connects me with other people and, in an abstract way, with the universe as a whole. Along with this has come a (slightly) diminished fear of death—though I don't look forward to it. I sense that these feelings are not mine alone but common to those who meditate, though of course not exclusively to them. Let me close with a few examples of people who in their own ways express some aspect of this phenomenon that I have gathered under the chapter title "Toward a Connected Universe."

DIVORCE AND RECONCILIATION

Of all the fractured relationships we encounter in our ordinary lives, divorce is one of the most ubiquitous and painful. If you think about it, two people meet, fall in love, plan a life together, share their dreams, and intend quietly or passionately, gently or fervently—and sometimes against objective odds—to live happily ever after. And yet, sooner or later, things begin to go wrong: The fabric frays, then tears, and finally ruptures. Sometimes this happens amicably but all too often not. It sometimes seems as though no two people can hate each other as much as those who have loved and lost each other.

Joe and Gillian had such a marriage, which broke up after a few years, during which a lovely daughter had been born. As with many couples in their situation, they had not planned to raise her under two roofs, and neither was satisfied with their joint-custody arrangement, to say the least. As Joe saw it, Gillian was always looking to renegotiate arrangements.

At the time of the story I am about to tell, Joe, a financial analyst about forty years old, had been practicing TM for about a year. One evening Gillian called him and said she wanted to renegotiate the terms of the custody once again. Joe felt the blood rushing to his face and was about to launch into a tirade when he checked himself. "This isn't a good time for me to discuss this," he said. "Let me call you back later." Then he sat down to meditate. As he did, he felt his body settle down and, strangely, he began to feel compassion for Gillian. "She seemed upset," he thought. "She seemed stressed."

Joe emerged from his meditation feeling rested and ready to call Gillian. He listened to her thoughts about her new proposal, without interrupting or rebutting her suggestions. Instead, he asked some questions about how the new custodial arrangement would work, and as Gillian kept talking, Joe could hear her settle down. She then said, "Who am I talking to? You don't sound like the same person." The custody situation remained unchanged. In reviewing this interaction, Joe told his TM teacher, "Before meditating, the problem felt like scaling Mount Everest. Afterward it felt just like climbing a regular mountain—one I'd scaled many times before."

RAY DALIO: SEEING THE BIG PICTURE

I had last interviewed Ray Dalio formally for *Transcendence*, and his views of TM and its role in his life can be found in chapter 15. Although he was even then a leading business figure, having founded the biggest hedge fund in the world, in the intervening five years he has attained iconic status. His insights into markets and international finance are legendary. Leaders in the arenas of finance, politics, and policy reach out to him regularly for advice, and he in turn has sought out the opinions of leading scientists and other wise people in order to better understand humanity's role in the universe. When I interviewed him for this book, he shared with me some of what he has learned in the course of his explorations.

I asked whether in the last five years he had noticed any continuing changes in his state of mind or the way in which he viewed his life in the world that he would ascribe to his ongoing TM practice. Here's how he replied:

> Yes. I think it's a result of a complementary relationship between my own personal evolution and my TM practice. I think that as one goes through various stages of life, particularly as one gets older and rises above one's own personal circumstances, more and more one sees things as patterns rather than as individual events. That higher-level perspective comes from observing many things happen over and over again. Your perspective evolves, and I think it's greatly facilitated by meditation. As I've continued to transcend and progress over the past five years, I have seen my perspective ascending and myself living in the context of that new perspective. I look down at things as though from above, and see them within a greater context. And that ascending and change in perspective is happening because of my own evolution operating together with meditation.

COMPASSION ON THE STREETS OF NEW YORK CITY

We have met Richard Friedman in earlier chapters. He is a psychiatrist, *New York Times* columnist, and a friend who decided to learn TM after reading *Transcendence*. He had been practicing TM regularly for four years when I asked him whether he thought it had affected his feelings toward others and toward the universe as a whole. His answer was unequivocal: yes. He elaborated as follows:

I've always been empathic with people I know. In the last two years, however, I am much more aware of people around me—strangers— and wonder about their stories. People who look upset and used to irritate me—for example, because they were screaming. I am now more in tune with their suffering. I see them more as individuals and don't dismiss them as a category. I am more forbearing.

As the inhabitants of many big cities know, the teeming crowds and press of strangers bumping up against you induce a certain guardedness, which can be highly adaptive. TM helps lower the barriers safely, allowing a greater sense of fellowship—as Richard goes on to describe.

I commute to work on the subway from Union Square, the number 6 line in Manhattan, which is like a sardine can during the early morn- ing commute. Now when I now go on the subway, I let the crowd kind of wash me into the car, then out of the car and up the steps. I do nothing to resist. And all the while I sit and read or stand and read, seemingly unbothered. That would have been an unusual experience for me in the past. I normally would have been put out. I'd have found it aversive and not wanted to go back on the subway in those condi- tions. But now it doesn't bother me at all.

At the same time, I feel more sensitized to the world around me, more interested and porous—less in a bubble. Sometimes, when I am lucky enough to get a seat on the subway, I look at strangers and imagine what their lives are like. I see a painter with house paint all over his dungarees and think how hard it must be to have to paint on such a hot day; or a woman wearing too much makeup, and I'll won- der how painful it must be to worry so much about one's attractive- ness. In the past, all these people would have blurred into one undifferentiated mass. Now I see them as distinct individuals.

He feels more empathy toward people he sees on the street, who are obvi- ously having a hard time. "I actually stop and feel some sorrow and wonder, 'How did they get there?' I take in more of what's going on around me. Things don't pass by me in a blur as they used to."

Richard's account of the humanizing effect of TM on the experience of living in New York City is by no means unique, as evidenced by this report from a fellow New Yorker.

I live in a city where most people navigate through their lives locked within personal barriers that they have constructed to protect themselves. I know, because I was one of them. But since I began meditating, I notice that I am much more comfortable being open and available to whatever experience I am having, whether it's on a subway, in a shop or restaurant, or just walking down the street. Sometimes I am overwhelmed with the sense of connectedness I feel among us all. At the same time, being a New Yorker, I am not blind to potential threat—it's just that I don't live as much on the defensive as I used to. What I am finding is that many people, whom I would not have even seen before, are quite beautiful—and also wanting to make a connection, even if it is just a passing smile of acknowledgment.

To return to Richard Friedman, the changes in his feelings toward others since he has started to meditate have also influenced his clinical work, where he is more patient. His partner has also observed his greater empathy and decreased defensiveness—and appreciates these changes.

As he has continued to meditate, Richard has had a growing sense of communication with a larger world: "An immanent, ineffable state—fleeting glimpses from time to time of contact with something shot through with light." In tandem with these experiences Richard has felt less self-conscious and less concerned about his value to the world. As he puts it, "I feel less skin in the game with regard to what I have done or accomplished, and what I have left to do. Something about those concerns feels less salient. It's as if there are bigger concerns out there—not that I know what they are, just that they are there."

Along with these changes, Richard, like many other meditators (myself included), feels less worry about death. He also feels less certain about what happens after death. I have often seen such changes develop in meditators, and they seem to represent a greater comfort with being part of a wider universe. One might think that this idea would be threatening in its implied diminution of our human importance, but in general that has not been so. Instead, there is a sense of comfort that comes with being part of a larger, more connected universe.

Results of our meditator survey were consistent with the anecdotal observations reported in this chapter. When asked, "Since starting to meditate, have you felt a greater connection with your community, the world, or even the universe?" 85 percent of respondents said yes. Perhaps that explains why a large majority of respondents (72 percent) reported feeling less afraid of death since starting to meditate.

*   *   *

Once again we see themes emerge that speak to a connection with a larger universe, which include a decreased fear of death. In Ray's case, the connection has also taken the form of extensive philanthropy through his family foundation. He has given, not only of his money and time, but also the gift of meditation to people in every stratum of society. He has given it to people suffering from cancer, to those who are really poor and downtrodden in various ways, and to schools in disadvantaged neighborhoods where children are severely stressed on a daily basis. At the other end of the spectrum, he has given the gift of TM to leaders of industry and finance and other prominent people. The idea behind this strategy is that by helping people at high levels of responsibility to become less stressed and more enlightened, millions of others will benefit indirectly.

A CLOSING NOTE

Some people might think of meditation as selfish or self-indulgent. Based on the many meditators I have known and interviewed for this book, I would maintain that the opposite is true. In listening to the stories of fellow meditators, I have been impressed by how many people have freely donated their time, money, expertise, and creativity to help others achieve the gifts of the Super Mind—as well as to many other causes.

In closing, let me offer this Chinese proverb, which expresses the relationship between personal growth and the health of the world far better than I can:

> When there is light in the soul, there is beauty in the person
> When there is beauty in the person, there is harmony in the house
> When there is harmony in the house, there is order in the nation
> When there is order in the nation, there is peace in the world

And so we come to the end of our journey, our exploration of consciousness. I thank you for accompanying me on the adventure and bid you farewell with the conviction that the end of one adventure is surely the beginning of the next.

APPENDIX 1

ANSWERS TO QUESTIONS ABOUT THE SUPER MIND
AN EXPERT'S PERSPECTIVE

In the course of researching this book, I've found a number of questions that arise again and again. Here they are—with answers from Bob Roth, who has been teaching TM all over the world for over forty-five years.

NORM ROSENTHAL: I ALWAYS ENJOY YOUR DESCRIPTION OF HOW TRANSCENDING IS LIKE MOVING DOWN INTO THE OCEAN. CAN YOU SHARE THAT WITH THE READERS ONCE AGAIN?

Bob Roth: You are on a small boat in the middle of the Atlantic Ocean, and suddenly your boat is being walloped by massive, forty-foot waves. Alarmed, you might think, "The whole ocean is in upheaval!" Maybe. But not the *whole* ocean. Because if you could somehow do a cross section of the ocean, you would realize that even when its surface is engulfed by these forty-foot waves, the ocean, in reality, is over a mile deep. And the depth of the ocean is virtually silent.

Active on the surface, silent at the depth—this is an excellent metaphor for the mind. The surface of the mind, the thinking mind, is like the surface of the ocean—sometimes calm but often turbulent. In terms of Transcendental Meditation, we hypothesize that, just as there is silence deep within the ocean, deep within every human being there is a level of the mind that is *already* calm, settled, and silent. You don't have to believe in it, nor do you have to push out thoughts to create the calm because it's always there: settled, silent, and wide awake. Science calls this level the state of "restful alertness." According to ancient meditation texts, this level is also the source of an individual's unbounded creativity, intelligence, energy, and happiness. It is your own inner self. The texts call it the "source of thought," "pure consciousness," "transcendental consciousness," or "the fourth state of consciousness."

What is remarkable—and most unexpected—is that anyone can access that field through Transcendental Meditation easily and effortlessly.

TM doesn't require any concentration or control of the mind; nor do you have to even believe in it for it to work.

HOW LONG DO YOU MEDITATE FOR?

Adults meditate for twenty minutes twice a day, sitting comfortably in a chair, with your eyes closed. Kids meditate for less time.

ABOUT HOW MANY PEOPLE WOULD YOU SAY YOU HAVE TAUGHT TO MEDITATE IN YOUR CAREER AS A TM TEACHER?

Several thousand. I am one of more than ten thousand specially certified TM teachers in the world. All told, more than eight million people of all ages, nationalities, and walks of life have learned the Transcendental Meditation technique.

WHAT PERCENTAGE OF THOSE PEOPLE WOULD YOU ESTIMATE HAVE SUCCEEDED IN EXPERIENCING TRANSCENDENCE (THE FOURTH STATE OF CONSCIOUSNESS)?

I know this is hard to believe, but everyone I have taught—and everyone who learns TM from a certified teacher—experiences the fourth state of consciousness, either clearly or as a glimpse. This can be for a split second, or over a more sustained time, but transcendence is a regular feature of TM.

WHAT ARE THE BIGGEST OBSTACLES TO PEOPLE EXPERIENCING TRANSCENDENCE WHEN THEY START TO MEDITATE?

The definition of "transcend" is to "go beyond." So in every meditation you do go beyond the surface, excited level of thinking to a quieter, more settled level of thought. And then as you continue to meditate, over the twenty minutes, you will periodically transcend, or settle down, to the *next* quieter level of thinking—and so on.

If the question is what are the obstacles that might prevent people from experiencing "transcendental consciousness," then the answer is stress in the physiology. If your body has a backlog of "stored up" stress or tension, this could slow the process of transcending for a bit. But the deep rest gained during the practice allows those stresses to be dissolved, which then allows the mind to settle down in subsequent meditations. The only other obstacle would be not meditating regularly. In other words, you have to *do it*! You have to take the few minutes, ideally twice a day every day, to meditate. If you do that, the rest is automatic.

ON AVERAGE HOW LONG DOES IT TAKE FOR PEOPLE TO TRANSCEND AFTER LEARNING TM—AND WHAT IS THE RANGE?

Well, that is hard to quantify, because everyone's physiology is different. If a person suffers from trauma or toxic stress, it could take a bit longer, maybe a week or more. That said, everyone, no matter who they are or what stress they live under, *will* transcend. Everyone will go beyond the excited levels of thought to quieter, more settled levels of mind— and that's within the first few days. I must emphasize that transcending is not a flashy experience. It is quite simple and natural. We are just settling down to our own quiet, inner, unbounded self.

IS THERE ANYBODY WHO CANNOT LEARN TM OR FOR WHOM TM WOULD NOT BE SUITABLE?

I have been teaching TM for more than forty years, to thousands of people, and I can say honestly and confidently that everyone who completed the four-day course is able to meditate. And the same would be true for any certified TM teacher.

DOES EVERYONE CONTINUE TO MEDITATE, EVERY DAY, TWICE A DAY?

Many do. Some meditate once a day, and some meditate irregularly. But that is a matter of choice, and whenever they do meditate, they tell me they derive very real, very positive benefits.

I HAVE SEEN PEOPLE LEARN TO MEDITATE AND THEN STOP ALTOGETHER— OFTEN EVEN WHEN THEY KNOW THEY HAVE BEEN HELPED! WHY DO PEOPLE DO THIS?

There are two main reasons, in my experience. People who stop may have hit a rough spot in their life—a dire sickness in the family, upheaval at work, or a big life transition. What's more, they tell me in retrospect that it was during those times that they know they should have been meditating! The second reason is that people stop meditating correctly. They inadvertently introduce into the practice some effort, some concentration or control of the mind. As soon as they do that, they are no longer practicing TM, so the experience is no longer effortless, no longer enjoyable. It is no longer relaxing and rejuvenating. However, I do find that most people who stop end up coming back to it—and for good reason: a few minutes of effortless meditation can give you a full day of clearer thinking and increased focus, greater energy, and improved resilience. That's a pretty good trade-off!

WHAT ARE THE BEST STRATEGIES FOR GETTING THEM BACK ON THE HORSE?

In the end, everyone decides for him- or herself. Maybe they remember how much better they felt during the day, or how much better they slept at night, when they were meditating regularly. Or maybe they realize how tired or irritable or less happy they feel now that they are not taking the time to recharge their batteries, so to speak. Something like that. Then they reach out to their TM teacher or local TM center for a refresher. The refresher is free, and it only takes a few minutes to get back on track. Once they are meditating properly again, they will quickly regain the benefits.

OF THE PEOPLE YOU HAVE TAUGHT, WHAT PERCENTAGE WOULD YOU SAY EXPERIENCE SOME DEGREE OF SUPER MIND DEVELOPMENT?

In truth, everyone. When you transcend and you experience that field of inner silence, then the growth of equanimity, of creativity, focus, and intelligence in your daily life is both automatic and natural. And those are the expressions of the development of the Super Mind. And remember, the Super Mind is not some comic-book, "Supermanish" experience. Rather it is the unfolding of who we are naturally when we are not shrouded in stress or fatigue, and when we are using more of our brain potential. Super Mind is a big term for a simple reality. It is who we are, naturally.

WHAT FORMS DOES SUPER MIND DEVELOPMENT MOST COMMONLY TAKE?

The neuronal connections between the frontal lobes and the rest of the brain are strengthened during TM, and those connections are then maintained naturally during daily activity. So beyond sleeping better and having more energy and clearer thinking, one of the first sustainable signs will be that you are less reactive to outer irritants—e.g., people who push your buttons. You are more "field independent," which means you "know" yourself better. You are more comfortable in your own skin, and are therefore less influenced by outside pressures and social habits that may be destructive to your health and life, such as drinking excessive alcohol. Basically, you are happier and more content inside, more energized and confident outside. Another sign that people report is that life gets easier, smoother, and more enjoyable. It is less of a struggle, less of a battle. Things just seem to go your way more often. That is hard to quantify, but that's the experience.

HOW LONG ON AVERAGE DOES IT TAKE FOR A PERSON WHO LEARNS TO MEDITATE TO DEVELOP THE FIRST GLIMPSES OF THE SUPER MIND?

It differs for different people, based on their life experiences. For people with more stress, it may take a little longer. But it starts from the first meditation.

HOW DOES THE SUPER MIND RELATE TO COSMIC CONSCIOUSNESS?

The fully developed Super Mind *is* Cosmic Consciousness—it is the natural and spontaneous coexistence of the inner silence of the transcendent inner Self with the outer dynamism of daily life.

ARE THERE ANY FURTHER THINGS YOU WOULD LIKE TO TELL THE READERS ABOUT TRANSCENDENCE OR THE SUPER MIND?

The ability to transcend is natural to every human being. Just as we can get worked up about something—and our blood pressure and cortisol levels can spike dramatically and the amygdala or fear center in the brain gets hyperaroused—we can meditate and settle down naturally in the other direction. We can move naturally toward increasing inner calm and ease— and blood pressure and cortisol levels decrease markedly and the amygdala resets itself to normal. In the same way, the Super Mind is the birthright of every human being. It is not, I will emphasize again, *not* something otherworldly. It is who we are when we are not blanketed by accumulated stress, tension, and fatigue. TM eliminates those blocks, wakes up the brain, and allows us to live our full potentiality. And we can live this way without any associated philosophy, belief system, or change in lifestyle.

WHY CAN'T I LEARN TM FROM A BOOK?

I get this question a lot because most meditations you *can* learn from a book or a tape. But not with TM. This is because Transcendental Meditation is tailored for the individual. You learn to meditate in personal instruction with a certified teacher who will give you a "mantra" or sound, and then teach you how to use it properly, to facilitate the "transcending" process. With your own teacher you can have your questions answered to your satisfaction, eliminating confusion and doubts. Plus you will have the ongoing support of your teacher—or any one of the thousands of certified teachers in the world—to ensure you are meditating properly for the rest of your life.

DOES IT TAKE A LONG TIME TO LEARN TM?

It takes about sixty to ninety minutes a day over four consecutive days to learn to meditate. Basic TM courses with follow-up programs are offered in TM centers all over the world.

WHAT IS THE CURRENT FEE FOR TM TRAINING?

The current course fee for an adult is $960, and if a spouse or partner learns at the same time, the fee for the second person is $720. The fee for college students is $480, while for high school students and younger, the fee is $360. TM is a nonprofit educational organization, and those funds are used for three things: (1) to pay the salaries of certified TM teachers, (2) to help cover the rent and administrative costs of thousands of local TM centers around the world, and (3) to provide a lifetime of follow-up instruction at no additional fee for every single person who learns to meditate anywhere in the world.

IF THIS IS NOT AFFORDABLE, ARE THERE ANY MEASURES THAT AN INTERESTED PERSON CAN TAKE TO OBTAIN A REDUCED FEE?

Yes, absolutely. Just as any public or private college or educational institution offers grants, scholarships, loans, and payment plans for individuals who cannot afford the tuition, the local TM centers offer similar opportunities. For more information, you can go to www.tm.org.

I UNDERSTAND THAT ADVANCED TECHNIQUES CAN BE HELPFUL IN FACILITATING THE DEVELOPMENT OF THE SUPER MIND. IS THAT CORRECT AND, IF SO, WHAT CAN YOU TELL THE READERS ABOUT ADVANCED TECHNIQUES?

Learning TM is like planting a seed and watering it regularly. The plant grows. If you want, you can add some fertilizer to the plant after every few months to help the plant grow a bit faster. That is what the advanced techniques are like: adding some strength to the practice so that all the benefits of TM—the growth of the Super Mind—are accelerated. Your regular TM practice is the main thing, but advanced techniques are a valuable addition.

AND WHAT IS THE VALUE OF WEEKEND RETREATS?

Weekend retreats, or "residence courses," are great! They are usually held at a nearby quiet, comfortable resort hotel or in-residence facility. Here you have the opportunity, in a structured course environment, to deepen your experiences of daily meditation; practice light yoga postures; explore intriguing ideas on meditation, consciousness, brain development, life, etc.; and meet interesting, successful people. Such weekend retreats are the ideal vacation: you have a great time and you come home rested and refreshed. Local TM centers also often hold one-day retreats at a local hotel where you can get a good "mini vacation" but without having to leave home for an entire weekend.

CAN YOU TELL US ABOUT THE TM-SIDHI PROGRAM?

Once you have completed four advanced-technique courses you are eligible to apply for the TM-Sidhi program. Maharishi introduced this program based upon the ancient meditation text called the Yoga Sutras of Patanjali. The first half of this book describes TM—the process of effortless transcending to gain access to transcendental consciousness, the fourth state of consciousness, which lies deep within the mind of every human being. The second half of the book describes techniques, or "sutras," to allow any meditator to consciously enliven this deepest level of the mind. Such techniques accelerate the development of consciousness, such as increased energy, creativity, focus, happiness, etc., by helping to more quickly stabilize the inner silence of transcendence as it moves into the intensifying dynamism and demands of daily life. The substantial benefits of the TM-Sidhi program have also been documented by research, as well as by the personal experiences of tens of thousands of people who practice the program today, including physicians, business leaders, athletes, seniors, and students. It's definitely worth pursuing if you are interested.

IS THERE ANYTHING ELSE YOU WOULD LIKE TO ADD?

There is a spectrum as to how creative, intelligent, focused, etc., we are at any given moment. On one end, when we are under enormous stress and not responding well to the pressure, we freeze up. We can't remember our lines in a play, the answers to an exam; we can't make the free throw in a tight basketball game we have made a million times in practice. On the other end are those amazing moments when we are in a splendid zone when everything flows effortlessly, seamlessly, even joyfully. We are in perfect communication with the person we love, the words for a short story or poem flow spontaneously out on a page, one putt drops after another in a close golf game. Those moments, if we even have them, may be so rare that we remember them for a lifetime. But they *do* exist. And the purpose of Transcendental Meditation over the millennia has been to give any individual, no matter his or her religion, culture, or educational background, access to a transcendental level of the mind where creativity and intelligence feel limitless. And as a result of regular meditation, we begin to live every aspect of our life in a natural, powerful, unified flow with every other part of our life. Those special moments arise more often. As the Super Mind develops to the point of full realization, it is possible to live life "in the zone" 24/7. In the past we thought such moments were unique and fleeting. But the purpose of meditation has always been to make that a regular feature of our daily life.

CONSCIOUSNESS INTEGRATION QUESTIONNAIRE
NORMAN E. ROSENTHAL, MD; FRED TRAVIS, PHD; GERRY GEER

CONSCIOUSNESS INTEGRATION QUESTIONNAIRE INTRODUCTION

Thanks for being willing to take a look at the Consciousness Integration Questionnaire (CIQ). The purpose of this questionnaire is to obtain information about experiences that some people have after they start to meditate. Almost all the questions refer to the period of time since you started to meditate.

Although almost all the questions refer to the period of time since you started to meditate, this questionnaire is also useful as a baseline measure. If you have not yet started to meditate, simply ignore that opening clause to most of the questions, and answer them to reflect how you have been in the past year. That way you will be able to evaluate how your scores vary over time, including what impact, if any, meditation may have on them.

Frequency Scale	please rate the average frequency over the past year		
1. Rarely (less than once a year)	**5.** Regularly (+/- once a week)	**7.** Very often (at least once a day)
2. Infrequently (+/- once a year)	**6.** Often (> once a week, <daily)	**8.** Almost continuously (most of the day)
3. Occasionally (few times a year)		**9.** Continuously
4. Sometimes (+/- once a month)	← one point ↑ two points	↑ three points

INSTRUCTIONS FOR SCORING CONSCIOUSNESS INTEGRATION QUESTIONNAIRE

1. Answer questions 4 through 31 by noting "yes" or "no."
2. **All "no" responses are scored as zero for the purpose of determining your final score.** Item numbers 17, 18, 29, 30, and 31 do not count toward your final score and are included only for the sake of completeness and for your interest.
3. For those items that you marked "yes," give yourself a score of

Frequency Scale	please rate the average frequency over the past year		
1. Rarely (less than once a year)	**5.** Regularly (+/- once a week)	**7.** Very often (at least once a day)
2. Infrequently (+/- once a year)	**6.** Often (> once a week, <daily)	**8.** Almost continuously (most of the day)
3. Occasionally (few times a year)		**9.** Continuously
4. Sometimes (+/- once a month)	← one point ↑ two points	↑ three points

one point, two points, or **three points** corresponding to how frequently it applies to you, using **COLUMNS 1, 2,** or **3** in the **Frequency Scale** key at the top of each page.

4. Add up your scores for items **4 through 9** to arrive at your total **"state of consciousness"** score.

5. Add up your score for items **10 through 28** to arrive at your total **"life impact"** score.

CONSCIOUSNESS INTEGRATION QUESTIONNAIRE

NORMAN E. ROSENTHAL, MD; FRED TRAVIS, PHD; AND GERRY GEER

- Name (optional)
- Today's date:
    - Day _____
    - Month _____
    - Year _____
- If we have follow-up questions, may we be in touch?
    - ❏ Yes
    - ❏ No
- If it is okay to be in touch, please provide e-mail address.
- What city and country do you live in? _____
- Gender:
    - ❏ Male
    - ❏ Female
- Age: _____
- Highest educational level:
    - ❏ High school
    - ❏ Partial college
    - ❏ Graduated college
    - ❏ Graduate degree

Frequency Scale | please rate the average frequency over the past year		
1. Rarely (less than once a year)	**5.** Regularly (+/- once a week)	**7.** Very often (at least once a day)
2. Infrequently (+/- once a year)	**6.** Often (> once a week, <daily)	**8.** Almost continuously (most of the day)
3. Occasionally (few times a year)		**9.** Continuously
4. Sometimes (+/- once a month)	← one point ↑ two points	↑ three points

- What is your current occupation? _____
- Code (if this has been provided to you) _____

1. How long have you been doing TM?
   Years _____
   Months _____

2. On average, how often do you meditate?
   _____ times per week

3. On average, how long do you meditate for each session?
   _____ minutes

EXPERIENCES RELATED TO YOUR STATE OF CONSCIOUSNESS

4. While meditating, have you experienced periods of time that are different from ordinary waking experience—often silent and calm without thoughts?
   ❏ Yes
   ❏ No

If yes, how frequently? (Please refer to above frequency scale)

Please feel free to describe these experiences.

_____

_____

_____

_____

5. Since starting to meditate, have you felt a sense of inner stillness even during times of activity?
   ❏ Yes
   ❏ No

Frequency Scale | please rate the average frequency over the past year

1. Rarely (less than once a year)   **5.** Regularly (+/- once a week)   **7.** Very often (at least once a day)

2. Infrequently (+/- once a year)   **6.** Often (> once a week, <daily)   **8.** Almost continuously (most of the day)

3. Occasionally (few times a year)   **9.** Continuously

4. Sometimes (+/- once a month)   ← one point   ↑ two points   ↑ three points

If yes, how frequently? (Please refer to above frequency scale)

Please feel free to describe these experiences.

_____

_____

_____

_____

EXPERIENCES RELATED TO YOUR STATE OF CONSCIOUSNESS

6.   Since starting to meditate, have you felt that the "real you" is somewhat separate from the ups and downs of your daily life?
  ❑   Yes
  ❑   No

If yes, how frequently? (Please refer to above frequency scale)

Please feel free to describe these experiences.

_____

_____

_____

_____

7.   Since starting to meditate, have there been times in which you have experienced the world around you in more vivid, richly colorful, or fine-grained detail?
  ❑   Yes
  ❑   No

If yes, how frequently? (Please refer to above frequency scale)

Frequency Scale | please rate the average frequency over the past year

1. Rarely (less than once a year)	**5.** Regularly (+/- once a week)	**7.** Very often (at least once a day)
2. Infrequently (+/- once a year)	**6.** Often (> once a week, <daily)	**8.** Almost continuously (most of the day)
3. Occasionally (few times a year)		**9.** Continuously
4. Sometimes (+/- once a month)	← one point ↑ two points	↑ three points

Please feel free to describe these experiences.

_____

_____

_____

_____

_____

8. Have you noticed any continuing influence of such vivid experiences in your daily life?
    ❑ Yes
    ❑ No

If yes, how frequently? (Please refer to above frequency scale)

Please feel free to describe these experiences.

_____

_____

_____

_____

_____

9. Since starting to meditate, have you noticed any changes in the quality of your sleep or in your experiences during sleep?
    ❑ Yes
    ❑ No

If yes, how frequently? (Please refer to above frequency scale)

Please feel free to describe these experiences.

_____

_____

_____

_____

_____

Frequency Scale | please rate the average frequency over the past year

1. Rarely (less than once a year)   **5.** Regularly (+/- once a week)   **7.** Very often (at least once a day)

2. Infrequently (+/- once a year)   **6.** Often (> once a week, <daily)   **8.** Almost continuously (most of the day)

3. Occasionally (few times a year)   **9.** Continuously

4. Sometimes (+/- once a month)   ← one point   ↑ two points   ↑ three points

10. Since starting to meditate, do you feel you have become more mindful of your own inner experiences or of the world around you?
    - ❏ Yes
    - ❏ No

If yes, how frequently? (Please refer to above frequency scale)

Please feel free to describe these experiences.

_____

_____

_____

_____

11. Since starting to meditate, have you noticed any change in your level of well-being?
    - ❏ Yes
    - ❏ No

If yes, how frequently? (Please refer to above frequency scale)

Please feel free to describe these experiences.

_____

_____

_____

_____

12. Since starting to meditate, have you noticed that you feel less upset by, or recover faster from, unpleasant or negative experiences?
    - ❏ Yes
    - ❏ No

Frequency Scale | please rate the average frequency over the past year

1. Rarely (less than once a year)	**5.** Regularly (+/- once a week)	**7.** Very often (at least once a day)
2. Infrequently (+/- once a year)	**6.** Often (> once a week, <daily)	**8.** Almost continuously (most of the day)
3. Occasionally (few times a year)		**9.** Continuously
4. Sometimes (+/- once a month)	← one point ↑ two points	↑ three points

If yes, how frequently? (Please refer to above frequency scale)

Please feel free to describe these experiences.

_____

_____

_____

_____

_____

13. Since starting to meditate, have you noticed any change in your reactions to pleasant or positive experiences?

❏ Yes

❏ No

If yes, how frequently? (Please refer to above frequency scale)

Please feel free to describe these experiences.

_____

_____

_____

_____

_____

14. Since starting to meditate, have you noticed that you don't get as overly attached to things—or emotionally overinvolved in things—as you did before?

❏ Yes

❏ No

If yes, how frequently? (Please refer to above frequency scale)

Please feel free to describe these experiences.

_____

_____

_____

_____

_____

Frequency Scale | please rate the average frequency over the past year

1. Rarely (less than once a year)   **5.** Regularly (+/- once a week)   **7.** Very often (at least once a day)

2. Infrequently (+/- once a year)   **6.** Often (> once a week, <daily)   **8.** Almost continuously (most of the day)

3. Occasionally (few times a year)   **9.** Continuously

4. Sometimes (+/- once a month)   ← one point   ↑ two points   ↑ three points

15. Since starting to meditate, do you feel you are more fully present in your day-to-day life, more in the moment, or more engaged?

    ❏ Yes

    ❏ No

If yes, how frequently? (Please refer to above frequency scale)

Please feel free to describe these experiences.

_____

_____

_____

_____

_____

16. Since starting to meditate, when you have been involved in specific activities, have you felt more completely engaged and focused, in "the zone," or in a state of "flow?"

    ❏ Yes

    ❏ No

If yes, how frequently? (Please refer to above frequency scale)

Please feel free to describe these experiences.

_____

_____

_____

_____

_____

17. Since starting to meditate, have you been less afraid of death?

    ❏ Yes

    ❏ No

Frequency Scale | please rate the average frequency over the past year

1. Rarely (less than once a year)   **5.** Regularly (+/- once a week)   **7.** Very often (at least once a day)

2. Infrequently (+/- once a year)   **6.** Often (> once a week, <daily)   **8.** Almost continuously (most of the day)

3. Occasionally (few times a year)   **9.** Continuously

4. Sometimes (+/- once a month)   ← one point   ↑ two points   ↑ three points

Please feel free to describe.

_____

_____

_____

_____

18. Since starting to meditate, have your ideas about the possibility of life after death changed in any way?

    ❏ Yes

    ❏ No

Please feel free to describe.

_____

_____

_____

_____

19. Since starting to meditate, do you feel more content with who you are and what you have?

    ❏ Yes

    ❏ No

If yes, how frequently? (Please refer to above frequency scale)

Please feel free to describe these experiences.

_____

_____

_____

_____

Frequency Scale | please rate the average frequency over the past year

1. Rarely (less than once a year)	**5.** Regularly (+/- once a week)	**7.** Very often (at least once a day)
2. Infrequently (+/- once a year)	**6.** Often (> once a week, <daily)	**8.** Almost continuously (most of the day)
3. Occasionally (few times a year)		**9.** Continuously
4. Sometimes (+/- once a month)	← one point ↑ two points	↑ three points

20. Since starting to meditate, do you feel more empowered to be your authentic self?
    - ❏ Yes
    - ❏ No

If yes, how frequently? (Please refer to above frequency scale)

Please feel free to describe these experiences.

_____

_____

_____

_____

_____

21. Since starting to meditate, have you noticed any improvement in your work or other endeavors?
    - ❏ Yes
    - ❏ No

If yes, how frequently? (Please refer to above frequency scale)

Please feel free to describe these experiences.

_____

_____

_____

_____

_____

22. Since starting to meditate, is it easier to get things done?
    - ❏ Yes
    - ❏ No

If yes, how frequently? (Please refer to above frequency scale)

Frequency Scale | please rate the average frequency over the past year

1. Rarely (less than once a year)   **5.** Regularly (+/- once a week)   **7.** Very often (at least once a day)

2. Infrequently (+/- once a year)   **6.** Often (> once a week, <daily)   **8.** Almost continuously (most of the day)

3. Occasionally (few times a year)   **9.** Continuously

4. Sometimes (+/- once a month)   ← one point   ↑ two points   ↑ three points

Please feel free to describe these experiences.

_____

_____

_____

_____

_____

23. Since starting to meditate, have you noticed changes in your productivity or creativity?
    ❑ Yes
    ❑ No

If yes, how frequently? (Please refer to above frequency scale)

Please feel free to describe these experiences.

_____

_____

_____

_____

_____

24. Since starting to meditate, have you made healthier choices in your daily life, e.g., discontinued bad habits or initiated good habits?
    ❑ Yes
    ❑ No

If yes, how frequently? (Please refer to above frequency scale)

Please feel free to describe these experiences.

_____

_____

_____

_____

_____

Frequency Scale | please rate the average frequency over the past year

1. Rarely (less than once a year)	**5.** Regularly (+/- once a week)	**7.** Very often (at least once a day)
2. Infrequently (+/- once a year)	**6.** Often (> once a week, <daily)	**8.** Almost continuously (most of the day)
3. Occasionally (few times a year)		**9.** Continuously
4. Sometimes (+/- once a month)	← one point ↑ two points	↑ three points

25. Since starting to meditate, have you noticed changes in your relationships with others?
    - ❏ Yes
    - ❏ No

If yes, how frequently? (Please refer to above frequency scale)

Please feel free to describe these experiences.

_____

_____

_____

_____

_____

26. Since you started to meditate, has anyone commented on changes in you?
    - ❏ Yes
    - ❏ No

If yes, how frequently? (Please refer to above frequency scale)

Please feel free to describe these experiences.

_____

_____

_____

_____

_____

27. Since starting to meditate, have you noticed any changes in your financial circumstances?
    - ❏ Yes
    - ❏ No

If yes, how frequently? (Please refer to above frequency scale)

Frequency Scale | please rate the average frequency over the past year		
1. Rarely (less than once a year)	**5.** Regularly (+/- once a week)	**7.** Very often (at least once a day)
2. Infrequently (+/- once a year)	**6.** Often (> once a week, <daily)	**8.** Almost continuously (most of the day)
3. Occasionally (few times a year)		**9.** Continuously
4. Sometimes (+/- once a month)	← one point ↑ two points	↑ three points

Please feel free to describe these experiences.

_____

_____

_____

_____

_____

28. Since starting to meditate, do you feel you have been luckier or that things have gone your way more than before without you having to put any extra effort into them?

    ❑ Yes
    ❑ No

If yes, how frequently? (Please refer to above frequency scale)

Please feel free to describe these experiences.

_____

_____

_____

_____

_____

29. Since starting to meditate, have you felt a greater connection with your community, the world, or even the universe?

    ❑ Yes
    ❑ No

If yes, please feel free to describe.

_____

_____

_____

_____

_____

Frequency Scale	please rate the average frequency over the past year		
1. Rarely (less than once a year)	**5.** Regularly (+/- once a week)	**7.** Very often (at least once a day)	
2. Infrequently (+/- once a year)	**6.** Often (> once a week, <daily)	**8.** Almost continuously (most of the day)	
3. Occasionally (few times a year)		**9.** Continuously	
4. Sometimes (+/- once a month)	← one point ↑ two points	↑ three points	

30. Since starting to meditate, if you have noticed positive changes in yourself or your life, have these changes continued to grow over time? For example, have they become more frequent or continuous the longer you have meditated?

    ❑ Yes
    ❑ No

If yes, please feel free to describe.

_____
_____
_____
_____

31. Since starting to meditate, have you had any kind of peak or heightened experience of consciousness not covered in the rest of the questionnaire?

    ❑ Yes
    ❑ No

If you have, please share it here:

_____
_____
_____
_____

NOTES

CHAPTER 1

1. According to Vedic tradition, there are seven states of consciousness. The three basic states include waking, sleeping, and dreaming. Beyond those three there are:

   Transcendental Consciousness: the experience of the transcendent—the Self—in the silence of meditation.

   Cosmic Consciousness: the experience of the transcendent in activity. The light of the transcendent, or Self, is maintained naturally throughout the waking state as well as in the sleep and dream states of consciousness.

   Refined Cosmic Consciousness emerges through a process of development of the senses and the emotions. Here you experience the finest levels of your environment. Your love, compassion, and appreciation for friends, family, humanity, and the whole manifest world are at their maximum. At this stage, the Vedic maxim "the world is my family" becomes a living reality.

   Unity Consciousness, Maharishi has said, is the state of full self-actualization, full enlightenment. In this state you experience transcendental reality, not just within yourself, but within everyone and everything.

2. Rosenthal, N. E., et al. Seasonal affective disorder: A description of the syndrome and preliminary findings with light therapy. *Archives of General Psychiatry* 41 (January 1984): 72–80; Rosenthal, N. E. *Winter Blues: Everything You Need to Know to Beat Seasonal Affective Disorder* (Guilford, 2013).

3. Matthew 7:16, as translated in the *World English Bible* (Rainbow Missions, 2000).

CHAPTER 2

1. Dehaene, S. *Consciousness and the Brain: Deciphering How the Brain Codes Our Thoughts* (Viking, 2014), 7–8.

2. Dennett, D. *Consciousness Explained* (Back Bay Books, 1991).

3. Dehaene, S. *Consciousness and the Brain*, 115–60.

4. Lazar, S. W., et al. Meditation experience is associated with increased cortical thickness. *Neuroreport* 16 (17) (November 28, 2005): 1893–97.

5. Pearson, C. *The Supreme Awakening: Experiences of Enlightenment Throughout Time—And How You Can Cultivate Them* (Maharishi University of Management Press, 2013), 42.

6. See note 1 for chapter 1.

7. Travis, F. T., and Shear, J. Focused attention, open monitoring, and automatic self-transcending: Categories to organize meditations from Vedic, Buddhist and Chinese traditions. *Consciousness and Cognition* 19 (4) (December 2010): 1110–18.

8. Brasington, L. *Right Concentration: A Practical Guide to the Jhanas* (Shambala, 2015).

9. I gave Leigh Brasington the following description of transcendence and asked him which if any of the eight *jhanas* corresponded to transcendence.

It is a state of calm alertness, in which boundaries of space and time disappear. It has therefore been called a state of boundlessness. Although one is alert and conscious, there is no specific content to the consciousness. It has therefore been called pure consciousness. It is also blissful. Physically, transcendence is accompanied by relaxation of the muscles and slowing of the breath.

Here is his response, in which he deconstructs my description into components, and matches each with a corresponding *jhana* (numbered according to the *jhana* stage):

NR: It is a state of calm alertness, in which boundaries of space and time disappear.

LB: This is indeed like J5—the realm of infinite space, though time doesn't disappear necessarily in J5—only if you are deeply concentrated.

NR: It has therefore been called a state of boundlessness.

LB: This fits the "infinite" part of J5 and J6.

NR: Although one is alert and conscious, there is no specific content to the consciousness.

LB: In J5 the content of the consciousness is a huge space. There is a very clear object. People who are visual see it. This does not fit J5.

LB: In J6 there is no specific content to the consciousness. And it's a huge consciousness. This fits J6.

NR: It has therefore been called pure consciousness. It is also blissful.

LB: J5 and J6 (as well as J7 and J8) are neutral—no bliss, just a strong equanimity. This does not fit any of J4 or J5–J8.

NR: Physically it is accompanied by relaxation of the muscles and slowing of the breath.

LB: This does not fit any of J5–J8. The description of J5 starts, "By passing beyond all bodily sensations. . . ." There is no body awareness in J5–J8. This does fit J2–J4, however. But there is nothing infinite in J1–J4.

> So although there are many aspects in common between transcendence as experienced in TM and the *jhanas*, no *jhana* really matches all these aspects.

CHAPTER 3

1. Suzuki, S. *Zen Mind, Beginner's Mind.* (Weatherhill, 1970), 21.

2. *Bhagavad Gita,* translated by Maharishi Mahesh Yogi (Arkana Penguin Books, 1967), 133.

CHAPTER 4

1. Lao-Tzu (translated by Star, J.). *Tao Te Ching: The New Translation from Tao Te Ching: The Definitive Edition* (Tarcher Cornerstone, 2008).

2. Maharishi Mahesh Yogi. *The Science of Being and Art of Living* (Plume-Penguin, 1995) 32–33.

3. Lynch, D. *Catching the Big Fish: Meditation, Consciousness, and Creativity* (Tarcher Penguin, 2006).

CHAPTER 5

1. Travis, F. T., and Pearson, C. Distinct phenomenological and physiological correlates of "consciousness itself." *International Journal of Neuroscience* 100 (2000): 77–89. The figure showing the GSR finding in question is on page 85.

2. Wehr, T. A. Effect of seasonal changes in daylength on human neuroendocrine function. *Hormone Research* 49 (3–4) (1998): 118–24.

3. Wehr, T.A., et al. Conservation of photoperiod-responsive mechanisms in humans. *American Journal of Physiology* 265 (Regulatory, Integrative Comparative Physiology 34, 1993): R846–57.

4. Travis, F. T., and Arenander, A. Cross-sectional and longitudinal study of effects of Transcendental Meditation practice on interhemispheric frontal asymmetry and frontal coherence. *International Journal of Neuroscience* 116 (2006): 1519–38; Travis, F. T., et al. A self-referential default brain state: Patterns of coherence, power, and eLORETA sources during eyes-closed rest and Transcendental Meditation practice. *Journal of Cognitive Processing* 11 (2010): 21–30; and Travis, F. T. Transcendental experiences during meditation practice. *Annals of the New York Academy of Sciences* (2013): 1–8.

5. Ludwig, M., et al. Brain activation and cortical thickness in experienced meditators. Doctoral dissertation, California School of Professional Psychology, Alliant International University, San Diego, 2011.

6. Harung, H. S., and Travis, F. T. Higher mind-brain development in successful leaders: Testing a unified theory of performance. *Journal of Cognitive Processing* 13 (2) (2013): 171–81.

7. Harung, H. S., et al. Higher psycho-physiological refinement in world-class Norwegian athletes: Brain measures of performance capacity. *Scandinavian Journal of Medicine and Science in Sports* 21 (1) (2011): 32–41.

8. The relationship between TM, brain changes, and performance is reviewed in Harung, H. S., and Travis, F. T., *Excellence Through Mind-Brain Development: The Secrets of World-Class Performers* (Gower, 2015).

CHAPTER 6

1. Maitri Upanishad, VI., 19–23.

CHAPTER 7

1. Maharishi Mahesh Yogi. Audio file, Rishikesh, India, February 15, 1968; Pearson, *Supreme Awakening*, 170–87.

2. My colleagues and I encountered a similar situation shortly after we described seasonal affective disorder (SAD). It emerged that seasonality—the tendency to display emotional and behavioral changes with the seasons—exists on a spectrum ranging from those with very little change to those with extreme change. In order to document the degree of seasonality in an individual or group, we needed to create a scale. The result was the Seasonal Pattern Assessment Questionnaire (*Winter Blues*, 2013), which has been widely used in research. Likewise, we have now created the Consciousness Integration Questionnaire, which has yielded useful information that I share with you in this chapter. Also, the questionnaire may prove valuable for others wishing to understand the development of consciousness and its effects.

3. We received 607 usable responses after "cleaning up" the data by removing duplicates and questionable responses, such as the individual who gave his age as 111 years. We cannot provide a response rate since we only have the numerator (the number of people who responded) but not the denominator (the total number of people to whom the request went out).

Several limitations of this survey must be acknowledged: First, it applied only to those practicing TM at the time of the survey. Although it is possible that respondents might have practiced other forms of meditation as well or previously, we did not specifically ask about this. I do not, however, suspect that this was a major confounding variable, as the target group clearly identified themselves as TM practitioners. Second, the respondents cannot be said to be representative of TM practitioners as a whole. For example, they might be more diligent or interested in TM—or might have had greater benefits from it—than the average TM practitioner. Finally, we did not inquire about any drugs of the kind that might alter states of consciousness, though I strongly doubt whether that was a significant factor since TM practitioners as a group disdain the use of mind-altering drugs.

4. https://www.surveymonkey.com.

5. Demographics, Background Characteristics, and Transcendental Meditation Behaviors:

CHARACTERISTICS	TOTAL SAMPLE (N=607)
Age	N=607
Mean (SD) Median Range	52.68 (14.87) 56.0 16–100
Gender, % (N)	N=607
Male	47.8% (290)
Female	52.2% (317)
Education, % (N)	N=607
High School	5.1% (31)
Partial College	13.7% (83)
College Graduate	31.6% (192)
Graduate Degree	49.6% (301)
Occupation, % (N)	N=602
Employed	76.1% (458)
Student	6.3% (38)
Homemaker	1.0% (6)
Retired	15% (90)
Not Employed	1.7% (10)
Geographic Location, % (N)	N = 568
USA	78.7% (447)
South Africa	19% (108)
Other	2.3% (13)

CHARACTERISTICS	TOTAL SAMPLE (N=607)
USA Regions	N = 417
Northeast	19.4% (81)
Midwest	22.8% (95)
South	33.1% (138)
West	24.7% (103)
Years Practicing TM	N=607
Mean (SD) Median Range	15.48 (17.61) 4.0 0–56
Frequency of Practicing TM (Times per Week)	N=607
Mean (SD) Median Range	11.54 (4.2) 14.0 0–28
Length of TM Session (Minutes)	N=607
Mean (SD) Median Range	27.94 (18.63) 20.0 0–180

6. As you can see in the CIQ, we asked people to rate all items they endorsed on a nine-point frequency scale (see appendix 2). In order to simplify analysis, we collapsed these nine levels of frequency into three: infrequent, often, and very often. Some items did not lend themselves to frequency analysis (specifically items 17, fear of death; 18, possibility of life after death; 29, greater connection with community, etc.; 30, continued growth over time; 31, peak experiences not covered elsewhere).

7. Level of coherence for a cluster of items is measured by a statistic called "Cronbach's alpha," which was 0.84 for the State of Consciousness scale, and 0.93 for the Impact on Life scale (in both cases when evaluated taking frequency of item into account). In general, Cronbach's alpha levels of 0.4 to 0.65 are regarded as adequate, 0.65 to 0.85 as good, and over 0.85 as excellent. The level of coherence for State of Consciousness variables is therefore on the cusp between good and excellent, and that for the Impact on Life scale is excellent. Throughout our calculations, we have found that taking frequency into account (as opposed to simply considering responses on a yes-no basis) improves the Cronbach's alpha level, and therefore report the results using this type of calculation throughout. The results using bimodal responses are generally only slightly less good and still fall into the "good" range. The advantage of having such good Cronbach's alpha levels is that it allows one to add the item scores to create a sum total for each scale.

8.   Factor Analysis for Impact on Life Scale: Rotated Factor Matrix

COLUMNS	1	2	3
CIQ #	IN THE ZONE	INTERNAL GROWTH	SUPPORT OF NATURE
10		.74	
11	.32	.59	
12		.67	
13	.32	.60	.33
14		.59	.36
15		.38	
16	.50	.42	.35
19	.52	.44	.37
20	.49	.42	
21	.72	.33	.33
22	.74	.32	
23	.70		.35
24	.34		.53
25	.44	.37	.47
26			.42
27			.59
28			.67

The above columns show the results of the factor analysis for the Impact on Life items (numbers in column 1 represent item numbers on the CIQ). The numbers under each column show how strongly each item loads to the factors indicated by columns number 1, 2, and 3 above. These represent the three factors: in the zone, internal growth, and support of nature, respectively. Even though items 19 (Do you feel more content with who you are and what you have?) and 20 (Do you feel empowered to be your authentic self?) load slightly more strongly on factor 1 (in the zone) than on factor 2 (internal growth), we have elected to classify them under the latter factor because they seem to belong more logically there. The numbers shown in bold represent the items that load most strongly or, in the above two cases, most logically to each factor. The missing numbers correspond to items that don't have frequencies associated with them, and were therefore left out of this analysis.

9.   Multivariate Analyses for State of Consciousness Scale

	STATE OF CONSCIOUSNESS FREQUENCY SCALE	
R-squared = .46	OR	95% CI
Age	-.24	-.84–.35
Gender	.10	-.40–.60
Geographic Location	-.25	-.89–.40
Frequency of Practicing TM	.07*	.005–.13
Years Practicing TM	.04**	.02–.06
Impact of TM Scale	4.32**	3.78–4.85
*p≤0.05; **p≤0.001		

Respondents who practice TM more frequently throughout the week are more likely to experience a higher score on their State of Consciousness scale. Likewise for those who have practiced TM for more years.

Note that a third variable, the impact of TM on one's life, has an even more powerful correlation with the State of Consciousness score than either duration or frequency of meditation.

10.   Multivariate Analyses for Impact of TM Frequency Scale

	IMPACT OF TM FREQUENCY SCALE	
R-Squared = .43	OR	95% CI
Age	-1.19	-2.75–.38
Geographic Location	-.09	-1.79–1.60
Length of TM Session	1.96	-1.31–5.24
Frequency of Practicing TM	.28**	.11–.45
Years Practicing TM	.08**	.04–13
State of Consciousness Scale	10.98**	9.60–12.37
*p≤0.05; **p≤0.001		

Respondents who practice TM more throughout the week and have practiced TM for more years are more likely to experience a greater impact of TM on their lives. Additionally, individuals with a higher score on the State of Consciousness scale are more likely to have a higher frequency in their impact of TM.

If you examine the factors determining the State of Consciousness (as opposed to the Impact on Life, discussed above), you will notice a powerful correlation between Impact on Life and State of Consciousness. As has often been said, correlation does not mean causation. Since each major factor predicts the other, it is a matter of interpretation as to which comes first. My inclination is to hypothesize that the growth of consciousness predicts the impact of TM on a person's life, especially since years of observation by TM experts and teachers have led to that hypothesis. Nevertheless, the opposite hypothesis could be true. Also, the two scales may well feed back on each other, as I suggest in the body of the chapter.

CHAPTER 8

1. Sapolsky, R. M. *Why Zebras Don't Get Ulcers* (Holt, 2004).
2. Anderson, J. W., et al. Blood pressure response to Transcendental Meditation: A meta-analysis. *American Journal of Hypertension* 21 (2008): 310–16.
3. Orme-Johnson, D. W., et al. Neuroimaging of meditation's effect on brain reactivity to pain. *Neuroreport* 17 (12) (2006): 1359–63.
4. Goleman, D. J., and Schwartz, G. E. Meditation as an intervention in stress reactivity. *Journal of Counseling and Clinical Psychology* 44 (3) (1976): 456–66.
5. Schneider, R. H., et al. Long-term effects of stress reduction on mortality in persons ≥55 years of age with systemic hypertension. *American Journal of Cardiology* 95 (2005): 1060–64.
6. Schneider, R. H., et al. Effects of stress reduction on clinical events in African Americans with coronary heart disease: A randomized controlled trial. *Circulation* 12 (2009): S461.
7. Castillo-Richmond, A., et al. Effects of stress reduction on carotid atherosclerosis in hypertensive African Americans. *Stroke* 31 (2000): 568–73.
8. B-mode ultrasound is a technique in which the machine scans a plane through the body, which can be viewed as a two-dimensional image on the screen.
9. O'Connell, D., and Alexander, C., eds. *Self-Recovery: Treating Addictions Using Transcendental Meditation and Maharishi Ayur-Veda* (Harrington Park Press, 1994).
10. Peeke, P. *The Hunger Fix: The Three-Stage Detox and Recovery Plan for Overeating and Food Addiction* (Rodale, 2013).
11. Volkow, N. D., et al. Food and drug reward: Overlapping circuits in human obesity and addiction. *Current Topics in Behavioral Neurosciences* (October 21, 2011).
12. Duhigg, C. *The Power of Habit: Why We Do What We Do in Life and Business* (Random House, 2014).
13. Herron, R. E., and Hills, S. L. The impact of the Transcendental Meditation program on government payments to physicians in Quebec: An update. *American Journal of Health Promotion* 14 (5) (2000): 284–91.

CHAPTER 9

1. Hains, A. B., and Arnsten A. F. T. Molecular mechanisms of stress-induced prefrontal cortical impairment: Implications for mental illness. *Learning & Memory* 15 (2008): 551–64.
2. Grosswald, S. J., et al. Use of the Transcendental Meditation technique to reduce symptoms of attention deficit hyperactivity disorder (ADHD) by reducing stress and anxiety: An exploratory study. *Current Issues in Education* 10 (2) (2008).

3. Travis, F. T., et al. ADHD, brain functioning, and Transcendental Meditation practice. *Mind and Brain* 2 (1) (July 2011): 73–81.
4. Monastera, V. J., et al. The development of a quantitative electroencephalographic scanning process for attention deficit-hyperactivity disorder: Reliability and validity studies. *Neuropsychology* 15 (1) (2001): 136–44.
5. Travis, F. T., et al. ADHD, brain functioning, and Transcendental Meditation practice, 73–81.
6. So, K., and Orme-Johnson, D. W. Three randomized experiments on the longitudinal effects of the Transcendental Meditation technique on cognition. *Intelligence* 29 (2001): 419–40.
7. Iliff, J. J., et al. Implications of the discovery of brain lymphatic pathways. *Lancet Neurology* 14 (10) (October 2015): 977–79.
8. Xie, L., et al. Sleep drives metabolite clearance from the adult brain. *Science* 342 (6156) (October 18, 2013): 373–77.
9. Orme-Johnson, D. W., and Barnes, V. A. Effects of the Transcendental Meditation technique on trait anxiety: A meta-analysis of randomized controlled trials. *Journal of Alternative Complementary Medicine* 20 (5) (May 2014): 330–41.
10. So, K., and Orme-Johnson, D. W. Three randomized experiments on the longitudinal effects of the Transcendental Meditation, 419–40.
11. One useful way to combine the results of several small studies is by a technique called meta-analysis (Hunter, J. E., and Schmidt, F. L. *Methods of Meta-analysis* (Sage, 1990). This approach applies statistical methods that analyze and combine results from independent studies, taking into account all pertinent information. The pooled data are usually measured as "effect sizes," which reflect the overall magnitude of what you are looking for—in this case the degree to which anxiety predicts subsequent cardiovascular disease. Researchers often employ meta-analysis to combine the results of clinical trials and report effect sizes to describe the difference between experimental and control treatment conditions. In behavioral sciences, an effect size is considered to be large at 0.8 units or more, medium at 0.5 units, and small at 0.2 units (Cohen, J., *Statistical Power Analysis for Behavioral Sciences* [Academic Press, 1977]).
12. Bandy, C. L., et al. Meditation training in rook cadets increases resilience (personal communication, 2015).
13. Beck, A. T., et al. An inventory for measuring depression. *Archives of General Psychiatry* 4 (1961): 561–71.
14. Marteau, T. M., et al. The development of a six-item short-form of the state scale of the Spielberger State-Trait Anxiety Inventory (STAI). *British Journal of Clinical Psychology* 31 (3) (September 1992): 301–6.
15. Heuchert, J. P., and McNair, D. M. *Profile of Mood States*, 2nd ed. (MHS Psychological Assessments and Services, 2004).
16. Bartone, P. T. Test-retest reliability of the dispositional resilience scale-15, a brief hardiness scale. *Psychological Reports* 101 (3) (December 2007): 943–44.

CHAPTER 10

1. Bannister, R. *The Four-Minute Mile* (Lyons Press/Globe Pequot Press, 2004), 167–73.
2. King, B. J., with Chapman, K. *Billie Jean* (Harper & Row, 1974), 197–201.
3. Pearson, C. *Supreme Awakening*, 244.
4. Ibid., 172.
5. Csikszentmihalyi, M. *Flow: The Psychology of Optimal Experience* (Harper Perennial Modern Classics, 2008).

CHAPTER 11

1. Rosenthal, N. E. *The Emotional Revolution: How the New Science of Feelings Can Transform Your Life* (Citadel/Kensington, 2002), 215–19.
2. Thoreau, H. D. *Walden and Other Writings* (Bantam Books, 1982), 188. This quote comes from *Walden*, "Sounds."

CHAPTER 12

1. *Bhagavad Gita*, trans. Maharishi Mahesh Yogi (chapter 2, verse 47), 133.
2. Norwood, R. *Women Who Love Too Much* (Pocket Books, 1997).
3. Rosenthal, N. E. *The Gift of Adversity: The Unexpected Benefits of Life's Difficulties, Setbacks, and Imperfections* (Tarcher, 2013), 314.
4. Maharishi Mahesh Yogi. Excerpted from a lecture in August 1970 at Humboldt State University, Arcata, California.
5. James, W. *The Varieties of Religious Experience* (Touchstone/Simon and Schuster, 1997), 302.

CHAPTER 13

1. Rosenthal, N. E. *Winter Blues*, 239–41.
2. Sula, M. *Don't Let Your Mind Go* (Balboa Press/Hay House, 2014).

CHAPTER 14

1. Khoury, B., et al. Mindfulness-based therapy: A comprehensive meta-analysis. *Clinical Psychology Review* 33 (2013): 763–71; Hoffman, S. G., et al. The effect of mindfulness-based therapy on anxiety and depression: A meta-analytic review. *Journal of Consulting and Clinical Psychology* 78 (2) (April 2010): 169–83; Goyal, M., et al. Meditation programs for psychological stress and well-being: A systematic review and meta-analysis. *JAMA Internal Medicine* 174 (3) (2014): 357–68; and Rutledge, T. Meditation intervention reviews (comment on above article). *JAMA Internal Medicine* 174 (3) (2014): 1193.
2. Brook, R. D., et al. Beyond medications and diet: Alternative approaches to lowering blood pressure. *Hypertension* (2013). The report is available at http://hyper.ahajournals .org/content/early/2013/04/22/HYP.0b013e318293645f.full.pdf.
3. Ameli, R. *25 Lessons in Mindfulness: Now Time for Healthy Living* (American Psychological Association, 2014).
4. Ibid., 5.
5. Hanh, T. N. *Peace Is Every Step: The Path of Mindfulness in Everyday Life* (Bantam, 1992).
6. Kabat-Zinn, J. *Full Catastrophe Living: Using the Wisdom of Your Body and Mind to Face Stress, Pain, and Illness* (Bantam Dell, 2005).
7. Travis, F. T., and Shear, J. Focused attention, open monitoring, and automatic self-transcending: Categories to organize meditations from Vedic, Buddhist and Chinese traditions, 1110–18.
8. Gunaratana, B. H. *Mindfulness in Plain English* (Wisdom Publications, 2002), 7.
9. https://www.tm.org.
10. Killingsworth, M. A., and Gilbert, D. T. A wandering mind is an unhappy mind. *Science* 330 (2010): 932.

11.   Raichle, M. E., et al. A default mode of brain function. *Proceedings of the National Academy of Sciences* 98 (2001): 676; Christoff, K., et al. Experience sampling during fMRI reveals default network and executive system contributions to mind wandering. *Proceedings of the National Academy of Sciences* 106 (2009): 8719; and Buckner, R. L., et al. The brain's default network. *Annals of the New York Academy of Sciences* 1124 (2008): 1.

12.   Tolle, E. *The Power of Now: A Guide to Spiritual Enlightenment* (Namaste/New World Library, 2004), 56–57.

13.   Travis, F. T., et al. A self-referential default brain state, 21–30.

14.   Brewer, J. A., et al. Meditation experience is associated with differences in default mode network activity and connectivity. *Proceedings of the National Academy of Sciences* 108 (2001): 20254–59.

15.   Simon, R., and Engstrom, M. The default mode network as a biomarker for monitoring the therapeutic effects of meditation. *Frontiers in Psychology* 6 (June 2015), article 776.

16.   Travis, F. T., et al. A self-referential default brain state, 21–30.

CHAPTER 15

1.   Maharishi Mahesh Yogi. *Third Day Checking,* DVD.

2.   Attwood, J. A., Atwood, C., and Dvorak, S. *Your Hidden Riches: Unleashing the Power of Ritual to Create a Life of Meaning and Purpose* (Penguin Random House, 2014).

3.   Gladwell, M. *Blink: The Power of Thinking Without Thinking* (Little Brown, 2007).

4.   Covey, S. *The 7 Habits of Highly Effective People: Powerful Lessons in Personal Change* (Simon and Schuster, 2013).

5.   Forbes/Pharma and Healthcare. April 27, 2015. This can be found at: http://www .forbes.com/sites/alicegwalton/2015/04/27/transcendental-meditation-makes-a-comeback-with-the-aim-of-giving-back/.

6.   Josh Zabar's blog on this topic can be found at: http://www.tm.org/blog/meditation /a-look-into-transcendental-meditation/.

7.   Frankl, V. E. *Man's Search for Meaning* (Beacon Press, 2006).

8.   Cattaneo, L., and Rizzolatti, G. The mirror neuron system. *Archives of Neurology* 66 (5) (May 2009): 557–60.

9.   Dalio, R. Principles (2011). PDF available at: http://www.bwater.com/Uploads/ FileManager/Principles/Bridgewater-Associates-Ray-Dalio-Principles.pdf.

10.   Covey, S. *7 Habits of Highly Effective People.*

11.   Ludwig, M., et al. Brain activation and cortical thickness in experienced meditators.

12.   Travis, F. T., et al. A self-referential default brain state, 21–30.

13.   Travis, F. T., et al. Patterns of EEG coherence, power, and contingent negative variation characterize the integration of transcendental and waking states. *Biological Psychiatry* 61 (2002): 293–319.

14.   Hill, N. *Think and Grow Rich* (Ballantine Books, 1960).

CHAPTER 16

1.   Bartels, M. Genetics of wellbeing and its components satisfaction with life, happiness, and quality of life: A review and meta-analysis of heritability studies. *Behavior Genetics* 45 (2) (2015): 137–56.

2.   Myers, D. H. "Emotions, Stress, and Health," in *Psychology,* 11th ed. (Worth Publishers, 2015), 479–87.

3.   Ibid.
4.   Bartone, P. T. Test-retest reliability of the dispositional resilience scale-15, 943–44.
5.   Bandy, C. L., et al. Meditation training in rook cadets increases resilience.
6.   Epstein, S., and Meier, P. Constructive thinking: A broad coping variable with specific components. *Journal of Personality and Social Psychology* 57 (2) (August 1989): 332–50.
7.   Myers, D. H. "Emotions, Stress, and Health."
8.   Rosenthal, N. E. *Emotional Revolution.*
9.   Maslow, A. "Self-actualizing People: A Study of Psychological Health," in *Motivation and Personality*, 2nd ed. (Harper and Row, 1970).
10. Shostrom, E. L. An inventory for the measurement of self-actualization. *Education and Psychological Measurement* 24 (2) (1964): 207–18.
11. Alexander, C. N., et al. Transcendental Meditation, self-actualization, and psychological health: A conceptual overview and statistical meta-analysis. *Journal of Social Behavior and Personality* 6 (5) (1991): 189–247.

CHAPTER 17

1.   James, W. *Varieties of Religious Experience*, 17.
2.   Maharishi Mahesh Yogi. *Mallorca*, 1972.
3.   Rosenthal, N. E. *Gift of Adversity.*
4.   Ibid., 174.
5.   Ibid., 235–36. I learned about the "silver lining" exercise from Chris Germer, a psychologist affiliated with Harvard University.
6.   James, W. *Varieties of Religious Experience*, 172.

CHAPTER 18

1.   Travis, F. T., et al. Patterns of EEG coherence, 293–319.
2.   Tolle, E. *Power of Now.*
3.   Travis, F. T., and Arenander, A. Cross-sectional and longitudinal study of effects of Transcendental Meditation practice on interhemispheric frontal asymmetry and frontal coherence.
4.   Travis, F. T., et al. Patterns of EEG coherence, 293–319.
5.   See notes 8–10 for chapter 6.
6.   Baruss, I., and Moore, R. J. Measurement of beliefs about consciousness and reality. *Psychology Reports* 71 (1992): 59–64.
7.   Gibbs, J. C., et al. *Moral Maturity* (Erlbaum, 1992).
8.   Marteau, T. M., et al. The development of a six-item short-form of the state scale of the Spielberger State-Trait Anxiety Inventory (STAI), 301–6.
9.   International Personality Item Pool: items are freely available at: http://ipip.ori.org/ipip/.
10. Travis, F. T., et al. Psychological and physiological characteristics of a proposed object-referral/self-referral continuum of self-awareness. *Consciousness and Cognition* 13 (2004): 401–20.
11. Mason, L. I., et al. Electrophysiological correlates of higher states of consciousness during sleep in long-term practitioners of the Transcendental Meditation program. *Sleep* 20 (2) (1997): 102–10.
12. Note that the three groups in the study by Mason et al. were not fully matched for age. The long-term meditating group was on average older than the other groups, in

part—as might be expected—because the longer you meditate, the older you get. Mason and colleagues used statistical measures in an attempt to factor out the age difference and concluded that the central findings survived these statistical challenges.

CHAPTER 19

1. James, W. *Varieties of Religious Experience*, 301.
2. Lawrence, D. H. *Complete Poems* (Viking Press, 1964).
3. James, W. *Varieties of Religious Experience*, 313–14.
4. Bucke, R. *Cosmic Consciousness: A Study in the Evolution of the Human Mind* (Innes & Sons, 1905).
5. Evans, J. *Philosophy for Life and Other Dangerous Situations: Ancient Philosophy for Modern Problems* (New World Library, 2012).
6. White, F. *The Overview Effect: Space Exploration and Human Evolution*, 2nd ed. (American Institute of Aeronautics and Astronautics, 1998).
7. Tolle, E. *Power of Now*, 4.
8. James, W. *Varieties of Religious Experience*, 299–301

CHAPTER 20

1. Rumi (translated by Barks, C.). *The Essential Rumi* (HarperOne, 1995), 36.
2. Isaiah 2:4, as translated in the *English Standard Version of the Bible* (Good News, 2001).

ACKNOWLEDGMENTS

I am grateful to many people who helped bring this book to fruition. I owe thanks to Bob Roth, to whom the book is dedicated: friend, colleague, and TM mentor, he was actively engaged in every step of the book's development; to Ray and Barbara Dalio, for their invaluable support; to my official editors Mitch Horowitz of TarcherPerigee and Elise Hancock, my wise friend on whose unfailing red pen I have come to rely; and my unofficial editors Craig Pearson, Mario Orsatti, Richard Friedman, and Bill Stixrud, for carefully reading earlier versions of the manuscript and offering sage advice. Fred Travis was generous with his encyclopedic knowledge of the science of TM, and always there to help.

The David Lynch Foundation and TM community were boundlessly supportive: Vicki Broome, my original TM teacher, offered advice and encouraged South African meditators to participate in a survey using the Consciousness Integration Questionnaire, which was an essential part of gathering information for the book. In the United States, other TM teachers encouraged their students to participate, which resulted in over six hundred responses. Special thanks in this regard to Jeanne and Tom Ball, Donna Brooks, Carla and Duncan Brown, Mark Cohen, Gerry Geer, Katie and Roger Grose, Lynn Kaplan, and many others whose names never came to my attention. Sam Katz helped set up SurveyMonkey, Shebna Garcon assisted with handling the data, and Randi Williams provided expert statistical advice.

Sam Johnson was my able tour guide in Fairfield, where I met with Nancy Lonsdorf, Ed Malloy, Jay Marcus, David and Rhoda Orme-Johnson, Keith and Samantha Wallace, and Ziv Soferman (via Skype), all of whom offered their own unique angles on TM and consciousness. A special thanks to Vernon Katz and Judy Booth for their knowledge and wisdom.

For help in educating me about mindfulness, thanks goes to Rezvan Ameli, Leigh Brasington, and Chris Germer.

Many helped in multiple ways that space does not permit to detail, but all are remembered distinctly and with gratitude. Some kindly granted me interviews. Others provided background information, yet others much-needed support. I thank Lindsey Adelman, Kevin Ashley, Mark Axelowitz, Carole Bandy, Casey Benjamin, Chuck Bliziotis, Natane Boudreau, Peter Bracken, Richard Broome, Andrew Cannon, Bennett Connelly, Paul Dalio, Megan Fairchild, Suzanne Fierston, Katie Finneran, Carolyn Grayson, Linda Green, Joanne Grigas, Ken Gunsberger, John Hagelin, Todd Hardin, Michael Heinrich, Sharon Isbin, Hugh Jackman, Isabell Jansen, Melody Katz, Brian Lavin, Dianne Leader, Ian Livingstone, Marcia Lorente, Linda Mainquist, Dan McQuaid, Kristina Nikolova-Dalio, Niyazi Parim (Neo), Pamela Peeke, Greg Polakow, Lynn Stallings, Temple St. Clair, Stephen Sufian, Mirela Sula, Randi Williams, Josh Zabar, Walter Zimmerman, Barry Zito, and Dave Zobeck.

Finally, for their support and love I am deeply grateful to Wendy and Desmond Lachman, Susan Lieberthal, Josh and Liana, and—as always—Leora.

INDEX

Tables are indicated by numbers in italics.